THE NEW INTERNATIONAL COMMENTARY ON
THE NEW TESTAMENT — F. F. Bruce, *General Editor*

THE FIRST AND SECOND EPISTLES TO THE THESSALONIANS

THE FIRST AND SECOND EPISTLES
TO THE THESSALONIANS

THE ENGLISH TEXT WITH INTRODUCTION.
EXPOSITION AND NOTES

by

LEON MORRIS, B.Sc., M.Th., Ph.D.
Vice-Principal, Ridley College,
Melbourne

WM. B. EERDMANS PUBLISHING CO.
GRAND RAPIDS, MICHIGAN, U.S.A.

U.S.A.

WM. B. EERDMANS PUBLISHING CO.

GRAND RAPIDS 3, MICHIGAN

First published 1959
Second printing, March 1964
Third printing, February 1968
Fourth printing, June 1970
Fifth printing, March 1973
Sixth printing, March 1975

ISBN 0-8028-2187-1

The Scripture text used in this commentary is that of the American Standard Version of 1901. This text is printed in full for the sake of readers who do not read Greek; the expositions are, however, based upon the Greek text.

PHOTOLITHOPRINTED BY GRAND RAPIDS BOOK MANUFACTURERS, INC.
GRAND RAPIDS, MICHIGAN, UNITED STATES OF AMERICA

CONTENTS

ABBREVIATIONS

Accidence	—	*A Grammar of New Testament Greek* by J. H. Moulton, Vol. II, *Accidence and Word-Formation*, ed. by W. F. Howard (Edinburgh, 1919)
AV	—	Authorized Version
ARV	—	American Revised Version
Bicknell	—	Commentary on I & II Thessalonians by E. J. Bicknell in *The Westminster Commentaries* (London, 1932)
Bull. Ryl. Lib.	—	Bulletin of the John Rylands Library, Manchester
Calvin	—	Commentary on I & II Thessalonians by John Calvin (the edition used is that published by Eerdmans, Grand Rapids, 1948)
DB	—	*Dictionary of the Bible*, ed. J. Hastings, 5 vols. (Edinburgh, 1898–1904)
Denney	—	Commentary on I & II Thessalonians by James Denney in *The Expositor's Bible* (London, 1892)
Dewailly and Rigaux		*Les Épitres de Saint Paul aux Thessaloniciens*, traduites par L.-M. Dewailly et B. Rigaux
EB	—	*Encyclopedia Biblica*
ExT	—	*The Expository Times*
ExGT	—	*The Expositor's Greek Testament*
Findlay (CBSC)	—	Commentary on I & II Thessalonians by G. G. Findlay in *The Cambridge Bible for Schools and Colleges* (Cambridge, 1891)
Findlay (CGT)	—	Commentary on I & II Thessalonians by G. G. Findlay in *The Cambridge Greek Testament* (Cambridge, 1911)
Frame	—	Commentary on I & II Thessalonians by J. E. Frame in *The International Critical Commentary* (Edinburgh, 1912)
Grimm–Thayer	—	*A Greek-English Lexicon of the New Testament*, being Grimm's *Wilke's Clavis Novi*

	Testamenti; translated, revised, and enlarged by J. H. Thayer (Edinburgh, 1888)
Idiom Book	— *An Idiom Book of New Testament Greek* by C. F. D. Moule (Cambridge, 1953)
JBL	— *Journal of Biblical Literature*
JThS	— *Journal of Theological Studies*
LAE	— *Light from the Ancient East* by A. Deissmann (London, 1927)
Lightfoot	— *Notes on Epistles of St Paul* by J. B. Lightfoot (London, 1904)
LXX	— The Septuagint
Milligan	— *Commentary on I & II Thessalonians* by G. Milligan (London, 1908)
MM	— *The Vocabulary of the Greek Testament* by J. H. Moulton and G. Milligan (London, 1930)
Moffatt	— Commentary on I & II Thessalonians by J. Moffatt in *The Expositor's Greek Testament*, Vol. IV (London, 1910)
Neil	— Commentary on I & II Thessalonians by W. Neil in the *Moffatt New Testament Commentaries* (London, 1950)
Proleg.	— *A Grammar of New Testament Greek* by J. H. Moulton, Vol I, Prolegomena (Edinburgh, 1906)
RSV	— Revised Standard Version
S-BK	— *Kommentar zum Neuen Testament aus Talmud und Midrasch* by H. L. Strack and P. Billerbeck (München, 1922–8)
Syntax	— *A Syntax of the Moods and Tenses in New Testament Greek* by E. de W. Burton (Edinburgh, 1955)
TWNT	— *Theologisches Wörterbuch zum Neuen Testament*, ed. G. Kittel and G. Friedrich (Stuttgart, 1933–)

Translations of the New Testament by R. Knox, J. Moffatt, J. B. Phillips, W. G. Rutherford and A. S. Way are cited by the use of the author's name.

THE FIRST EPISTLE TO THE THESSALONIANS

EDITOR'S FOREWORD

With the publication of this Commentary from the pen of Leon Morris of Australia—the eighth volume of the *New International Commentary on the New Testament* to appear—the circle of international participation is again happily enlarged. What is primarily in view in expressing gratification at this development, it may be noted, is not that search for an Australian representative led to Dr. Morris but rather that the discovery of his eminent scholarly and literary qualifications resulted in the extension of the circle to include a contributor from another continent. His favorable response to the invitation extended to him and the gracious spirit of cooperation which came to expression as the project developed have been sources of genuine satisfaction and pleasure to the editor.

The author was brought up in New South Wales where, after specializing in natural science, he taught for a period in this field. His principal interest became theology, however, and he undertook preparation for service as a clergyman in the Church of England in Australia. This service, beginning in 1938, included pastoral and missionary activities before he was called in 1945 to labor as Vice-Principal of Ridley College in Melbourne, a position he still holds. He qualified for the London B.D. and M.Th. degrees as an external student, and received his Ph.D. from the University of Cambridge in England following two years of residence there as a Travelling Fellow of the Inter-Varsity Fellowship.

The reputation of Dr. Morris as a biblical scholar has been established especially by his penetrating and illuminating work, *The Apostolic Preaching of the Cross*, which has attracted wide attention in the English-speaking world since its publication in 1955. Favorable notice has also been given his solid contributions to leading theological journals. That in addition to competence as a scholar he possesses exceptional gifts as a popular expositor has been fully demonstrated. The evidence of this is to be found especially in his exposition of the Thessalonian Epistles (1956) and of I Corinthians (1958) published as contributions to the *Tyndale New Testament Commentaries*, but mention may also be made here of his noteworthy devotional study of Matthew 26–28, *The Story of the Cross*, published in 1957. His recent popular study of the New Testament teaching on the deity and humanity of Jesus Christ in *The Lord from Heaven* (1958) provides still another demonstration of his theological insight and literary skill.

In a recent issue of *The Expository Times* (April 1957) Vincent Taylor, in reviewing Morris' *Tyndale* Commentary, gave enthusiastic expression to his admiration of both its contents and style, and declared: "One could wish that he had written a full-scale commentary on the Greek text." At the time that this comment appeared in print Dr. Taylor could not know that this larger project had been undertaken and that the manuscript had just come into the editor's hands! One may confidently hope, accordingly, that the present volume, which has allowed the author full scope for the application of his talents for research and exposition, will win not only Dr. Taylor's approval but also that of many a discriminating reader besides.

As this Commentary goes forth it is with the prayer that it may contribute to the end that the message of the Apostle Paul to the Thessalonians—a message which dwells richly upon the Christian's hope, but also, in this very connection, emphasizes the meaning and earnestness of his calling in the present world—may lay fresh hold upon the minds and hearts of men in our day. Thus we may be constrained to redeem the time even as we contemplate that salvation is nearer than when we first believed and that the ends of the ages have come upon us.

NED B. STONEHOUSE

Note: Upon the death of Ned B. Stonehouse, November 18, 1962, F. F. Bruce accepted the publishers' invitation to become General Editor of this series of New Testament commentaries begun under the very able and faithful scholarship of Professor Stonehouse.

The Publishers

AUTHOR'S PREFACE

When I was invited to contribute the volume on Thessalonians to this series I must confess to some hesitation. I was well on the way with my Tyndale Commentary on these Epistles, and was not at all sure that it was expedient for one man to write twice within such a short space on the same subject. What led me to respond to Dr. Stonehouse's gentle insistence was the consideration that in my work on the preceding commentary I had gathered a mass of information which the limitations of space precluded me from using. The longer commentary gave scope for this, as did the different method. It should be made clear that this is not a longer edition of the other commentary. It is a completely new work. The approach is different (though I have not felt it necessary to differ from myself at every point).

I would like to express my appreciation of the invitation extended to me by Dr. Stonehouse to contribute to this series, and also of his kindly interest in the progress of the work. As in the case of the earlier commentary, I owe much to the commentators whose works have been before me. The footnotes bear witness to my many indebtednesses. Finally, I would like to pay tribute to my colleagues on the staff of Ridley College. They have given me constant encouragement, and have made many suggestions.

LEON MORRIS

13

INTRODUCTION

I

THE FOUNDING OF THE CHURCH AT THESSALONICA

In response to the vision of the man of Macedonia Paul turned his back on Asia Minor and became the first known Christian missionary to preach in Europe. It is probable that this step did not seem so momentous to him as it does to us, for he simply passed from one province of the Roman Empire to another. But it set the course of Christianity westwards. In time Europe would become Christian.

Associated with Paul were Silas, Timothy, and Luke. There may have been others but, if so, we have no knowledge of them. The little band followed Paul's usual practice of seeking out strategic centers from which the new faith might radiate out to the surrounding districts. They preached with success in Philippi, a Roman colony, and the most important town in the district adjacent to their landfall. The mission there concluded with something very like a riot (Acts 16:22). The preachers were scourged and imprisoned. Their jailor was dramatically converted after an earthquake in the middle of the night. In the morning Paul and Silas as Roman citizens refused to accept summary release. The incident ends with the lordly praetors bringing the humble preachers out of their prison and requesting them to leave the city.

The preachers[1] then made for Thessalonica. They passed through Amphipolis and Apollonia (Acts 17:1), but there is no record of preaching in either center. It is clear that Paul was seized with the importance of Thessalonica, and wished to establish the church there. This was the largest and most important city in Macedonia, and the capital of the province. Its situation halfway

---

[1] Paul and Silas are both mentioned as having been at Thessalonica. We do not hear of Timothy between the time Paul took him "to go forth with him" at Lystra (Acts 16:1–3) and his being left at Beroea with Silas when Paul went on to Athens (Acts 17:14). But the natural presumption that he had journeyed all along with Paul and Silas is strengthened by the fact that he is joined with these two in the superscriptions of both Epistles to the Thessalonians.

between the Adriatic and the Hellespont and at the head of the Thermaic Gulf, coupled with its fine harbor, made it the natural outlet for the trade of Macedonia, and a center where many roads met. The great Via Egnatia, the Roman highway to the East, passed through it. As Meletius long ago said, "So long as nature does not change, Thessalonica will remain wealthy and fortunate."[2] To this day it is a flourishing center.

The city had a long history. In early days the hot springs had given the name Therma to the settlement alongside them. In 315 B.C. Cassander named the place Thessalonica, after his wife who was half sister to Alexander the Great. It is possible that he renamed the old city, but it seems more probable that this was a new foundation near to Therma, for Pliny the Elder speaks of the two cities as existing together. But in time Thessalonica became increasingly prosperous and swallowed up the older center. When the Romans conquered Greece they recognized the importance of the city by making it the capital of one of the four parts into which they divided Macedonia. When later they altered the system and made a single province, Thessalonica became capital of the whole. During the first civil war the city was Pompey's headquarters, but in the second it was wise enough, or fortunate enough, to side with Anthony and Octavian. When they emerged victorious Thessalonica was rewarded by being made a free city. Its rulers were called "politarchs" as Luke tells us in Acts 17:6, 8, and as we see from inscriptions. While there were undoubtedly many Romans there, the city remained basically a Greek city. Included among the extraneous elements in the population was a strong Jewish community. The Jews had a synagogue, whereas in Philippi there was only a *proseuche*, which probably means an open-air place where they were accustomed to meet for prayer.

Thus Thessalonica had everything we would expect to attract Paul from what we know of his missionary methods.[3] It is not at all surprising that he made his way there soon after coming to Macedonia. As was his custom, he began by attending the syna-

---

[2] Cited by J. B. Lightfoot, *Biblical Essays* (London, 1893), p. 255.

[3] Cf. the discussion by Roland Allen in Ch. II of *Missionary Methods, St. Paul's or Ours* (London, 1930). He says, for example, "Thus at first sight it seems to be a rule which may be unhesitatingly accepted that St. Paul struck at the centres of Roman administration, the centres of Hellenic civilization, the centres of Jewish influence, the keys of the great trade routes" (p. 23).

gogue and preaching there (Acts 17:2). This he did for "three sabbath days," which sets us the problem of the length of his stay. The impression we get from Acts 17 is that it was at the end of this period that the riot took place which ended Paul's activities in Thessalonica. But in I Thess. 2:7–11 we read that Paul worked hard at manual work, and this might well indicate a longer period. So also with the reference in Phil. 4:16 to the gifts sent by the Philippian church while Paul was at Thessalonica. The usual interpretation of this verse is that they sent twice. It is not probable that this would take place within the period covered by "three sabbaths," which, allowing for some days before the first and after the third Sabbath, would give us rather less than a month.

Most commentators find a solution to the difficulty in thinking that the three Sabbaths refer to the period of Paul's activities in the synagogue. After that Paul continued his mission, preaching elsewhere, and he may have been there as long as six months.[4] This may be so. The chronology of Paul's life is difficult, and we cannot be certain about many points. But it seems that the period may well have been just short of a month as Acts tells us.[5] In the first place, the preaching was in the nature of a short campaign; it was not a prolonged affair.[6] It is clear from the Epistles that, while Paul had given a good deal of teaching, there was much he had not been able to say. In the second place, Paul may well have had to go to work even if his stay was only about a month. We have no reason for thinking that he was a man of means, and to have a month without income is a luxury that not all can afford. In the third place, it is not at all certain that the Philippian passage means

---

[4] This is Ramsay's estimate, *St. Paul the Traveller and the Roman Citizen* (London, 1930), p. 228.

[5] Frame accepts a period "not longer than three weeks," though allowing the possibility of a longer stay (p. 7). Bicknell prefers to think of Paul as spending "a few weeks" on "a direct mission to the heathen" after his three Sabbaths' preaching in the synagogue (p. xiii).

[6] "St. Paul and Silas must not be compared to men who preach to a heathen population tolerably well satified with its creed, or seek to convince minds which are not especially interested, and do not share in the general point of view of the missionaries, but rather to 'revival preachers' such as Wesley or Whitefield, who understood and were understood by their hearers, and had a definite message for a clearly felt want. For such men three weeks is long enough for anything; certainly it is long enough to create a considerable body of fervent believers among men who are dissatisfied with their own position—and that is exactly what the God-fearers were" (K. Lake, *The Earlier Epistles of St. Paul* [London, 1919], p. 65).

that the friends at Philippi sent twice to him. The expression occurs in I Thess. 2:18, and in the note there I have suggested that the Philippian passage means "both [when I was] in Thessalonica and more than once [when I was in other places] you sent...." Even if it does mean "twice" it is not at all beyond the bounds of possibility that this should take place within the space of a month, though admittedly unlikely. In the fourth place, Acts gives careful information as to the circumstances of Paul's preaching in places like Corinth, Ephesus, and Rome. It tells us in each case when he turned from the Jews to the Gentiles. It is not impossible that this was overlooked at Thessalonica, but Luke's method is such that this is unlikely.

It seems then that we cannot say with certainty how long Paul and his companions preached in the city. But it was certainly a short period, and may have been as little as about a month. The preaching was strikingly successful. From Acts we learn that it centered on the necessity for the Christ to suffer and to rise from the dead, and on the identity of Jesus with this Christ. "Some" Jews were converted, as were "a great multitude" of "devout" Greeks, and "not a few" of the chief women.[7] The largest group among the converts was thus derived from the Gentiles who had attached themselves loosely to the synagogue. These people were dissatisfied with the moral laxity and the intellectual absurdity of polytheism. In their search for something better they turned to Judaism, and at this time they were to be found attending Jewish synagogues in most places. It was among this group that Christianity everywhere found its most ready adherents. In this new faith they found the satisfying monotheism and the lofty morality which drew them towards Judaism, without the intense nationalism, the legalism, and the ritual requirements which they found so uncongenial. In Thessalonica, as in other places, this group gave the gospel a ready welcome. Nothing is said, either in Acts or the Thessalonian Epistles, about the social class of the converts, except for the statement that some of the "chief women" believed (Acts 17:4). But from Paul's stress on manual labor, and from the nega-

---

[7] There is evidence that women occupied a position of greater prominence in Macedonia than was common in the ancient world. See Ramsay, *op. cit.*, p. 227, and Lightfoot on Philippians, pp. 55 f. The latter cites inscriptions on monuments erected in honor of women by public bodies, and other relevant data.

tive fact that he does not find it necessary to warn the Thessalonians about the perils of riches, we might fairly deduce that most of them were from the lower classes.

The members of the synagogue reacted to the success of the Christian mission with violence. They gathered "certain vile fellows of the rabble" (Acts 17:5), and stirred up a riot. They attacked the house of a certain Jason, expecting to find the preachers there. When they were unsuccessful they dragged Jason and some of the believers before the politarchs. They accused Jason of harboring "these that have turned the world upside down" (Acts 17:6), and went on to complain that they affirmed Jesus to be king. This was the kind of accusation which might well proceed from the Jews with their understanding of the royal functions of the Messiah. It may also reflect some of the second-advent preaching of the apostles. It was a very damaging accusation to be made in a free city, for the countenancing of treason might lead to the loss of all her privileges. That there was no substance in the allegations is plain, for the politarchs simply took security of Jason and others and released them. The believers promptly sent Paul and Silas away to the next large town, Beroea.

It is not easy to make out just what was implied in the taking security[8] of these men. It is usually held that Jason was no longer to shelter Paul and his company, but Acts does not say this. The big difficulty in the way of this is that from I Thess. 2:17 f. it is plain that Paul anticipated that he would return. Therefore it does not seem possible that Jason had agreed to keep him away. It is more probable that Jason and his friends were bound over in general terms. They were to keep the peace, and in the circumstances of the moment all agreed that Paul and his companions had better leave the city quickly. This explains the sudden departure, and also Paul's expectation that he would return.

---

[8] MM say: "The neut. *ἱκανόν* is common = 'bail,' 'security,'" and they cite examples of its use, e.g. "unless indeed they persuade the chief usher to give security for them until the session"; "security is demanded by the tax-gatherers."

II

OCCASION AND PURPOSE OF I THESSALONIANS

Paul's next preaching place after Thessalonica was Beroea. Here he found the Jews much less prejudiced, and when he and Silas preached in the synagogue, they received their word, and checked it against the Scripture. As a result many Jews believed as well as the Gentile adherents of the synagogue. But the Thessalonian Jews heard what was happening and some of them came to Beroea. There they stirred up so much trouble that Paul sailed away to Athens, though his helpers, Silas and Timothy, stayed on.

Having arrived at Athens, Paul sent for Silas and Timothy to come to him quickly. But he was so stirred by the idolatry he saw that he could not wait for their arrival before proclaiming the gospel, both in the synagogue and in the market place. His preaching aroused interest and won some converts. But for the most part the cultured Athenians found the resurrection a stumbling block.

We have every reason for thinking that Paul was a discouraged man when he came to Corinth, his next port of call. Fanatical opponents had brought about his forcible ejection from three successive preaching places, in each case just when it seemed as though his work was to be crowned with success. After that he had gone to Athens, the capital city of Greece, and had been met by mockery. In later days he recalled that he arrived at Corinth "in weakness, and in fear, and in much trembling" (I Cor. 2:3).

But not long after this Silas and Timothy came to him from Macedonia, bringing news of his converts there. They told him that despite all difficulties the new believers were standing firm. Their story was such that Paul could not but be encouraged. He saw his setbacks in their right perspective, and realized afresh that God was with him, that he was God's messenger, and that the blessing of God was upon the work he was doing. He received new strength. Inspired by this news he gave himself over to the vigorous proclamation of the gospel that was to mean so much to Corinth in the following days. This we gather from Acts 18:5: "When Silas and Timothy came down from Macedonia, Paul was constrained by the word, testifying to the Jews that Jesus was the Christ." Paul's first letter to the Thessalonians reflects this mood of

20

relief and exultation. We see in it something of what these Thessalonian friends meant to Paul. He wrote to express his concern for them and his joy in them. It is not certain that Silas as well as Timothy had been to Thessalonica, but we know that the latter had been there (I Thess. 3:6) and that recently. One or both of these friends brought Paul news of the Thessalonian church. I Thessalonians was the reaction to the need thus revealed. While in general Paul was thrilled at the progress made by this church, the report showed that there were certain things which were wrong, and certain difficulties they were facing. He wrote accordingly to correct and encourage them.

It is clear from both Acts and I Thessalonians that the principal opposition to the church at Thessalonica came from the implacable Jewish community in that city. They probably were able to enlist a certain amount of Gentile support, but the Jews were the mainspring of the constant opposition. One part of their campaign was a personal attack on Paul himself. They urged that he had no real love for his converts (else why did he not come back to them?), and that he had never been motivated by any genuine concern for them, but only by the desire for personal profit. At that period there were many wandering preachers, both of philosophy and religion. They made a living by imposing on the credulity of those whom they could persuade to listen to them.[9] It was easy to impugn Paul's sincerity,[10] and to class him with these familiar wandering charlatans. Could his enemies have been successful in this campaign of slander Paul would have been hopelessly discredited,[11] and the message he preached along with him.

---

[9] Cf. M. Dibelius: "Paul's mission might easily have been confused by the public with the activities of wandering speakers, mendicant philosophers, pseudo-prophets and sorcerers. Therefore the missionary's first concern had to be to dissociate himself from them by emphasising that his aims were not self-seeking" *(Studies in the Acts of the Apostles* [London, 1956], p. 156). See also notes on I Thess. 2:1 ff.

[10] "It is clear that in the early days of the Church the device of discrediting the teachings of a prominent man by throwing doubt on his motives and conduct was perfectly understood and efficiently practised" (K. and S. Lake, *An Introduction to the New Testament* [London, 1938], p. 135).

[11] All the more would this be so if, as Lake suggests *(Earlier Epistles,* pp. 70, 76), the failure of Paul and Silas to appear before the politarchs meant that the treasonable nature of Christianity had been settled by default. It would mean that some of the blame for the persecutions might plausibly be attributed to Paul.

Findlay reconstructs the calumnies of the slanderers thus: "These so-called apostles of Christ are self-seeking adventurers. Their real object is to make themselves a reputation and to fill their purse at your expence. They have beguiled you by their flatteries and pretense of sanctity . . . into accepting their new-fangled faith; and now that trouble has arisen and their mischievous doctrines bring them into danger, they creep away like cowards, leaving you to bear the brunt of persecution alone. And, likely enough, you will never see them again!"[12] Had the Thessalonians come to accept this (and the amount of attention Paul gives it may indicate that some were being influenced) the effect on the church must have been disastrous. Thus Paul devoted a considerable amount of space to the refutation of such slanderers. He insisted on the purity of his motives. He pointed to the way he and his companions had steadfastly refused to take anything from the Thessalonians, but had worked hard day and night to support themselves. He protested his love for his converts.

In addition to the campaign of the Jews there was opposition from the Gentiles as we see from I Thess. 2:14 f. Paul wrote to encourage his friends to stand fast in the face of such persecution.

Apart from these external trials there were within the church some erroneous views on the second advent which were causing trouble. It is clear that the converts, while they knew the essentials, were yet imperfectly informed about this doctrine. Paul wrote to give them that fuller information they needed. Some had evidently gathered the impression that the *Parousia* was imminent. Christ would come and take them *all* to Himself. But then some of them died, and that raised a problem. Did it mean that the deceased would miss their share in the events of that great day? Did it perhaps throw discredit on the whole idea of the *Parousia?* Paul wrote to set their minds at rest and to give them the true teaching.

Another false inference that was drawn by some from the thought of the imminence of the second coming was that it was unnecessary for them to do any work. This in turn meant that they had to live on the charity of their fellows, and that they became idle busybodies. The full development of this tendency is seen in the Second Epistle, but we find its beginnings in the First (I Thess. 4:11 f.). Paul sought to set such people on the right track.

---

12 Findlay, CGT, pp. xxxiv f.

A further point about the second coming may well have concerned the possibility of knowing just when it would be. At any rate, Paul thought it necessary to remind them that there was no knowing when it would take place (I Thess. 5:1 ff.), which seems to indicate that some had been concerned about the point.

It is likely that in trying to deal with the problem the zeal of the leading members of the congregation had outrun their tact. Some of the rank and file were offended, and were beginning to have a low opinion of them. Paul counselled the church at large to hold their leaders in high esteem "for their work's sake" (I Thess. 5:13).

A feature of life in a Greek city of the first century was its laxity in matters of sexual morality. Converts were taught that in Christ things were different. But the pressure from their environment to revert to the old easy behavior must have been very strong. Paul accordingly includes a section encouraging them to stand firm in the right way (I Thess. 4:4 ff.).

There are other things that he speaks of which may indicate some measure of irregularity. Thus in I Thess. 5:19 f. he speaks about the Holy Spirit in a way which may indicate that some had frowned on the enthusiasm of members who were more Spirit-led.[13] But in the foregoing we will have most of the matters which seem to have weighed with the great Apostle as he wrote to his friends. The great thing was that he wrote in exultation of spirit, having just heard the good news of the way in which they were standing fast. He wrote to let them know how thankful he was. He wrote to let them know of his tender concern for them. He wrote to encourage them in the face of the opposition, even persecution, that still confronted them. He wrote to give them fuller information about matters in which their zeal had outdistanced their knowledge. He wrote to put them further along the Christian way that meant so much to him and to them.

---

[13] Cf. Lightfoot: "An unhealthy state of feeling with regard to spiritual gifts was manifesting itself. Like the Corinthians at a later day, they needed to be reminded of the superior value of 'prophesying,' compared with other gifts of the Spirit which they exalted at its expense" (*op. cit.*, p. 264). Most, however, feel that the Thessalonian error was different. There the danger was of "quenching" the Spirit (1 Thess. 5:19). See the notes *ad loc*

III

Occasion and Purpose of II Thessalonians

Paul's First Epistle was dispatched, and it was successful in doing some of the things he set out to do. For example, he had defended his personal integrity, and since there is no repetition of this in II Thessalonians we may fairly assume that his readers had taken this in. But the same was not true of every point.

Thus in I Thessalonians Paul had had much to say about the second coming. He had stressed that this will take place suddenly. Either from misunderstanding this, or from some other source, some of the Thessalonians had concluded that the day of the Lord had already come. Paul heard of this, perhaps from the people who had delivered his letter when they returned to him, and he wrote accordingly to correct such a false impression. This second Epistle is largely concerned with the second coming, and Paul gives information about the Man of Lawlessness which would show that the coming of the Lord could not be as yet.

When he first wrote, Paul knew of certain people whose second-advent speculations had led them to give up their work and live lives of meddlesome idleness. They had not been persuaded by his short reference to their case, and accordingly he devotes considerable space to them. He points out the importance of quiet work. He urges them to follow the example that he and his companions had set in working for their living so that they would not be a burden on others. But he apparently feels it unlikely that all will heed him, so he gives instructions as to how the church is to treat the disobedient.

These two topics, the second coming and the idlers, are the principal ones of this Epistle. Paul takes advantage of the fact that he is writing to give further encouragement to the believers in their continuing difficulties, to request their prayers and to give general counsel.

IV

The Date of the Epistles

I Thessalonians was written not long after Timothy reached Paul (I Thess. 3:6), and not long after he himself had left his converts (I Thess. 2:17). From I Thess. 3:1 f. we learn that Paul sent Timothy to Thessalonica from Athens, so that Timothy must have joined him in the capital city. From Acts 18:5 we find that Timothy also joined him in Corinth. This meeting would be within a few months of Paul's departure from Thessalonica, and would, therefore, be quite soon enough to fit in with I Thess. 2:17. There is no way of saying with absolute certainty whether the Epistle was written just after Timothy came to him in Athens or in Corinth, but on the whole the latter is more likely. The situation envisaged in the Epistle must have taken a little time to develop. People died. Strange ideas about the second coming appeared. Jewish propaganda and Gentile persecution made their presence felt. Paul also speaks of the widespread reputation of the Thessalonian church (I Thess. 1:8; cf. 4:10), and we must allow time for this to eventuate. The Epistle can hardly come after Paul's stay in Corinth, for he was there for eighteen months (Acts 18:11), but he speaks of being separated from the Thessalonians "for a short season" (I Thess. 2:17). We conclude that Paul wrote from Corinth at the time indicated in Acts 18:5.

Now it happens that one of the important dates for a determination of New Testament chronology is associated with just this period. Acts 18:12 refers to the proconsul Gallio. This same man referred a question to the Emperor Claudius, and the Emperor's reply is found on an inscription at Delphi. The date given is the 12th year of Claudius' power as a tribune, and after his 26th acclamation as Emperor. His 12th year was from Jan. 25, 52 to Jan. 24, 53. The date of the 26th acclamation is not known exactly, but the next acclamation, the 27th, took place before Aug. 1, 52. That means that the Emperor's decision would have been given in the months preceding this. Thus it must have been during the earlier rather than the later part of the year 52. It was the custom for proconsuls to assume their office in early summer, which makes it unlikely that Gallio began his term in 52. It does not seem possible for him to assume office, come across the difficulty, refer the question to Claudius, and receive his answer in the time. He must have been in office a year earlier, i.e., in 51.

Acts 18 does not say at what stage of Gallio's proconsulship Paul was brought before him, though it seems as though it was early. The great Apostle was in Corinth for a period of eighteen months (Acts 18:11), but again, we do not know at what point in this period he came before Gallio. Clearly he had exercised a considerable ministry by then. Yet it was not at the very end of his time there, for he stayed in Corinth after this incident "yet many days" (Acts 18:18). All in all it seems likely that Paul had been in Corinth for rather more than a year before Gallio's arrival. Probably the best we can do is to say that Gallio assumed office early in the summer of 51, and that Paul came to Corinth in the first half of the preceding year. I Thessalonians would thus have been written in the early part of the year 50.

It will be obvious that this date must be taken as approximate only. To the uncertainties already noted must be added another. Proconsuls sometimes had two years in office instead of one. Thus Gallio may have been at Corinth earlier than we have so far allowed. The date of the Epistle may vary a year or two from our date. But it will hardly vary more than that. Almost all commentators are agreed that the Epistle must be dated in the early 50's.[14]

As we have already seen, there is every indication that the Second Epistle followed within a period of weeks after the First. The same sort of situation is envisaged, and the same sort of advice given. Another point confirmatory of the early date arises from the fact that Paul is recorded in Acts 20:1 f. as visiting Macedonia, as going through those parts and giving much exhortation. II Thessalonians must come before this, for it is hard to think of so similar a situation to that in I Thessalonians emerging again after Paul had had opportunity of dealing with it in person. Now Corinth is the only place we know of where Silas and Timothy were with Paul during the period up to Acts 20. Thus II Thessalonians as well as I Thessalonians was written from this city. This brings the dates together. It seems impossible to assign II Thessalonians to any other period.

It is worth pointing out that this puts the Thessalonian Epistles among the earliest that Paul wrote. There are some scholars who date Galatians earlier than these, but none, I think, would place any of the other Pauline epistles so early. These are among the oldest Christian writings that we have.

---

[14] Kirsopp Lake quotes and discusses the inscription and other relevant texts in *The Beginnings of Christianity*, Vol. V (London, 1933), pp. 460–64.

V

THE AUTHENTICITY OF I THESSALONIANS

This letter claims to be from Paul (1:1, 2:18), and it is Pauline both in language and in ideas. The author's associates, Silas and Timothy, we know from Acts to have been with Paul on his second missionary journey. The letter must be early for various reasons.[15] Church organization is apparently in a very early stage. It is difficult to think of anyone writing after Paul's death putting forth in Paul's name a statement that might be understood as meaning that the *Parousia* would take place during the Apostle's lifetime (I Thess. 4:15). The question of the fate of believers who died before the *Parousia* must have been answered fairly early in the church's life. Yet it is impossible to think of anyone but Paul putting it out in early times. How could it possibly gain a circulation while the Apostle was still engaged in vigorous work, travelling among the churches and well able to denounce it? (Yet we must bear in mind that the possibility of forgery seems to be implied by II Thess. 2:2, and the explanation of the autograph in II Thess. 3:17.)

Moreover, the letter is as well attested as we could reasonably ask. It is not the kind of letter which would be quoted often. This explains its absence from the few sub-apostolic writings that have come down to us (though there are some similarities of language which may be more than coincidence[16]). But it was accepted as sacred Scripture by Marcion (c. 140 A.D.). It is included among the canonical books in the list given in the Muratorian Fragment (a list of the books accepted as canonical some time after the middle of the second century, probably at Rome). The Epistle is definitely quoted by Irenaeus (c. 180 A.D.) and later writers.

It hardly seems the kind of letter which would be forged. Why

---

[15] Cf. the verdict of F. C. Burkitt: "There was plenty of pseudepigraphical literature in late-Judaism and among the early Christians, but the unauthentic document betrays itself by marks of a later date. Exactly the reverse is the case with the Thessalonian Letters" *(Christian Beginnings* [London, 1924], pp. 129 f.).

[16] Milligan, for example, though discounting "the frequently-cited passages from the Apostolic Fathers" is of opinion that "two passages in Ignatius, and one in the *Shepherd of Hermas* may perhaps be taken as showing acquaintance with its contents" (p. lxxii).

should anyone produce a letter like this? What did he aim to do thereby? The letter reads naturally as the reaction of Paul to the situation we have outlined in an earlier section. But it seems completely out of character as a forgery foisted on the church to serve some devious purpose of the forger.

Nothing very considerable can be set over against all this. Some of the Tübingen school regarded the Epistle as unauthentic, but they stand practically alone. Their reasons for rejecting the Epistle fail to commend themselves. Thus we find the objection that it is not doctrinal enough, or again, that it shows too close dependence on I and II Corinthians. These two surely cancel each other out, for the former means it is not Pauline enough, and the latter that it is too Pauline! Neither carries conviction, nor do others that are alleged.

No more convincing is the suggestion that the letter cannot be an authentic writing of the Apostle because there are serious discrepancies between it and Acts. For example, I Thess. 2:7 ff. gives us a picture of Paul working at his trade, and this is said to be incompatible with the statement of Acts 17:2 that he preached in the synagogue at Thessalonica on three Sabbaths. We have already examined this in considering the circumstances of the first preaching in the city, and we have seen no necessary contradiction. Paul may have stayed in Thessalonica no longer than Acts indicates. Or, if we feel that a longer period is required, Acts may give us the length of his synagogue preaching. It is the same with the allegation that the two contradict each other since Acts 17:4 speaks of the converts as both Jews and Gentiles, while I Thess. 1:9, 2:14 refer to Gentiles only. Or that Acts 18:5 speaks of Silas and Timothy as coming to Paul at Corinth, whereas I Thess. 3:1 f. shows that Timothy was with Paul for a time in Athens. As B. Clogg says, "Discrepancies of this nature prove little except that the authors of Acts and of I Thessalonians wrote independently of each other."[17] Neither is giving the complete story, and we must make use of both. But to say that both must in all points tell all they know is so obviously false as to need no refutation.

We conclude, then, that there is no real reason for doubting the authenticity of this epistle.[18]

---

[17] *An Introduction to the New Testament* (London, 1940), p. 21.

[18] Cf. McGiffert: "If one accepts any of Paul's epistles there is no good reason for denying the authenticity of 1 Thess." (EB, col. 5041).

VI

THE AUTHENTICITY OF II THESSALONIANS

As in the case of the First Epistle there are good reasons for thinking of II Thessalonians as authentic. It has early attestation, for Polycarp, Ignatius, and Justin all seem to have known it, possibly also the writer of the Didache. It is found in the Marcionite canon and in the Muratorian Fragment. It is quoted by name by Irenaeus and later writers. As with I Thessalonians, the mention of Silvanus and Timothy as associates of the author, and the obviously early date of the writing favor Pauline authorship. II Thessalonians emerged into church history associated unequivocally with I Thessalonians. It claims to have been written by Paul, and the language and theology are Pauline. It is difficult to think of a suitable motive for a forger (notice that, since II Thess. 3:17 claims to be Paul's signature, forgery is the only alternative to authenticity. We cannot think of someone putting out in good faith a sample of Pauline teaching). It is difficult to think of a reason for making the letter resemble I Thessalonians so closely. It is difficult to think of a forger entering so fully into the mind of Paul as to produce a writing so redolent of the Apostle as this one.[19] There is also the point that had we not I Thessalonians we would hardly call in question the authenticity of II Thessalonians. It is rather strange to call in question an Epistle which has all the hallmarks of a genuine Pauline writing on the grounds that it is similar to another Pauline writing.

For reasons such as these most scholars have not hesitated to accept this writing. In recent times, however, attention has been focussed on certain matters which raise doubts. While not many would go so far as to pronounce the Epistle non-Pauline, a number of scholars feel perplexed. The principal points are the following.

(1) There is what Neil speaks of thus: "The problem of the letter is one of accounting for the similarity to and difference from a letter written by the same hand, to the same people, only a short

---

[19] Cf. Milligan: "Not only are there abundant traces of the Apostle's characteristic phraseology and manner, as has been clearly shown by Dr. Jowett and others, but the whole Epistle reflects that indefinable original atmosphere which a great writer imparts to his work, and which, in this instance, we are accustomed to associate with the name of St. Paul" (p. lxxx).

while before."[20] Sometimes II Thessalonians repeats I Thessalonians not only in general ideas, but also in the actual words that are employed. The objection is that such an outstanding man as Paul would not find it necessary to repeat himself. He would, if he had to say the same thing, say it in different words, so that deliberate imitation is the explanation. At the same time there are differences, such as those on eschatology, which we shall notice in the next section. The thought then is that the ideas are not the ideas of Paul, and they are expressed in language which is a deliberate imitation of that of the great Apostle.[21]

In the first place it must be rejoined to this that the general similarity to Pauline style is very close indeed. It is very difficult to envisage a forger who could imitate Paul's language so very closely. Pauline words and phrases and constructions are everywhere. So are Pauline ideas. If Paul wrote II Thessalonians not so very long after I Thessalonians it would not be surprising if sometimes words and phrases were repeated,[22] especially if, as Neil thinks possible, he read through "the customary draft copy of his first letter before writing the second."[23] This would be the more likely in that he had to bear in mind what was written in I Thessalonians, because some of it had been misunderstood.

It must also be borne in mind that the extent of the resemblance is easy to exaggerate. It is natural for there to be close resemblances in such places as the opening and the close, and indeed, in the general structure of the letters. It is natural also for an author to come close to repeating himself when he is writing on the same

---

[20] P. xxi.

[21] Cf. the objection of Johannes Weiss: "the majority of critical scholars are doubtful of the genuineness of 2 Thess.; for, since they only read it in the shadow of 1 Thess., it appears to them as an insignificant and empty copy of 1 Thess." (cited by T. W. Manson, *Bull Ryl. Lib.*, Vol. 35, pp. 436 f.).

[22] Bicknell (in another connection) adduces a number of similarities between passages in Romans, I, II Corinthians, and Galatians, and comments: "In fact every Epistle is full both of ideas and expressions to which parallels can be found in the rest. It is only natural that a writer should tend to express himself in much the same terms when dealing with similar situations. In pastoral work even the most original of teachers falls into certain habits of style and phrasing" (p. xxv).

[23] *Op. cit.*, p. xxiii. Frame cites Zahn as the originator of the suggestion (p. 53). McGiffert thinks that "the genuineness of the second epistle can be maintained, in fact, only by assuming that Paul had a copy of 1 Thessalonians in his possession, and that he read it over again shortly before writing 2 Thessalonians" (EB, col. 5045).

subjects twice within a matter of weeks or even months.[24] But the suggested parallels do not cover more than about one-third, which is strange in a deliberate imitation. And even so, more or less identical language is used in different ways. For example, there are marked resemblances between the ways in which Paul describes his hard manual labor in the two letters. But in the first he does it to show his love for his converts, while in the second it is to bring out the force of his example. This kind of thing is more likely to be due to a writer's free handling of familiar expressions than to slavish imitation by a forger.[25] There is, moreover, the point that the resemblances are to I Thessalonians. Why should a later imitator confine himself to this Epistle and not make use of Paul's major writings?

The differences are no more conclusive. Thus Paul's comments on the Man of Sin (or Lawlessness) in the second letter are different from anything he has to say in the first. But the difference does not amount to an incompatibility. It is no more than a man might add as a supplement to what he has already said on the subject. It is the same with the other differences that are brought forward.

This combination of likeness and difference is interesting, and there may be more to it than at present appears. But the point is that it does not prove difference of authorship. Such a man as Paul was quite capable of both.

(2) The eschatology of II Thessalonians is said to be different from that of I Thessalonians. The simplest way of putting this is to say that in the First Epistle the coming of the Lord is thought of as about to take place very soon and very suddenly. But in the Second Epistle it will be preceded by signs, like the great rebellion and the appearance of the Man of Lawlessness.

But to state this hypothesis is virtually to refute it, for it is a commonplace in apocalyptic literature that the Lord's coming is to be sudden, and yet that it will be preceded by signs. We find this in the Gospels and in Revelation, to name no other. It should

---

[24] Moffatt points out that the similarities might be explained "by the hypothesis ... that his mind was working still along the lines of thought voiced in the former epistle, when he came to write the latter." This, he says, "can be illustrated from any correspondence" (ExGT, vol. IV, p. 14).

[25] Cf. Frame: "Apart from the formal agreements in the main epistolary outline, the striking thing is not the slavish dependence of the author of II on I, but the freedom with which he employs the reminiscences from I and incorporates them in original ways into new settings" (p. 47).

31

also not be overlooked that Paul's warning in I Thess. 5 not to be unprepared when the day comes may well imply a knowledge of premonitory signs.

A similar objection is that the people to whom II Thessalonians was written obviously knew a good deal about the *Parousia*, for even the teaching about the Man of Lawlessness is given them only by way of reminder, and not as communicating new information (2:5). Such people would hardly be in ignorance of such fundamental teaching on the subject as is given in I Thess. 4:13 ff. But again the objection does not get us far. In the short time that he was in Thessalonica Paul could not give all the teaching on the second coming that he would have wished. Many matters were certainly left ungrasped by the Thessalonians. It is entirely natural that eager new converts should have fastened their attention on such an outstanding figure as the Man of Lawlessness without appreciating the fact that some of their number would die before the great day. Indeed they may well not have given this matter any thought at all before the decease of some of their number forced it on their notice.

Other objections turn on the Man of Lawlessness. Thus some urge that this figure does not appear elsewhere in Paul and therefore we cannot accept the idea as Pauline. To say this is to refute it. We cannot dismiss an idea because Paul produces it once only. For that matter it does not occur elsewhere in the New Testament. But Paul had an eager, questing mind. He is more likely to have seized on the truth concerning this being than some at least of his contemporaries. There is no real objection here.

A variant of this objection dates the origin of the idea of the Man of Lawlessness too late to put it within the time of Paul. This objection maintains that the whole idea of the Man of Lawlessness is based on the Nero redivivus myth. After Nero's death in 68 A.D. there appeared a number of people who claimed to be that emperor come to life once more. They were discredited, but the idea persisted that one day Nero would come back to life. Then he would put himself at the head of the forces of evil. The myth came to have a supernaturalistic tinge. Nero was held to be demonic as well as human. Now if the portrait of the Man of Lawlessness was drawn from the Nero redivivus myth, obviously Paul could not have drawn it. The idea did not gain currency till after his death. But the idea of the anti-Christ is far older than the Nero redivivus myth, as Bousset, for example, has shown. It goes back long before the time of Paul, and there is no reason for holding that II Thessalonians 2 is based on the late myth. Consequently the objection falls to the ground.

Thus we see that there are various ways of putting the objection from eschatology, but none of them is decisive.[26] The eschatological teachings in the two epistles are not contradictory, but complementary.

(3) There are some who think that a difference of authorship is indicated by the fact that whereas I Thessalonians is warm and friendly in tone, II Thessalonians is cold and rather formal. The difference is difficult to sustain. Frame points out that the vehement self-defense in the First Epistle accounts for a good deal of its warmth, and that if this were omitted the differences in tone "would not be perceptible."[27] Again, the coldness alleged in the tone of II Thessalonians is very largely due to a few expressions. Thus Paul says, "We are bound to give thanks to God always for you, brethren," and adds, "even as it is meet" (II Thess. 1:3). But this is probably to be understood as a protestation that his praise of them in the First Epistle was no more than was right (see notes *ad loc.*). Again, the objection that we meet authoritative commands (II Thess. 3:6, and elsewhere) overlooks the fact that throughout that whole section there is an undertone of genuine brotherly warmth. Paul is very concerned to bring back into full fellowship some whose conduct had raised a barrier. But he is just as loving as he is authoritative.

Thus, while admittedly II Thessalonians is slightly cooler in tone than the First Epistle, it does not seem as though the difference amounts to much. Even if we were to grant all that the objectors put forward it still would prove little. Writers are not always in the same mood, and we have no reason for thinking of Paul as an

---

[26] Moffatt cites Baur's admission: "It is perfectly conceivable that one and the same writer, if he lived so much in the thought of the Παρουσία as the two epistles testify, should have looked at this mysterious subject in different circumstances and from different points of view, and so expressed himself regarding it in different ways." Moffatt proceeds, "This verdict really gives the case away. Such variations are hardly conceivable if both epistles emanated from a later writer, but they are intelligible, if Paul, living in the first flush and rush of the early Christian hope is held to be responsible for them" (*op. cit.*, p. 14).

[27] P. 35.

exception. Moreover, as we saw in the opening section, there is good reason for thinking that when he wrote I Thessalonians Paul was experiencing a joyful reaction from a time of discouragement. It would not be surprising if a later letter failed to reproduce such a mood, especially if it revealed that some had failed to give heed to instructions given in that first letter. Moreover, we know from II Thess. 3:2 that Paul was in a somewhat difficult situation when he wrote that letter.

Thus it does not seem as though any of the objections is compelling. There is none for which an answer does not lie ready to hand. There is, accordingly, no reason why we should not accept the positive evidence and accept this Epistle as an authentic writing of Paul.

VII

The Relationship Between the Two Epistles

Granted that the two Epistles are both authentic there are still some unusual features, such as those noted in the previous section. A number of ideas have been put forward in the attempt to explain them.

1. *A Divided Church*

A suggestion of Harnack's, adopted by Kirsopp Lake, was that at Thessalonica the church was divided into two sections meeting separately, a Jewish and a Gentile church. I Thessalonians is written to the Gentile church, and II Thessalonians to the Jewish church.[28]

In favor of this view it is pointed out that Gentiles seem to be the recipients of the First Epistle (see, for example, the turning from idols in 1:9, and the distinction between "your own countrymen" and the Jews in 2:14). In the Second Epistle there is said to be a much stronger Jewish flavor, with appeals couched in Old Testament language. A second point depends on the acceptance of ἀπαρχὴν as the true reading instead of ἀπ᾽ ἀρχῆς in II Thess. 2:13.

---

[28] See for this view Kirsopp Lake's article in ExT, Vol. xxii, pp. 131-3; his *The Earlier Epistles of St. Paul* (London, 1919), pp. 83 ff.; and K. and S. Lake, *An Introduction to the New Testament* (London, 1938), pp. 134 f.

"God chose you as a first fruit" instead of "God chose you from the beginning." The Thessalonians were not the first converts in Macedonia, nor Paul's first converts, so the term does not fit the church well. But the Jews were the first converts in Thessalonica, so the term might apply to them over against the Gentiles. The case is more or less completed by drawing attention to the "all" in I Thess. 5:26 f. It is felt that something must lie behind this insistence that *all* be greeted, and that the letter be read to *all*. The autograph in II Thess. 3.17 was "to avoid the danger which he foresaw of one of the two parties in the Church impugning the authenticity of the other's Epistle."[29]

This evidence is not compelling. The Jewish coloring of II Thessalonians is not at all decisive. There is not one quotation from the Old Testament in this Epistle. While admittedly some of the language, particularly in the section dealing with the *Parousia*, is reminiscent of that in the Old Testament, it is significant that Plummer's close scrutiny of both Epistles for traces of Septuagint language reveals that this is "less conspicuous" in the Second Epistle than in the First.[30] But in any case Old Testament language is not at all decisive for a Jewish destination. Paul cites the Old Testament most frequently of all in the Epistle to the Romans, addressed to a church which was predominantly Gentile. Not much can be built on a variant reading, especially when, as here, most editors prefer the alternative. Again, the "all" at the end of I Thessalonians is not emphatic, and is capable of being explained otherwise. Paul desired that his greetings should embrace everybody, and that there should be no doubt as to his desire (see the notes *ad loc.*). Lake's explanation of the autograph is not at all convincing.

Thus the evidence in favor of the theory is not strong. There are also strong reasons against it. The most important of these is the impossibility of thinking that Paul would have acquiesced in such a situation. We know from I Cor. 1:11 ff. that he was strongly opposed to disunity within a church. He did not hesitate to rebuke those who disturbed the unity of the churches. Again and again in his correspondence he speaks of the unity of those in Christ. It is

---

[29] K. Lake, ExT, Vol. xxii, p. 132.
[30] *A Commentary on St. Paul's Second Epistle to the Thessalonians* (London, 1918), pp. xvii ff.

impossible to understand his joy in the Thessalonians if they were divided so deeply that the two segments did not even worship together.

Quite apart from the Pauline attitude there is the fact that we do not know of any church divided in this way. While there are many things about the early church that we do not know there are also many that we do. And none of them gives countenance to the idea that the early Christians would anywhere have accepted a situation like that posited by Harnack and Lake. We should need very strong evidence for such a division, but the evidence we are offered is not at all convincing.

There are also some points about the Epistles themselves which militate against the theory. Thus the superscriptions are practically the same, which is strange if they were intended for different groups. Harnack was driven to suppose that "which are of the circumcision" has been lost from the superscription of II Thessalonians. Then we have such curious facts as Paul's praise of the Jewish churches in I Thess. 2:13 ff., in a section intended for the Gentile church. He goes on to praise them for imitating these Jewish churches. This for Gentiles who would not even meet together with the Jewish Christians in their own city!

Thus, despite the great names which are ranged behind this hypothesis, we must feel that it does not do justice to the facts.

2. *Co-Authorship*

Both Epistles tell us that the senders are "Paul and Silvanus and Timothy." Throughout the letters "we" rather than "I" is used (with a few exceptions). Some have thought accordingly that we might find a solution to our problems by thinking of one or other of Paul's helpers as being largely responsible for one or both of the Epistles, Silas being usually favored.

Now it is obvious that if we think of either Silas or Timothy as being responsible for both letters[31] we are in no better case than if we think of Paul as having written them both. Indeed the case is rather worse, for we have the similarity of style, language, and theology with other letters certainly written by Paul to account for.

---

[31] F. C. Burkitt thinks of Silas as having drafted both letters and read them to Paul, who added I Thess. 2:18 and II Thess. 3:17 (*op. cit.*, p. 132). But he does not really face the difficulty of how Silas made these two letters so very much like the letters which come from Paul.

It is more plausible to think of one of his coadjutors as having a larger place in II Thessalonians than in I Thessalonians. As we saw in earlier sections there is practically no disputing that Paul wrote I Thessalonians. What doubts there are center round the Second Epistle. But against such a solution are three things. The first is the similarity of style, language, and theology. How did Silas or Timothy achieve this? The second is II Thess. 3:17, which tells us that Paul signed this Epistle. The third is Paul's intense personal interest in his converts. The Corinthian correspondence shows that it was his habit to deal in person with even comparatively unimportant matters. It is not easy to think of him delegating to another the responsibility for dealing with a situation like that at Thessalonica.

Thus while this view is superficially attractive it will not bear critical examination. The facts point us to Paul as the author of both Epistles.

3. *Reversal of Order*

The letters as we have them are not dated, and they bear no obvious indication as to which was written first. Traditionally the Epistle we know as I Thessalonians has been held to be the older. But there are some scholars who hold that many of our problems receive a solution if we simply reverse the order and think of II Thessalonians as having been written first. The point is made that I Thessalonians is fuller and richer in content, so that when II Thessalonians is held to follow it it suffers by comparison, and hypotheses of copying and the like begin to appear. But if we think of II Thessalonians as a first letter it is an attractive piece of work. It does not deal fully with a number of topics and thus it calls for another letter which will amplify what it says and make clear points left in doubt.

Reasons which are urged as showing the priority of II Thessalonians are as follows:

(a) II Thessalonians shows the church undergoing sore trials and difficulties. I Thessalonians speaks of these as past.

(b) There are difficulties within the church which are mentioned in II Thessalonians as though the writers have just heard of them. Indeed they may have appeared but recently. But in I Thessalonians they are mentioned as though familiar to everyone, which points to a later stage.

(c)   Such a statement as that the Thessalonians have no need
to be written about "the times and the seasons" (I Thess. 5:1) is
very much in point if these people have already received II Thess. 2.

(d)   Paul draws attention to his signature in II Thess. 3:17, but
not at the end of I Thessalonians. Such a statement would be
needed at the end of a first epistle.

(e)   T. W. Manson thinks that the recurrence of "Now concerning" in I Thess. 4:9, 13; 5:1, is significant.[32] This same formula
is found in I Corinthians in the places where Paul is replying to a
letter, each time referring to a point raised in the letter. The
inference to be drawn is that Paul sent II Thessalonians. This,
however, did not deal with all the difficulties in the minds of his
readers. They accordingly wrote him back a letter, and I Thessalonians is his reply.

(f)   Some members of the Thessalonian church had died when
I Thessalonians was written. This is more likely if we have a
longer period.

(g)   The organization revealed in I Thess. 5:12 f. requires a
longer time interval than we have if I Thessalonians is first.

(h)   Lyle O. Bristol thinks the shortness of II Thessalonians is
significant. He reasons that I Thessalonians is a later elaboration
of the shorter epistle.[33]

These arguments, however, seem very vulnerable. So far from
the trials in question being over by the time I Thessalonians was
written, most students believe that one reason for that letter was
to give the believers encouragement so that they might endure the
trials before them. No real reason appears to exist for thinking
that the internal difficulties were new when II Thessalonians was
written apart from the words, "we hear of some that walk among
you disorderly" (II Thess. 3:11). This is not really a strong
argument, for the expression could just as easily follow what is
said in I Thessalonians as precede it. It is not necessary to postulate
II Thessalonians 2 as the background to the statement in I Thessalonians about "the times and the seasons." On any showing Paul

---

[32]   He does not, however, deal with the fact that in I Thess. 4:13 we have
not περὶ δέ but δέ... περί. It is at least doubtful whether this can be regarded
as an occurrence of a "formula."

[33]   ExT, Vol. LV, p. 223. He was answered by Edward Thompson, ExT,
Vol. LVI, pp. 306 f. Another who has argued for the reversal of order is
J. C. West, "The Order of 1 and 2 Thessalonians", JThS, Vol. XV, pp. 66–74.

spoke about the *Parousia* and attendant happenings during his preaching while he was yet in the city, and this is sufficient to explain any reference in I Thessalonians. The argument about the explanation of the autograph being required in a first epistle breaks down on the fact that Paul does not explain it in any other of his epistles, be they first or otherwise. He mentions the autograph in I Cor. 16:21; Col. 4:18, but gives no explanation of its significance. Clearly, some special reason is required in II Thessalonians, and it is given by II Thess. 2:2. There was a letter which purported to be from Paul. How could they know a genuine letter when they saw one? Paul tells them.

Manson's "Now concerning" is no more conclusive. There seems no reason why it should not refer to matters to which Timothy drew attention in his oral report. Moreover, we do not know that it was used only as a formula in replying to a letter. It certainly is not used in that way in Mark. 12:26; 13:32; John 16:11; Acts 21:25.[34] Its occurrence in I Corinthians does not prove that Paul used the expression in no other way. The deaths of some members does not call for a long period. Life is an uncertain business, and in any given group it is always possible for deaths to occur. The problem of the fate of the deceased could have arisen quite early. So with the organization. There is nothing in I Thessalonians which requires a lengthy period for its development. From Acts 14:23 we know that Paul appointed elders quite soon after establishing churches, and if he did that at Thessalonica that is all that is required. Moreover, there was no great interval between the two Epistles, and not much could have developed in the intervening period. The argument from the shortness of II Thessalonians proves nothing. There is no reason why a first epistle should be shorter than a second. Moreover, I Thessalonians is not an elaboration of II Thessalonians. Where the same point is treated in both letters (e.g., the loafers) the discussion is apt to be longer in II Thessalonians.

---

[34] Chalmer E. Faw, in an article entitled "On the Writing of First Thessalonians" in JBL, Vol. LXXII, pp. 217 ff., argues that the Thessalonians had sent a letter to Paul before I Thessalonians. He notices that the passages we have cited refer to replies to oral, not written communications. But, strangely, he does not notice that this demonstrates that the occurrence of the expression in I Thessalonians may just as well refer to the oral report brought by Timothy as to a hypothetical letter from the Thessalonians.

On the other hand, there are good reasons for thinking the traditional order to be the correct one.[35]

(a) Of the problems which occur in both letters, persecution, the second advent, the loafers, each seems to intensify as we pass from I Thessalonians to II Thessalonians. The natural line of development seems to be in this direction and not the reverse.

(b) A letter from Paul certainly preceded II Thessalonians (see 2:2, 15; 3:17). If I Thessalonians followed II Thessalonians we must postulate another Thessalonian Epistle now lost. It seems more natural to understand that II Thessalonians follows I Thessalonians, which letter incidentally does not mention any previous letter to its recipients.

(c) The general tone of I Thessalonians seems to be that called for by the situation we have outlined in an earlier section. If Paul experienced an exultation of feeling when his discouragement was removed by the good news from Thessalonica then a letter like I Thessalonians is called for. The slightly cooler tone of II Thessalonians is explained by the interval of time and the fact that some disregarded his injunctions. But if we reverse the order of the letters how shall we explain these things?

(d) In similar fashion the personal reminiscences which we find in I Thessalonians are perfectly natural in a first letter, and need not be repeated in another missive following soon after. It is more difficult to think of a first letter as lacking in such items, and then of their appearing in a later letter.

(e) There are some indications of a continuing growth in the spiritual stature of the Thessalonians. Thus in I Thess. 1:6 and 2:13 Paul refers to the converts as having accepted the gospel, while in II Thess. 1:3 he speaks of their faith as growing. In I Thess. 3:12 and 4:10 Paul prays that their love may abound and exhorts them to abound in love, while in II Thess. 1:3 he gives thanks for their love abounding. This sort of thing is not decisive, but it supports other indications that II Thessalonians is rightly put second.

(f) There is a small point in the teaching on eschatology.

---

[35] McGiffert thinks that the idea of the priority of II Thessalonians "is excluded by the literary relationship between the two epistles, which clearly points to the secondary character of the second, by the sharper tone of II Thess. in dealing with the disorderly (3:6 f.), and by the relation of the apocalyptic passage in 2:2 f. to I Thess. 4:13 f." (EB, col. 5039, n. 2).

I Thess. 4:17 gives what is apparently new teaching on believers being caught up to meet the Lord. Such teaching seems to be presupposed by the reference to "our gathering together unto him" which is assumed as familiar in II Thess. 2:1.[36]

(g) The section I Thess. 2:17–3:6 seems to presuppose that this is the first letter written by St. Paul to this church (so Milligan, Jowett, Dewailly and Rigaux, and others).[37]

Thus our conclusion is that sufficient reason has not been shown for rejecting the traditional order of these epistles. The evidence as we have it seems rather to indicate that the first letter in point of time was our I Thessalonians.

---

[36] On the whole question of the eschatology of the two Epistles Edward Thompson remarks, "The likelihood is greater that the Apocalypse of II Thessalonians grew out of I Thessalonians rather than the reverse" (op. cit., p. 307).

[37] J. Rendel Harris argued that I Thessalonians gives indications of a previous letter Paul sent, and to which the Thessalonians had replied (The Expositor, 5th Series, Vol. VIII, pp. 161—80). But his arguments do not carry conviction (see notes on I Thess. 2:13). In any case, he did not dispute the order of our I and II Thessalonians.

ANALYSIS OF I THESSALONIANS

I. GREETING, 1:1

II. PRAYER OF THANKSGIVING, 1:2-4

III. REMINISCENCES, 1:5-2:16
 1. Response of the Thessalonians to the original preaching, 1:5-10
 2. The preaching of the gospel at Thessalonica, 2:1-16
    (a) The purity of the preachers' motives, 2:1-6a
    (b) The preachers' refusal to accept maintenance, 2:6b-9
    (c) The preachers' behavior had been impeccable, 2:10-12
    (d) The message of the preachers was the word of God, 2:13
    (e) Persecution, 2:14-16

IV. THE RELATIONSHIP OF PAUL TO THE THESSALONIANS, 2:17-3:13
 1. Paul's desire to return, 2:17, 18
 2. Paul's joy in the Thessalonians, 2:19, 20
 3. Timothy's mission, 3:1-5
 4. Timothy's report, 3:6-8
 5. Paul's satisfaction, 3:9, 10
 6. Paul's prayer, 3:11-13

V. EXHORTATION TO CHRISTIAN LIVING, 4:1-12
 1. General exhortations, 4:1, 2
 2. Sexual purity, 4:3-8
 3. Brotherly love, 4:9, 10
 4. Earning one's living, 4:11, 12

VI. PROBLEMS ASSOCIATED WITH THE PAROUSIA, 4:13-5:11
 1. Believers who die before the Parousia, 4:13-18
 2. The time of the Parousia, 5:1-3
 3. Children of the day, 5:4-11

VII. GENERAL EXHORTATIONS, 5:12-22

VIII. CONCLUSION, 5:23-28

COMMENTARY ON I THESSALONIANS

I. GREETING, 1:1

1 Paul, and Silvanus, and Timothy, unto the church
of the Thessalonians in God the Father and the Lord
Jesus Christ: Grace to you and peace.

1 In every age there have been conventions in letter writing.
Thus in our own day we begin by saluting the addressee as "Dear,"
and conclude by assuring him that we are "Yours faithfully" or
"Yours sincerely" or the like. In the first century there was some
latitude, but a letter always began with the name of the writer,
followed by that of the addressee, and a greeting. Frequently
there was then some pious expression, such as a thanksgiving or a
prayer that the gods would keep the addressee in health.

It is important to notice that the first words of I Thessalonians
are in the form usual at the beginning of a letter of this period.[1]
What follows is not a theological treatise, but a real letter arising
out of the situation in which the Apostle and his friends find
themselves. Paul retains the conventional form, but he adapts it
both to the wider context of the Christian religion, and to the
narrower one of the particular situation in which he is writing.
The opening to this letter is the simplest Pauline form, but in it
we have all the elements which we see expanded in the openings
of the other epistles.

He begins by associating Silvanus and Timothy with himself.
The former was Paul's chief assistant on his second missionary
journey. When Paul and Barnabas quarreled over Barnabas'
suggestion that John Mark should accompany them on a second
visit to the churches they had founded, they separated. Paul
chose Silvanus (or Silas, as Luke calls him) as his helper. This

---

[1] For writing materials, procedure, etc., see Note A in Milligan's commentary, and Ch. III of A. Deissmann, LAE.

man came under notice previously as one of the two who took the decisions of the Council of Jerusalem to Antioch (Acts 15:22, 27). He is spoken of as one of the "chief men among the brethren" (Acts 15:22), and as a prophet (Acts 15:32). He seems to have worked harmoniously with Paul throughout the missionary journey, and Paul later recalled his faithful preaching (II Cor. 1:19). Among other places, he had, of course, preached at Thessalonica, and this accounts for his association with Paul in the greeting to the church which had come into being as a result of the mission there. After the second missionary journey Silvanus is mentioned once only, namely as Peter's amanuensis in the writing of the First Epistle of Peter (I Pet. 5:12).

Timothy was the son of a Greek father and a Jewish mother. He was not circumcised in infancy (the rite was carried out when Paul wanted to take him with him, Acts 16:1–3), but this does not mean that his spiritual education had been neglected. Both his grandmother and his mother were devout (II Tim. 1:5), and he had been instructed in the Scriptures from his childhood (II Tim. 3:14f.). He seems to have been somewhat timid in disposition, but Paul thought highly of him. He took him with him on missionary journeys, sent him on missions (Acts 19:22, I Cor. 4:17, Phil. 2:19), and associated him in the salutations in several letters (II Corinthians, Philippians, Colossians, I and II Thessalonians, and even the little letter to Philemon). In the account of the preaching at Thessalonica given in Acts 17 Timothy is not mentioned, but as we hear of him earlier and later in the same journey, and as he is joined in the greeting here and in II Thessalonians, we may safely assume that he was one of those who brought the gospel to Thessalonica.

There is some difference of opinion as to how far Silvanus and Timothy were concerned in the actual composition of the letter. In a comparable case, I Corinthians, Paul associates Sosthenes with him in the greeting. But by verse 4 he is using the first person singular, and though he sometimes returns to "we," for the most part it is clear that the letter came from Paul, his mention of Sosthenes being largely a matter of courtesy. When we find that in Thessalonians "we" is used almost throughout we may well feel that Silvanus and Timothy had a somewhat larger share in the letter than did Sosthenes in I Corinthians. Yet in I Thess. 3:1 Paul uses the plural (even in the adjective "alone"), where clearly he is referring to himself. This, taken with the practical difficulty of seeing how three people could combine to write such homogeneous letters as those before us, and the fact that the style is that of Paul's other letters, leads to the conclusion that Paul's is the hand behind these writings also. We need not doubt that he consulted the others, nor that they endorsed what he wrote. The steady use of "we" may be meant to associate the others more closely with these Epistles than was usually the case with Paul's collaborators. But Paul was chiefly responsible for the form the letter took.

Paul usually attaches some epithet to his name, like "apostle," or "servant of Jesus Christ." But to the Thessalonians he is just "Paul." There is no need to protest his position to these good friends.

This letter, like II Thessalonians, is addressed to "the church of the Thessalonians," a form of address not used elsewhere. It is difficult to see why this one church should be addressed differently from all the others. Perhaps in this early letter Paul has not yet settled into a regular style of addressing churches. Whatever the reason, this wording directs attention to the group of believers comprising the local church, whereas such a salutation as "unto the church of God which is at Corinth" (I Cor. 1:2) brings to our minds rather the great universal church as it is manifested in a particular place.[2]

The following words, "in God the Father and the Lord Jesus Christ," are almost certainly to be taken with "the church,"[3] and

---

[2] A point which does not seem to have been satisfactorily accounted for is that Paul addresses the church in his five earliest epistles (Galatians, I, II Thessalonians, I, II, Corinthians), and "the saints," "the brethren," or the like, in the later letters.

[3] The doubt arises because there is no τῇ before the phrase as we would have anticipated. Lightfoot notices the possibility accordingly of taking it with an understood χαίρειν or γράφουσι. However, New Testament usage in such matters is variable (such an article is lacking, for example, in 2:14, 4:16), and the sense of the passage is strongly in favor of the meaning we have adopted. It is Paul's habit to add some description of those to whom he writes. There is also the point made by Chrysostom that this particular ἐκκλησία had to be distinguished from πολλαὶ ἐκκλησίαι καὶ Ἰουδαϊκαὶ καὶ Ἑλληνικαί. We, with our associations, are apt to overlook the point that to the Greek speaking ἐκκλησία was a secular rather than a religious word. See further on 2:14.

In Frame's judgment the absence of the τῇ emphasizes the closeness of the attachment.

they bring us the characteristic of a Christian church. Christians are not simply people who have heard about God and trust Him. They live "in" Him day by day. All their deeds are done in Him. It is Paul's usual habit to speak of being "in Christ," though "in God" occurs, as in Col. 3:3.[4] But throughout these two Epistles he constantly associates the Father and the Son in the closest of fashions (cf. v. 3; 3:11–13; 5:18; II Thess. 1:1, 2, 8, 12; 2:16 f.; 3:5; and see the note on I Thess. 3:11). No higher view could possibly be taken of the Person of Christ.

In line with this is his application to Jesus of the title "Lord." This is the regular word for Jehovah in the Septuagint, the Greek translation of the Hebrew Old Testament, and in all probability it is from this source that we should derive Paul's usage, rather than from Hellenistic sources, where the term is in use for the god in the cultus of more than one deity. Yet Paul was not unmindful of the associations the term held for Gentiles. He employs a term which conveys to men the idea that Jesus is divine, be their background Jewish or pagan.

Jesus is the human name. Wherever it is used by itself it draws attention to the humanity of our Lord. The word is derived from the Latin, which in turn is from the Greek transliteration of the Hebrew "Joshua," an abbreviation for "Jehoshua," meaning "Jehovah is salvation" (cf. Matt. 1:21).

"Christ" is from the Greek equivalent of the Hebrew word "Messiah," or "anointed one." Though it had become something of a proper name it yet retained its Messianic associations. Jesus is the chosen One in whom God is well pleased to fulfill His purposes planned from of old. The combination of the three terms into one impressive title[5] gives us compactly a view of a Person who alone can be ranked with God.

The greeting is "Grace to you and peace." This is apparently

---

[4] E. Best has an exhaustive discussion of the expression "in Christ" in the first chapter of his book, *One Body in Christ* (London, 1955). He also discusses "in God" (p. 21 f.), though his conclusion that this "may merely indicate Paul beginning to feel after a theology" is hardly adequate. The Thessalonian correspondence gives no indication that its author was still feeling for his theology. Rather he was quite sure of his position.

[5] Neil adds an important point, "The whole name, therefore, *Lord Jesus Christ*, and the significance of each of its component parts and all of them in conjunction, was essentially pre-Pauline, the faith of the church from the beginning."

a new form originated by Paul. It is not found before him, and is in all his epistles. "Grace" is from the same root as the salutation commonly employed in Greek letters. It is possible, accordingly, that Paul is taking over and adapting the usual salutation. "Peace" is the usual Hebrew greeting, so that this opening appears to be a combination of the Hebrew and Greek forms.

But the change in the Greek form, though slight in sound,[6] is great in sense. It is a big step from "greeting" to "grace." Grace fundamentally means "that which causes joy,"[7] a shade of meaning we may still discern when we speak of a graceful action or the social graces. It comes to mean "favor," "kindness," and then especially God's kindness to man in providing for his spiritual needs in Christ. Thence it comes to signify what is due to grace, namely, God's good gifts to men, and finally the attitude of thankfulness which all this awakes within the Christian. As used in greetings it is the free gift of God that is meant, but the word necessarily evokes memories of the free gift on Calvary.

Peace among the Greeks meant much the same as it does with us, namely the absence of war or strife. But among the Hebrews it was a positive concept. When a Hebrew said, "Peace be to you," he did not mean, "I hope you won't get into a fight," but rather, "I pray that you may prosper." The Hebrew _shalom_ meant prosperity in the widest sense. The root is concerned with "wholeness." The man who enjoys peace is thus the one whose life is well rounded. Peace is regarded as a gift of God, and there is a very definite spiritual aspect to the completeness it denotes.[8]

Paul's greeting, then, reminds his friends that all is owed to God. It is in the nature of a prayer that His grace and His peace, with all the richness of the concepts denoted by these terms, may be granted to the Thessalonians.

---

[6] From χαίρειν to χάρις.

[7] χαρά.

[8] I have discussed the Biblical idea of peace in my _The Apostolic Preaching of the Cross_ (London and Grand Rapids, 1955), pp. 210–17. Notice also the point made by G. Aulen. In the New Testament sense peace "is a peace 'in spite of all' and in the midst of the struggle. Because the forgiveness which brings peace is an act of God received and held by faith, or, in other words, because peace depends on fellowship with God, it can exist in the midst of darkness and tumult" (_The Faith of the Christian Church_ [London, 1954], p. 310).

II. PRAYER OF THANKSGIVING, 1:2-4

2 We give thanks to God always for you all, making
mention *of you* in our prayers;
3 remembering without ceasing your work of faith and
labor of love and patience of hope in our Lord Jesus
Christ, before our God and Father;
4 knowing, brethren beloved of God, your election,

2 Paul almost invariably begins his letters with some form of
thanksgiving (for a conspicuous exception see Galatians). But his
is removed from the merely conventional by the careful insertion
of "to God," which makes it clear that this is no casual reference
to whatever gods there be. It is the one true God to whom he gives
genuine thanks. Far from the conventional also is the warmth of
feeling he displays. Paul's regard for his converts is deep and
sincere. He includes them all in the thanksgiving, which is a mark
of his satisfaction at their spiritual progress (contrast Corinthians
or Galatians). Paul rates thanksgiving very highly. He enjoins his
readers to give thanks in everything (5:18, and cf. II Cor. 4:15,
9:11 f.).

Frame takes "making mention"9 with "always," and understands it to mean, "Each time that they are engaged in prayer, the
writers mention the names of the converts." But this does not seem
justified. "Always" qualifies "give thanks," and indicates that the
thanksgiving is constant, not sporadic. While Paul is clearly
affirming that he and his companions prayed much for the Thessalonians we need not think that he could never pray without
bringing in a reference to them. It is not certain whether the word
rendered "without ceasing" should be taken with "making mention" or with "remembering." On the whole it seems probable that
it goes with the former.

3 The matter of the thanksgiving is threefold.10 First, "your

---

9 μνείαν ποιοῦμαι is found in Paul also in Rom. 1:9, Eph. 1:16, Philem. 4,
each time being used of prayer. μνεία means "remembrance" and the expression
could mean "to remember," as does the very similar expression μνήμην
ποιεῖσθαι in II Pet. 1:15. However, there are not wanting examples of its
use in secular authors in the sense of "to mention," and this gives better
sense here. Also the idea appears to be different from that conveyed by
μνημονεύοντες in the next line.
ἐπί signifies "at," "in the time of."
10 For the conjunction of ἔργον, κόπος, and ὑπομονή, and in that order,
cf. Rev. 2:2.

work of faith." There is no reason to doubt that the meaning of this is "your work which springs from faith." Grammatically other meanings are possible[11] (as, for example, Hendriksen shows), but none suits the context as well as this. Paul is very emphatic that salvation is a matter of faith, not works, and he uses the very strongest of expressions to make it clear that man is not saved by works at all. But when this truth is not in dispute he does not hesitate to speak of the good works that characterize the life of faith. Faith, for Paul, is a warm personal trust in a living Savior, and such a faith cannot but transform the whole of life, and issue in "work" of many kinds. The word "work" is very general and we are not wise to try to delimit it too closely.

"Labor of love" is apt to be misunderstood, for we use the expression to denote small services we render without hope of reward. But Paul's term is a strong one,[12] and he means that, out of love, they have labored to the point of weariness. The word expresses the cost of their love, not its result. With or without visible success, love gives itself unstintingly.

The Greeks had a number of words for love, and it is of interest that the Christians passed over all those in common use. They took up *agape*, a word rarely used before them, and made it their characteristic word for love. It rings through the New Testament. Not only did they have a new word, but they had a new idea, for, as John says, we can never know what *agape* is from any human activity, not even from love to God. It is known only from God's great love to us shown in the propitiation wrought out on the cross (I John 4:10).[13] We have food for thought here, for it may be that

[11] Moffatt renders "active faith," but this is to put the stress on πίστεως while the Greek puts it on ἔργου. The same criticism might be levelled at his "patient hope," though curiously he renders the intervening expression (exactly the same Greek construction) by "labor of love."

[12] His word is κόπος on which Milligan says: "As distinguished from ἔργον, κόπος brings out not only the issue of work, but the cost associated with it . . . It is thus here the laborious toil (Grot. *molesti labores*) from which love in its zeal for others does not shrink." See further on 5:12.

[13] Bicknell's additional note on love overlooks this. He begins with self-love and works outward. When he comes to the love of God he finds it surprising that the Scripture does not speak of the love of God in creation, but rather in the cross. The point is that his direction is wrong. ἀγάπη cannot be understood from any human activity. We only begin to know what it is when we contemplate Calvary.

The most thorough examination is A. Nygren's *Agape and Eros* (London, 1953). See also G. Quell and E. Stauffer, *Love* (London, 1949), the translation of their article on ἀγάπη in TWNT.

51

in our day, as in theirs, popular ideas of love are misleading. The Hollywood brand of love will never do if we wish to understand the New Testament.

The usual word for love among the Greeks was *eros*. This means basically romantic love, love between the sexes. Though it came to be used of other loves, this is its characteristic meaning from which all others are derived. Now there are two important points about a young man's love for a maid. Firstly, he thinks highly of his beloved. Whatever the opinion of others ("I can't imagine what he sees in her!"), he thinks she's wonderful. Then, his love includes the desire for possession. I have never yet met a young man who said: "I'm head over heels in love with so-and-so, and I don't care who marries her!" These two ideas, the love of the worthy and the desire for possession, are of the essence of *eros*. The result may be a crude lust, or it may be a high and pure emotion. It is no small praise of a man, for example, when we can say of him that he loves (in the sense of *eros*) the good. For that is to say that he regards it as the most worthy thing, and that he desires to make it his own day by day. This is a fine concept. But it is not the Christian idea of love.

God loves us, not because we are worthy, nor even, as some think, because He sees in us possibilities as yet unrealized. God loves us although He knows full well our complete unworthiness. He knows that, at best, our righteousnesses are as "filthy rags" (Isa. 64:6, AV). And still He loves us. He loves, moreover, without thought of advantage, for there is nothing that we can bring to Him who made all things. He loves because it is His nature to love. He loves because He *is* love. Continually He gives Himself in a love which is for the blessing of others, not for the enrichment of Himself.

Further, His love is not something which exists only in words. His is a love which costs. It is a love which is active, which we see in the cross. Indeed, it is only in the cross that we can really know what the love of a pure and holy God for sinners is.

God's love does not leave man alone. As soon as a man sees what *agape* really is, he is forced to a decision. He must either yield to that love to be transformed by it, or he must reject it. In the former case he is made anew. By the grace of God he begins to see men in a measure as God sees them, and to love them, not for any worthiness that they may have, but despite their unworthiness. He loves them, not for his own advantage, but for theirs. Either he does this, or he turns away, and by so doing condemns himself. *Agape* compels a man to a decision. But Paul is able to give thanks for the way the divine *agape* is being realized in the self-giving labor of the Thessalonians.[14]

The third point in the thanksgiving is "patience of hope." "Patience" is better rendered "stedfastness" as ARV mg. What is meant is not a quiet, passive resignation, but an active constancy in the face of difficulties. As William Barclay says: "It is the spirit which can bear things, not simply with resignation, but with blazing hope."[15] This springs from hope, that hope which is more than pious optimism. It is a solid certainty. In the New Testament hope is always something which is as yet future, but which is completely certain.

It is not absolutely clear whether we should take "in our Lord Jesus Christ" with "hope," or, as Neil, for example, does, with the whole of the preceding, including the work of faith and labor of love. In the latter case it would mean that the whole of the life of the believer is lived in Christ. While this is true, yet here Paul seems rather to be saying that the Christian hope is in Christ. The Thessalonian Epistles have a good deal to do with the second coming and associated events, and hope is very prominent in them. Similarly, "before our God and Father" is probably to be taken with "hope" rather than with the preceding.[16] The hope of the believer is in Christ, and it is also a hope which has reference to his standing before the Father, and not merely before men.

---

[14] Denney makes the point that passion is a necessary prelude to effective work. "The passion of the New Testament startles us when we chance to feel it. For one man among us who is using up the powers of his soul in barren ecstasies, there are thousands who have never been moved by Christ's love to a single tear or a single heart throb. They must learn to love before they can labour."

[15] *A New Testament Word Book* (London, 1955), p. 60. A little later he says, "George Matheson, who was stricken in blindness and disappointed in love, wrote a prayer in which he pleads that he might accept God's will, 'not with dumb resignation, but with holy joy; not only with the absence of murmur, but with a song of praise'. Only *hupomone* can enable a man to do that."

[16] It is unlikely that ἔμπροσθεν τοῦ Θεοῦ καὶ Πατρὸς ἡμῶν goes with μνημονεύοντες (as Findlay inclines to think, CGT), because it is so far from it in the sentence. More possible is it to take it with all the words τοῦ ἔργου . . . Χριστοῦ. But if we confine the reference of τοῦ Κυρίου . . . Χριστοῦ to ἐλπίδος it is difficult to avoid doing the same with the concluding expression.

This verse brings us that conjunction of faith, hope, and love which we find also in 5:8, Rom. 5:2-5, I Cor. 13:13, Gal. 5:5 f., Col. 1:4 f., Heb. 6:10-12, 10:22-24, I Pet. 1:21 f. First Corinthians 13:13 is especially important, for that chapter is about love, not faith or hope. Yet at the climax the other two appear quite naturally. It was apparently an accepted Christian practice to join the three together. While the linkage is found in several places, the order varies. In this verse hope is last as a climax, which is very fitting in an epistle in which hope is so much stressed.

Here we might notice a characteristic of Paul's writing. The sentence might well have finished at "hope," and it would have been well-rounded and complete. But Paul is not satisfied. He goes on to another thought and another, so that his sentence does not finish till the end of v. 5 (or even later, according to some). As Findlay says, "His thought flows on in a single rapid stream, turning now hither, now thither, but always advancing towards its goal. His sentences are not built up in regular and distinct periods; but grow and extend themselves like living things under our eyes" (CBSC).

4 Paul addresses his readers as "brethren beloved of God."[17] He is fond of the address "brethren," using it in these two Epistles twenty-one times. Brotherhood was a very real thing in the early church, composed as it was of men from every race and social condition, but with a preponderance of those from the depressed classes (I Cor. 1:26 ff.). Within the church they knew a real brotherhood. In view of much modern talk about "the brotherhood of man," and brotherhood within groups such as lodges, we should be clear on the New Testament teaching. The brethren are those "beloved of God," and they are elect. There is a sense in which all men may be thought of as brothers. The fraternity of a club or lodge may be very real. But in the sense that matters brethren are brethren in Christ. The Christian brotherhood is the fellowship of the redeemed.

Election is one of the great concepts of the Bible, and it looms large in both Testaments. It is often misrepresented (as in Burns's

---

[17] Usually when referring to men as "beloved of God" the word ἀγαπητός is used (e.g. Rom. 1:7). ἠγαπημένοι ὑπὸ τοῦ Θεοῦ is found here only in the New Testament (though II Thess. 2:13 and Jude 1 are similar), and the perfect passive participle stresses the continuing love which God shows to men.

dreadful caricature). God is pictured as an arbitrary tyrant, damning or saving men without rhyme or reason. Against all such views we must insist that election, as Paul's words imply, proceeds from the fact of God's great love (notice the connection between love and election also in II Thess. 2:13). It is not a device for sentencing men to eternal torment, but for rescuing them from it. Election protects us from thinking of salvation as dependent on human whims, and roots it squarely in the will of God. Left to ourselves we do not wish to leave our state of untroubled sinfulness. It is only because God first convicts us and enables us that we can make even the motion of wanting to turn from our sins. From Eph. 1:4 we see that this is no afterthought of God, no sudden change in His plans. He has chosen His own from before the foundation of the world. Nothing gives security to the idea of salvation like the concept of election. Salvation, from first to last, is a work of God. Well may the seventeenth of the Thirty-Nine Articles of the Church of England speak of the idea as "full of sweet, pleasant, and unspeakable comfort."

The word for election is always used in the New Testament of the divine action, though sometimes it is used of other things than election to salvation. For example, in Acts 9:15 it is election to the office of preaching that is meant. Lightfoot says it "is never used in the New Testament in the sense of election to final salvation," but in view of Rom. 11:5, 7, 28, this seems impossible to maintain. Here it is clearly God's choice of the Thessalonians to salvation that gives Paul matter for thanksgiving. Anything less is inadequate. He undertakes no explanation of what election is, so that the Thessalonians must have been familiar with the concept. It evidently formed part of the original preaching. Notice that Paul expresses himself as quite certain of the election of the Thessalonians.[18]

---

[18] Rutherford is surely wrong when he renders "the circumstances of your election". εἰδότες is a causal participle depending on εὐχαριστοῦμεν (so Frame, *et al.*), and Paul is giving thanks because he knows their ἐκλογήν. It is not the circumstances of their election, but the fact of it that evokes his thanksgiving.

The doctrine of election has not received the attention its Biblical importance warrants in modern theological discussions, though H. H. Rowley's *The Biblical Doctrine of Election* (London, 1952), is a welcome reminder of its importance. Loraine Boettner discusses election in Ch. XI of *The Reformed Doctrine of Predestination* (Grand Rapids, 1948).

III. REMINISCENCES, 1:5–2:16

1. RESPONSE OF THE THESSALONIANS TO THE ORIGINAL PREACHING, 1:5–10

5 how that our gospel come not unto you in word only, but also in power, and in the Holy Spirit, and *in* much assurance; even as ye know what manner of men we showed ourselves toward you for your sake.

6 And ye became imitators of us, and of the Lord, having received the word in much affliction, with joy of the Holy Spirit;

7 so that ye became an ensample to all that believe in Macedonia and in Achaia.

8 For from you hath sounded forth the word of the Lord, not only in Macedonia and Achaia, but in every place your faith to God-ward is gone forth; so that we need not to speak anything.

9 For they themselves report concerning us what manner of entering in we had unto you; and how ye turned unto God from idols, to serve a living and true God,

10 and to wait for his Son from heaven, whom he raised from the dead, *even* Jesus, who delivereth us from the wrath to come.

5 Paul proceeds to give his reasons for knowing that the Thessalonians are elect (mg. "because" is to be preferred to the text "how that." Paul is showing how he knows the Thessalonians to be elect, not showing in what the election consisted). In v. 5 these reasons are chiefly subjective, relating to the experience of the preachers. In v. 6 he turns to the effects in the lives of the Thessalonians.

He goes back to the time when he and his companions had first preached the gospel[19] in Thessalonica. On occasion he can refer to "the gospel of God" (2:8, 9, etc.), stressing the divine origin of

---

19 εὐαγγέλιον directs attention to the content of the message as good tidings, whereas κήρυγμα would stress rather the message as something given to be proclaimed, like the tidings of a herald. When Paul says the gospel "came" he draws attention away from the messengers to the divine activity.

the message. "Our gospel" directs attention rather to the fact that
the preachers had made it their own. Only out of his own experience of salvation through the atoning work of the Savior can the
preacher deliver a message which rings true, and is really his own.

Sometimes Paul had had the experience of being forbidden by
the Spirit to preach at all (Acts 16:6 f.). Sometimes he had spoken
rather fearfully and haltingly (I Cor. 2:3). It is a reasonable conjecture that in some of his discussions with the Jews he had felt
that it was hopeless. But his experience in preaching at Thessalonica was different. There Paul had been conscious that the
power of God was at work. There the preaching had not been "in
word only." Words alone are empty rhetoric. More than that is
required to save men's souls. Paul makes three points about the
preaching.

First, the gospel "came . . . in power." The verb points to some
vital force in operation, and the noun completes the thought. In
many places we see evidence that the gospel is power, for God is in
it (cf. Rom. 1:16). It is not simply that the gospel tells of power,
though this, too, is true. But when the gospel is preached God is
there and God is working. The gospel *is* power. Sinful men do not
wish to be told how to be better. They do not even wish to be told
that Christ has died for them, unless there is a work of grace in
their hearts. But whenever the gospel is faithfully proclaimed,
there is power. Not simply exhortation, but power.

Now there are various kinds of power, and not all work for good.
The second point, then, is that this power is associated with the
Holy Spirit. This is no evil power deluding men with false
promises. It is the Holy Spirit of God, leading them into the
salvation God has prepared for them.

The third point is that the gospel came "in much assurance."
There is no repetition of the "in" in the Greek. The effect is to link
these words very closely with the foregoing. Assurance is not some
human device whereby men persuade themselves. Rather it is the
result of the activity of the Holy Spirit working within believers.
Some have felt that the assurance meant here is that which came
to the converts as they put their trust in Christ, and this may not be
out of the Apostle's mind. But his primary meaning is the assurance
that the Spirit gave to the preachers, for Paul is dealing with the
way he and his companions came to know the election of the
Thessalonians. They had the assurance in their own hearts that,

as they were preaching, the power of God was at work. The Spirit was working a work of grace.[20]

Paul appeals to what the Thessalonians knew of the original mission.[21] Several times he recalls to their minds the manner of life of the preachers. It must have made a profound impression on the mixed population of the city. Here is evidence of the power he has just been talking about. While many in modern times will feel hesitant about directing attention to their own lives, it yet remains true that no preacher can expect a hearing for his gospel unless it is bearing fruit in his own life.

6 "Ye" is emphatic. The certainty that the Thessalonians were among the elect did not rest solely on the experiences of the preachers. There had been dramatic changes in the lives of the converts, and attention is now turned to this. The word order, imitators "of us, and of the Lord," is startling. But a moment's reflection shows that this must be the historical order. The missionary must show the new way in his life as well as in his words.[22] His converts will begin by imitating him and go on to imitate his Master. Paul has no hesitation in saying to the Corinthians, "I beseech you therefore, be ye imitators of me" (I Cor. 4:16), and again, "Be ye imitators of me, even as I also am of Christ" (I Cor. 11:1). The great example for Christians is that of Christ. If they imitate their teachers it is in order that they may be brought to imitate Him more closely thereby.

This is further explained[23] as "having received the word in much affliction, with joy of the Holy Spirit." The word for "received" is that used for the reception of a guest (as in Luke 10:8, 10; Heb. 11:31), and it includes the thought of giving a welcome.

From the beginning there had been opposition to the word in Thessalonica. Thus Paul refers to the welcome the converts had given to it "in much affliction." The word for "affliction" outside the Bible usually denotes literal pressure, and that of a severe kind.

---

[20]   πληροφορία means "full assurance." There were no lingering doubts.

[21]   καθώς introduces an explanation or amplification of the preceding, cf. I Cor. 1:6, III John 3.

[22]   Cf. Bicknell, "In so far as they are truly Christian, they [i.e. missionaries] represent not simply Christ's teaching but Christ's life."

[23]   δεξάμενοι is probably to be taken "as a participle not of antecedent action, 'when you had welcomed,' but of identical action, 'in that you welcomed'" (Frame).

The corresponding verb, for example, was used of pressing the grapes in wine-making till they burst asunder, and so metaphorically came to mean very great trouble. In the New Testament the noun is generally used in the figurative sense we see here. It is not mild discomfort, but great and sore difficulty. The Jews who stirred up a riot against Paul (Acts 17:5) and followed him to Beroea (Acts 17:13) would not have left the new converts unmolested, and there was further opposition from the local pagans (I Thess. 2:14). There is every reason for thinking that the Thessalonian Christians had been sorely tried.

But their affliction was "with joy of the Holy Spirit." It is certain that the believer will experience tribulation (John 16:33), but it is equally certain that he will have an inner serenity, even a joy, which nothing in the world can give and nothing in the world can take away (John 16:22). Suffering is always unpleasant, but for those who have been saved through the sufferings of their Lord it has been transformed.[24] As Lightfoot says, "The degree in which the believer is allowed to participate in the sufferings of his Lord should be the measure of his joy," and he draws attention to Phil. 1:29 and I Pet. 4:13. Paul and Silas knew something of this joy (cf. Acts 16:25), and so did those who, in an earlier day, went out from the council, "rejoicing that they were counted worthy to suffer dishonor for the Name" (Acts 5:41). See also II Cor. 7:4, 8:2, etc.

This transformation of suffering does not come about by autosuggestion, or any other human device. It is specifically said to be "of the Holy Spirit." We are reminded that joy is part of the fruit of the Spirit (Gal. 5:22). It is a striking illustration of the way in which the whole of a man's values are transformed by the power of God's Holy Spirit when he enters into the salvation bought for him at the price of the blood of the Son.

7 But the imitators in their turn were imitated[25] and that

---

[24] Dewailly and Rigaux make the point that sufferings, for the Christian, stimulate rather than diminish hope: "Tribulations, those of Acts 17:1-9 and those which followed, associate Paul and the Christians (3:3 f., 7) with the sufferings of Christ, and are the measure of their future rest (II Thess. 1:7); thus they stimulate hope rather than diminish it (Rom. 5:3-5, etc.)."

[25] On ὥστε γενέσθαι Milligan comments: "The inf. introduced by ὥστε is here consecutive, and points to a result actually reached and not merely contemplated ... this result being further viewed in its direct dependence

widely. Paul speaks of this with satisfaction. His word for "en-sample" is *tupos*, from which we get our word "type." Originally it denoted the mark left by a blow. There is an example of this in John 20:25, where it is translated "print." Then it came to be used of a figure stamped by a blow, like the design stamped on a coin. From that it came to denote any image, whether stamped or not (as in Acts 7:43), and then a pattern (Acts 7:44, Heb. 8:5). Next we find the ethical sense of a pattern of conduct, occasionally of a pattern to be avoided (I Cor. 10:6), but more usually, as here, of an example to be followed (Titus 2:7, I Pet. 5:3, etc.).[26] In the present passage the word is used in the singular. Paul is speaking of the church as a pattern community, rather than of the individuals comprising it as so many individual patterns.

They are an example "to all that believe in Macedonia and in Achaia." It is easy to pass over the significance of "all that be-lieve." Nowadays great stress is placed on good works of various kinds, especially on social service. Often the essence of Christianity is held to be in such things. Apostolic Christianity was in no danger of confusing the root with the fruit in this way. Thus throughout the New Testament the characteristic mark of the Christian is his faith—his dependence on Christ alone for all things. Naturally and unobtrusively Christians are referred to simply as "believers."

8 The measure of Paul's satisfaction with the progress of the Thessalonian church is the praise he here bestows on them. This is the only time he speaks of a church as a pattern to others, and he specifically makes the point that they are a pattern to other be-lievers. He is not simply contrasting them with pagans who know not the power of God. He begins by speaking of them as examples to Christians in Macedonia and Achaia, the two provinces into which Greece had been divided since 142 B.C.[27] Then he goes on to speak of the way the word of God has gone out from them into

---

upon the previously-mentioned clause." Where ὥστε is followed by the indicative the actuality of the result is stressed, but not its connection with the preceding.

[26] A further use of the word is found in Rom. 5:14, where Adam is spoken of as a "type" or "figure" of Christ.

[27] According to the best MSS both Μακεδονίᾳ and 'Αχαΐᾳ have the article in v. 7, so that they are considered in their separateness. Their being linked under one article in v. 8 points to the totality, all Greece.

every place. This reflects something of the strategic situation of Thessalonica, on the great highway, the Via Egnatia, and with a harbor giving ready access to many places by sea. Paul himself would know what was going on in Achaia, and Priscilla and Aquila had just come to Corinth from Rome (Acts 18:2), doubtless bringing news of what was reported there. There is thus solid basis for Paul's way of putting it.

He speaks of "the word of the Lord"[28] as sounding forth[29] from them. Throughout this Epistle he several times comes back to the thought that the gospel is in very deed the word of God to man. He does not hesitate to use the strongest of terms to indicate this. It is of the utmost importance that this part of his thought be grasped. If men think of the gospel only as another philosophy, as the result of the reflection of certain, admittedly profound, first-century thinkers on religious topics, they will never have the burning zeal which sent the first Christian preachers through the world to proclaim what God had done for man. It is because it is indeed "the word of the Lord" that has been committed to us, that we can and must present it without apology or amendment.

9 The effect of the faithful proclamation of the word by the Thessalonians was that Paul found it unnecessary to say anything about his mission to that city. Wherever he went, people of their own accord kept telling (continuous present) him of what had happened there.[30] In particular, they kept rehearsing the evidence of the conversion of the Thessalonians. It seems very probable that we have here an example of the common terminology among the early Christians for the success of a mission, for there is very little that is specifically Pauline about it. It is hard, for example, to

---

[28] ὁ λόγος τοῦ Κυρίου is found in Paul only here and in II Thess. 3:1, though it occurs in Acts, and similar expressions are frequent in Paul. It is, of course, common in the Old Testament. The genitive is subjective—"the word which comes from the Lord," rather than "the word which tells of the Lord."

[29] The verb ἐξήχηται is found only here in the New Testament. It is a vivid word, and expositors from Chrysostom on have often thought the imagery to have been derived from the sounding out of a trumpet, though some prefer to think of the rolling of thunder. Either way there is nothing apologetic about it! The perfect denotes the continuing activity, as does the use of ἐν rather than εἰς (though this cannot be pressed). The word is pictured as still sounding forth.

[30] The αὐτοί of v. 9 is in contrast to the ἡμᾶς of v. 8. It is not Paul and his companions who are spreading abroad the news about the Thessalonians.

imagine that Paul would give an account in his own words of people entering into a genuine Christian experience with no mention of their being justified by faith, and without any reference to the cross. It may fairly be said that these things are implied. But the point is that they are not expressed, and we think that Paul is likely to have expressed them. But if he is taking certain terms from the accepted missionary vocabulary[31] then the situation is explained.[32]

He makes three points. The first, "ye turned unto God[33] from idols."[34] Becoming a Christian involves a very definite break with non-Christian habits. Whatever our previous background has been there must be a turning from our idols. The act of conversion involves a change of direction of the will. There is a decisive happening, a re-orientation of the whole of life. This is so in every age, but especially was it true of Christians in the Greek world of the first century A.D. There is a sense in which the Greek as well as the Jew prepared the way for the coming of the gospel.[35] But the most characteristic thing was not the continuity, but the decisive

---

[31] Yet F. F. Bruce points out, with reference to the account in Acts 14:15 ff. of Paul's words to the men of Lystra, "his [namely, Paul's] description of the Thessalonians' conversion from paganism in 1 Thess. 1:9 f. presupposes preaching very similar to that given here at Lystra" (*New International Commentary on the Book of the Acts* [Grand Rapids, 1954], p. 293).

[32] εἴσοδον, rendered "entering in," is an unusual word in this connection. It may mean "the act of entering" (as Acts 13:24, see mg.), or "the means of entering" (II Pet. 1:11). The former would seem to be the meaning here, and perhaps "visit" would give the sense of it. "Welcome" (RSV, Rutherford) is not quite right (RSV renders the same word "visit" in 2:1). Though the expression is unusual, Deissmann is able to cite a parallel from a Latin letter of the second century A.D. (LAE, p. 198).

[33] Milligan thinks that, in the previous verse, "the definite τὸν Θεόν emphasizes 'the God' towards whom the Thessalonians' faith is directed in contrast with their previous attitude towards τὰ εἴδωλα." We need not doubt that there is such a contrast, but it is the general structure of the sentence that gives it and not simply the use of the article. The article is lacking in a similar passage in Gal. 4:8, and in any case Paul more often uses the article with Θεός than not. In this Epistle it has the article 27 times, and is without it 9 times.

[34] Neil has a pertinent comment on idol worship. "When we are inclined to stress the beauty and symbolism of paganism, and shed a tear over the shattered statues of the Acropolis or the Forum, we should remember that Paul condemned the whole system, root and branch—and he was there, and we were not .... The idols that moulded life were not the austere images of Pallas Athene and Apollo, but the obscene figures that desecrated public and private altars."

[35] Cf. the title of the book by G. H. C. McGregor and A. C. Purdy, *Jew and Greek: Tutors Unto Christ* (London, 1937).

break. As F. V. Filson reminds us, "In government, religion, business, amusement, labor, and social clubs the pagan world was built on the pattern of polytheism." But "the attitude of Apostolic Christianity to the polytheistic world was one of militant hostility."[36] There was no attempt to find a place for Christ in the polytheistic milieu. Such an idea was preposterous. No matter how greatly their habitual practices had to be changed, the Christians of the first century saw that there could be no place for an idol alongside Christ.

But becoming a Christian is not a negative thing as many caricatures of Christianity suppose. The second point is that the Thessalonians turned "to serve[37] a living and true God." The absence of the article with "God" does not indicate that Paul left open the possibility of the existence of other gods. His adjectives give emphatic expression to his monotheism. Rather, the form without the article puts the stress on the nature rather than the person of God. The converts had come to serve One whose nature it is to be God living and true. "Living" means not only alive, but active, as we see from Acts 14:15. It contrasts sharply with dead idols, "gods" who can do nothing (Ps. 96:5, 115:4 ff.). The living God orders all things both in heaven and on earth.

There is more than one word in Greek for "true" and that used here has a meaning like "genuine." Its opposite is not so much "false" as "unreal." Moffatt says it is " 'real' as opposed to false in the sense of 'counterfeit.' " Paul is affirming that the converts had begun to worship a real God in contrast to the shadowy and unreal beings which had previously claimed their allegiance.

10 The third point in their conversion is that they had come "to wait for his Son from heaven."[38] The word for "to wait" is found only here in the New Testament, and Grimm–Thayer

---

[36] *The New Testament Against Its Environment* (London, 1950), p. 30, and cf. n. 51.

[37] δουλεύω means "to serve as a slave," and indicates the completeness of the Christian's surrender to God. Paul often uses the metaphor of slavery to describe the Christian's service, though usually he speaks of being a slave to Christ (Rom. 1:1, and elsewhere). The word, according to Milligan, is not used in pagan literature in a religious sense.

[38] Some have seen in the plural οὐρανῶν a reference to the plurality of the heavens, as in the Rabbis and in II Cor. 12:2. However, singular and plural seem to be used in the New Testament without perceptible difference of meaning, and it would be unwise to press the plural here.

suggest that in addition to the thought of awaiting someone expected, it includes "the added notion of patience and trust." Findlay thinks it implies "*sustained* expectation" (CGT). The prominence given to the second coming is in sharp contrast to so much that calls itself Christianity in modern times. This doctrine is mentioned most frequently of all in the New Testament, there being, so I am told, a reference to it on the average once every thirteen verses from Matthew right through to Revelation. Its neglect in many quarters is something which cannot be countenanced from Scripture.

In this verse the stress is on the second coming, and it is all the more interesting to see the Son referred to as Him "whom he raised from the dead." Both before and after this are eschatological references. But the resurrection had caught the imagination of the first-century preachers. It was natural for them to think of Jesus as the One whom the Father had raised. We might notice also that this is the way the New Testament usually puts it, the raising being directly attributed to the activity of the Father.

The chapter concludes with the reminder that the deliverance effected by Jesus is one with permanent significance. The participle "delivereth" is a timeless present, much as though Jesus were being called "the Deliverer." Deliverance is from "the wrath to come." The idea of God's wrath is unwelcome to many moderns, and determined attempts are made to get rid of the whole idea. It is sometimes said that it has no foundation in the Old Testament, the prophets and psalmists being concerned only to point out that when men sin disaster inevitably follows. God's direct intervention is not stressed, so that a more or less impersonal process is being described. Such an attitude can be maintained only by neglecting a great number of important Old Testament passages. The prophets and the psalmists know nothing of an impersonal process of retribution. They see the hand of God everywhere, in the punishment of the wicked as well as in the rewarding of the good.

So is it in the New Testament. The fact that we sometimes come across expressions like "the wrath" (without express mention of God) should not blind us to the fact that in the thought of the New Testament writers there is no place for an impersonal agency which can act in independence of God, for "all things are of God" (II Cor. 5:18 and cf. Acts 17:28, I Cor. 8:6). But in any case the wrath is explicitly linked with God many times, e.g. John 3:36;

Rom. 1:18; 9:22; Eph. 5:6; Col. 3:6; Rev. 11:18; 19:15; 14:10, 19. There is also the singular difficulty of doing without the idea of the wrath of God. Are we to think of God as not caring about sin? Or not caring enough to act? Or, if we are asked to think of an impersonal activity of retribution, what is the meaning of such a thing in a genuinely theistic universe? To say that God has made man and his environment in such a way that, when man sins, inevitable consequences follow, means that God is responsible when these consequences do follow. It is not really possible to be rid of the idea of the divine wrath without sacrificing a very great deal that is important in our understanding of the ways of God, and the nature of God.

This is not to deny that wrath must be carefully understood. The wrath of God is no vindictive passion, and it does not imply lack of control, as in human wrath. But whenever we apply any term to God, even love, we must make the mental reservation: without the imperfections that characterize the human. Who can think that that puny thing that human love is at its best really gives us a picture of God's mighty love? But we have no hesitation in applying the term "love" to His activity. So with wrath. God's wrath is without the imperfections that seem bound up with the purest of righteous indignation among men. But it gives strong expression to the active opposition of a holy God for all that is evil. We cannot do without this conception.[39]

Paul speaks of "the wrath to come," which brings before us the eschatological wrath. The wrath of God is not only something which we see here and now. It will endure to the end of all things. It will be especially manifested in the end of all things. It is inevitable, a thought conveyed by the present participle—it is even now coming.[40]

---

[39] See further the discussion in Chs. IV and V of my *The Apostolic Preaching of the Cross* (London and Grand Rapids, 1955). The idea that wrath is not to be taken as describing God's attitude to men has been vigorously argued by C. H. Dodd in, for example, *The Bible and the Greeks* (London, 1935), and in his Moffatt Commentary on Romans 1:18. See further R. V. G. Tasker, *The Biblical Doctrine of the Wrath of God* (London, 1951); the Addendum in P. T. Forsyth, *The Work of Christ* (London, 1948); and the article on ὀργή in TWNT.

[40] Moffatt comments on this verse: "In preaching to pagans, the leaders of the primitive Christian mission put the wrath and judgment of God in the forefront ... making a sharp appeal to the moral sense, and denouncing idolatry .... Hence the revival they set on foot. They sought to set pagans straight, and to keep them straight, by means of moral fear as well as of hope."

COMMENTARY ON I THESSALONIANS

2. THE PREACHING OF THE GOSPEL AT THESSALONICA, 2:1–16

a. *The Purity of the Preachers' Motives, 2:1–6a*

1 For yourselves, brethren, know our entering in unto you, that it hath not been found vain:
2 but having suffered before and been shamefully treated, as ye know, at Philippi, we waxed bold in our God to speak unto you the gospel of God in much conflict.
3 For our exhortation *is* not of error, nor of uncleanness, nor in guile:
4 but even as we have been approved of God to be intrusted with the gospel, so we speak; not as pleasing men, but God who proveth our hearts.
5 For neither at any time were we found using words of flattery, as ye know, nor a cloak of covetousness, God is witness;
6 nor seeking glory of men, neither from you nor from others,

1 "For" usually links what follows with what immediately precedes, but on this occasion it goes back in thought to 1:9[1] (cf. the repetition of the unusual word rendered "entering in").[2] In 1:9 Paul cited outsiders as witnesses. Now he says that the Thessalonians needed no other to bear witness, for they themselves knew what had happened. "Yourselves" is emphatic, as is brought out by Rutherford's translation, "You at any rate have no need to be told."

This calling of the Thessalonians to witness was a masterly

---

[1] γάρ here is used in an unusual way. Milligan thinks it almost equivalent to "however," though he cites no parallels. A better position is that of Lightfoot: "the explanation of γάρ is to be sought rather in the train of thought which was moving in the Apostle's mind, than in the actual expressions: 'I speak thus boldly and confidently as to my preaching, *for* I have such a witness at hand. You *yourselves* know, etc.'" Grimm–Thayer deny that such an ellipse is ever found, but Liddell and Scott give it as an established usage.

[2] For "entering in" see n. 32 on p. 62.

67

defense. It is clear that Paul had been accused of insincerity. His enemies said that he was more concerned to make money out of his converts than to present true teaching. The accusation would be made easier in virtue of the well-known fact that itinerant preachers concerned only to feather their own nests were common in those days.[3] Paul was being represented as nothing more than another of this class of preaching vagrants. Paul's emphatic calling of the Thessalonians to witness did two things. In the first place it showed his confidence in them. He had no fear that they would succumb to the propaganda being put before them. In the second place it demonstrated that all the facts required for his vindication were facts of common knowledge. Neither Paul nor the Thessalonians had need to search for material to prove his *bona fides*. An accusation of insincerity could hardly stand in the light of such public knowledge of the man and his work.

There is some difference of opinion as to what is meant by the word rendered "vain." Some understand it to mean "fruitless" (cf. Way, "barren of results"), but this is denied by Milligan and Lightfoot, who understand it to refer rather to the character of the preaching. Hendriksen thinks of it as having the same sort of meaning as in Mark 12:3, and as signifying that Paul did not come to them empty-handed, but with something to give them. Frame's point of view is similar.

Against the first suggestion is the fact that the meaning of the word is rather "empty" than "ineffective." Against the last that it is the "entering in" rather than the preachers which is thus described. Our best understanding, then, is something like: "hollow, empty, wanting in purpose and earnestness" (Lightfoot). Paul is affirming as a well-known fact the purposeful manner of the visit.[4]

---

[3] "There has probably never been such a variety of religious cults and philosophic systems as in Paul's day. East and West had united and intermingled to produce an amalgam of real piety, high moral principles, crude superstition and gross license. Oriental mysteries, Greek philosophy, and local godlings competed for favour under the tolerant aegis of Roman indifference. 'Holy Men' of all creeds and countries, popular philosophers, magicians, astrologers, crack-pots, and cranks; the sincere and the spurious, the righteous and the rogue, swindlers and saints, jostled and clamoured for the attention of the credulous and the sceptical" (Neil, on v.3). Cf. also Dibelius, cited in n. 9 on p. 21.

[4] The lasting results achieved may also be indicated by the verb γέγονεν on which Frame remarks that it "denotes completed action; the facts of the visit are all in, and the readers may estimate it at its full value." Similarly

2 He had come from Philippi after being badly treated there. He had undergone physical hardship ("suffered before"), and to that had been added grievous insult ("been shamefully treated"). Acts 16 tells us that the physical suffering included flogging, and the placing of the feet in the stocks. On that occasion, when it had been suggested that the jailor should simply free Paul and Silas, the great Apostle had refused to leave until the praetors themselves had come to make amends for their treatment of Roman citizens. In his insistence on upholding the dignity of Roman citizenship we see something of the deep hurt that Paul had experienced in the indignities which had been heaped on him. So now, as he recalls those days, he uses a word which evokes memories of the insolence of those who had ill-treated him. The same verb is employed in Acts 14:5.

Time-servers would have been discouraged by such treatment. Not so the little band of preachers. They had come from this treatment at Philippi and had preached with boldness. The verb rendered "waxed bold" is full of interest. It comes from two words meaning literally "all speech." It denotes the state of mind when the words flow freely, the attitude of feeling quite at home with no sense of stress or strain. This attitude includes both boldness and confidence. The noun corresponding to the verb is sometimes rendered one way, sometimes the other. When it is used in the New Testament the verb always has to do with the proclamation of the gospel. The boldness and confidence it denotes are not natural attributes. Paul speaks of waxing bold "in our God." Because he lived "in" his God he was always at home, no matter what the outward circumstances, and thus always had that attitude of ready speech we have been thinking of. It was because he lived and moved in God (cf. Acts 17:28) that no hardship and no opposition was able to take away Paul's confidence and his courage (cf. II Cor. 4:7).

He proceeds to designate the message that had been proclaimed, "the gospel of God." There are occasions when it is proper to speak of the gospel as the gospel of men (Paul does this, e.g., in 1:5). Unless the gospel has been appropriated and so taken within a man that it is completely his own he cannot proclaim it with conviction. But from another point of view the gospel is not man's at all. It

---

Findlay thinks it "implies *a settled result* . . . their work has proved thoroughly successful. Its fruit is permanent" (CBSC).

does not take its origin in man, but in God. It originates in God and it tells about God and it invites men to take God's way of salvation. Accordingly, when Paul speaks of "the gospel of God" he turns men's thoughts away from anything of human contrivance to God's perfect way. This thought is one which he develops with power in this chapter, and he uses the phrase "the gospel of God" again and again (vv. 8 f., and cf. v. 13).

The opposition at Philippi of which Paul has spoken in the first part of the verse did not cease when he came to Thessalonica. There, too, as he preached it was "in much conflict." The word "conflict" is a vivid one. It is part of the vocabulary of athletics, where it means a contest or race. It is that from which we derive our word "agony." It denotes not a token opposition, a tepid struggle, but a very real battle.[5] It is used in I Tim. 6:12, II Tim. 4:7, of fighting the good fight of faith, and that is no half-hearted fight. The use of the word here reminds the Thessalonians that the opposition which Paul had met was intense, and his preaching had not been easy. How, in the face of this, could it be urged that he had only preached for what he could get out of it?

3 The accusation that Paul was no better than the usual run of wandering preachers clearly underlies his defense of his position in this verse. The noun rendered "exhortation" has the original meaning of "a calling to one's side," that is, to help. It acquires other meanings like entreaty, exhortation, encouragement (it is cognate with the word rendered "Comforter" in John 14:16, etc.). Here it means "appeal." It is the outward approach (whereas "the gospel of God" of the previous verse stresses the content of the message). Their appeal, says Paul, did not have its origin in "error." The word so translated sometimes means "deceit" (hence the rendering in AV), but in the New Testament it always seems to have the passive meaning, "error." Paul had been accused of being completely mistaken in his preaching.

---

[5] RSV renders "in the face of great opposition," but the word goes beyond opposition and denotes actual strife. Phillips' "whatever the opposition might be," obscures the fact that the conflict was actual, not potential. Moffatt, "in spite of all the strain," points us to an inward state, which Frame takes as highly possible. (Knox renders, "With great earnestness," but this seems wide of the mark.) The word ἀγών did tend in later Greek to mean a state of mind, but in this context the reference seems rather to outward opposition than to inward stress.

The second accusation was more serious. "Uncleanness" denotes moral impurity.[6] The charge is startling to modern ears, but it must always be borne in mind in interpreting early documents that sexual impurity was a regular feature of many of the cults of antiquity, especially those from the East. Ritual prostitution was carried on in connection with many temples, the idea being apparently that one effected union with the god by union with one of his "consecrated ones." The Jews frequently brought the accusation of immorality against the Christians.[7] It had apparently been suggested that Paul and his companions had been associated with such practices, and the charge is repelled decisively.

The third accusation is that of using trickery.[8] The word rendered "guile" originally had reference to catching fish by means of a bait. From this it was used of any piece of cunning. The wandering sophists and jugglers resorted to all manner of devices to attract people and so get their money. Not so the preachers. They had not endeavored to ensnare their hearers.

4 Over against each of the points in the last verse comes its refutation. Paul's preaching could not have proceeded from error, for he was entrusted by God with the message. He was not impure, for he had been approved by God. He was not a trickster, for he aimed at pleasing God, not men.

The word translated "approved" basically means "to test." At

---

[6] Hendriksen rejects this meaning in favor of avarice or the seeking or honor, as does Denney. However, neither cites examples of the word used in this sense, and only strong evidence would allow such a meaning to a word with the basic sense of "uncleanness". In Rom. 1:24 it seems much the same as a dishonoring of the body; in Gal. 5:19 and II Cor. 12:21 it is linked with fornication and lasciviousness; in Eph. 4:19 and 5:3, although πλεονεξία is joined with it, the context deals with impurity, and it is this the word seems to denote. It occurs in other passages where the context does not establish the meaning, but impurity fits them all. Frame says that ἀκαθαρσία "regularly appears directly with πορνεία or in contexts intimating sexual aberration." Findlay is impressed by the fact that Paul is not elsewhere charged with *fleshly* impurity. He argues for "uncleanness *of spirit*," and says that in classical Greek the word denotes "moral *foulness, dirty ways,* of any sort" (CGT).

[7] Such accusations, as the church grew, became part of the stock-in-trade of its enemies. See, for example, H. B. Workman, *Persecution in the Early Church* (London, 1906), pp. 157 ff. The Apologists continually refuted such slanders.

[8] The change in preposition from ἐκ with πλάνης and ἀκαθαρσίας to ἐν with δόλῳ switches the attention from origin to atmosphere. The appeal did not spring from error or from sexual depravity, nor was it conducted in an atmosphere of trickery.

the end of this very verse it is used in that sense ("proveth"). Moffatt, by translating "attested . . . tests," retains something of the word play of the original, as does ARV. But "to test" readily passes over to "to approve by test." Milligan points out that there is a technical use of the word: "to describe the passing as fit for election to a public office." In the New Testament it is often used in this way of approving.[9] The gospel is something of divine origin, and no man may take it upon himself to proclaim it. God chooses His messengers, and He tests them out before committing the gospel to their trust.[10] The verb is in the perfect tense, signifying not only a past approval, but a continuing one. "We stand approved" is the sense of it. It is out of this context that Paul and his companions habitually speak (continuous present).[11]

This is further brought out by an emphatic disclaimer of any attempt to please men. The verb rendered "please" broadened in late Greek into the idea of actual service. Moulton–Milligan can say: "For the idea of *service* in the interests of others which underlies several of the NT occurrences of this verb (I Th. 2^5 . . .), we may compare its use in monumental inscriptions to describe those who have proved themselves of use to the commonwealth." There is something of this meaning here. Paul, in fact, might serve men. But he never served with the aim simply of pleasing them. If he served men it was in the spirit of "ourselves as your servants for Jesus' sake" (II Cor. 4:5). So now his aim is given as rendering that service which would be well pleasing to God.

That this could not rest in merely outward deeds, but was concerned with inward motives, underlies the reminder that God tests men's hearts. We are apt to misunderstand references to the heart in the Scriptures, for we are fond of using the term to denote the affections. But the affections in ancient times were thought of as

---

[9] In the New Testament the implication, when the test is applied, seems to be that it will be surmounted successfully. By contrast πειράζω, which also means "to test," looks for a failure, and so the meaning passes over into "to tempt."

[10] The verb πιστευθῆναι rendered, "to be intrusted," reminds Deissmann of the Imperial Secretary for Greek correspondence, known as ὁ τὰς ῾Ελληνικὰς ἐπιστολὰς πράττειν πεπιστευμένος or τάξιν ἐπὶ τῶν ῾Ελληνικῶν ἐπιστολῶν πεπιστευμένος (LAE, p. 374). If we can think that Paul was glancing at such an exalted official we have another indication of the dignity of his office as preacher of the gospel.

[11] οὕτως answers to the preceding καθώς and is not the antecedent to the following ὡς.

located in the intestines (cf. "bowels of compassion"). The heart, even though occasionally it might be used in a sense not far removed from our own, stood for the whole of the inner life, comprising thought and will as well as emotions. Here the meaning is that God searches out the whole of our inner life. Nothing is hidden from Him.

In passing we might note that the plural, "our hearts," is unlikely to be an editorial plural. It associates Silas and Timothy closely with Paul in this great affirmation.

5 The "for" which begins this verse takes up the "for" of v. 3. What was true of the conduct of the Christian preachers in general was true of them at Thessalonica. "Neither at any time" covers the whole period. No room is left for exceptions.

Paul goes on to disclaim three specific defects. By inserting "as ye know" he calls the Thessalonians to witness to the truth of what he says. First of all he deals with "words of flattery." A literal translation of what he says here might run: "neither have we come to be in a word of flattery." The verb is one with a wide range of meaning. In this particular construction it seems to mean to enter whatever state is spoken of and stay in it (as in Rom. 16:7 of coming to be "in Christ," or in I Tim. 2:14 of Eve entering "into transgression").[12] He denies, then, that he and his companions had made flattery their method. "Flattery," though, is not quite the meaning. We can use this English term of remarks which, though insincere, are directed to the pleasure of the person being flattered. The Greek term has rather the idea of using fair words as a means of gaining one's own ends. It is a matter of using insincerity as an instrument of policy, as a means of persuading another to do one's will.

The second charge refuted also contains the idea of insincerity. The term "cloak" denotes a specious pretext which conceals the real motive. It is used of putting forward something that is plausible, and which might well be true in itself, but which is not the real reason for doing whatever deed is referred to. So here Paul denies that evangelism had been simply a cover for an underlying

---

12 The construction is γίνομαι ἐν. It indicates that the state entered was continuous, but not necessarily permanent. It is used of the incarnation in Phil. 2:7. Other examples are to be found in I Cor. 2:3, II Cor. 3:7.

covetousness. This latter term denotes more than love of money.[13]
It is derived from two words meaning "to have" and "more." It
signifies an eager desire for what one does not have. It is self-
interest in the widest sense (cf. Moffatt, "self-seeking"). It is
sometimes associated with impurity (Eph. 4:19, where it is translated "greediness," cf. Eph. 5:3), for in such sexual relations there
is the gratification of one's own lusts with a disregard for the rights
of others. It often signifies desire for material possessions (Luke
12:15). Basically it is idolatry (Col. 3:5), for it exalts self to the
highest position. It regards self with a veneration that amounts to
worship. A few verses further on Paul is to affirm that he and his
companions had given themselves unstintingly for the Thessalonians. Here he puts the negative side of it. They had had no selfish
motives in their mission.

It is worth stopping to reflect that this covetousness almost
invariably comes with a cloak. We never admit to covetousness.
Some specious reason can always be found to cloak our real
motive even from ourselves. We are warned to be rigorous in our
self-examination.

In the first part of this verse Paul denies using flattery and calls
the Thessalonians to witness that what he says is true. In the
second he avows the purity of his motives and invokes God as
witness. There can be no mistaking the intense seriousness with
which he writes, nor the depth of his conviction that the methods
and motives of the preachers would bear the closest scrutiny.

6ᵃ The third point Paul makes is that he and his associates
had not sought the esteem of men, whether of the Thessalonians
or of any others.[14] He has already said something very like this
in v. 4. There his point was that they did not pursue ends that
would have the approval of men. Here he claims that they did
not seek praise for themselves. The emphasis is rather on the
inner state of the preachers. "Glory" stands for the expression of
esteem, i.e. praise. The preachers did not look for this sort of

---

[13] Lightfoot on Col. 3:5 defines πλεονεξία as "greediness" or "entire
disregard for the rights of others." Milligan distinguishes the word from
φιλαργυρία "as the wider and more active sin."
[14] There is possibly no significance in the change of preposition from ἐξ
with ἀνθρώπων to ἀπό with ὑμῶν and ἄλλων, for the two are often used interchangeably in Hellenistic Greek. But if there is a difference ἐκ denotes the
ultimate source, and ἀπό rather the intermediate agent.

thing. They may well have received it, as they certainly deserved it, but Paul's point is that they did not seek it. Their motives were pure.[15]

b. The Preachers' Refusal to Accept Maintenance, 2:6b–9

when we might have claimed authority as apostles of Christ.

7 But we were gentle in the midst of you, as when a nurse cherisheth her own children:

8 even so, being affectionately desirous of you, we were well pleased to impart unto you, not the gospel of God only, but also our own souls, because ye were become very dear to us.

9 For ye remember, brethren, our labor and travail: working night and day, that we might not burden any of you, we preached unto you the gospel of God.

6b In the middle of his sentence Paul passes over to his next topic. He is concerned in the next three verses with the fact that the little band of evangelists had steadfastly refused to claim maintenance from those to whom they had preached. The line of argument is: that should show plainly enough that they had not been seeking to make money.

"We might have claimed authority" is the translation of a Greek expression which is patient of more than one meaning.[16] The noun means "weight," "burden," and AV can render "we might have been burdensome." The meaning appears to be that they, being apostles of Christ, had every right to be maintained by those to whom they preached. Paul frequently uses words cognate with that used here to denote this right to maintenance (e.g., v. 9, II Thess. 3:8, II Cor. 11:9, 12:16). It is a strong point with him that preachers have this right, even though he himself frequently forbore to exercise it.

But, of course, the meaning "weight" readily passes over into that of "importance." The word is quite often used in this sense (though not, apparently, in the New Testament; II Cor. 4:17 is the

---

[15] The change of connective from οὐδέ which links the members in v. 4 to οὔτε here may point to the qualities mentioned here as being more closely linked to each other than those in the earlier verse.

[16] The expression is ἐν βάρει εἶναι.

75

nearest approach). Nevertheless there are many who think this to be the meaning here. It would be quite in the Pauline manner to use the word with a hint at both meanings. But if he does this the primary emphasis seems to be on "burden," and thus the right to maintenance.[17]

He speaks of "apostles of Christ." We read of the appointment of the apostles in Mark 3:14 f. where Jesus chose twelve, "that they might be with him, and that he might send them forth to preach, and to have authority to cast out demons." This gives us the primary function of the apostles. They were to preach in Christ's name and perform certain miracles. After Judas fell the early church took steps to see that his place was filled. But they neither selected nor commissioned Matthias. They recognized that God had already chosen a successor (Acts 1:24), and when, in answer to their prayer, God showed who the new apostle was, they simply numbered him with the eleven (Acts 1:26). In the same strain Paul stressed that his apostolate was not of human origin (Gal. 1:1).

In the providence of God apostles were used to establish churches. Inevitably they became the leaders in the Christian church, and their prestige was great. In modern times many have inferred that they were the source of all authority to minister in the church, so that only those ministries which can claim direct descent from the apostles (those in the "Apostolic Succession") are to be thought of as valid. There is much that could be said about this,[18] but we content ourselves with noticing that this is a function which the New Testament does not ascribe to the apostles. In the words of Christ, as we have seen, the primary functions are preaching and healing, and these remain primary throughout the New Testament.

7 There is a first-class textual problem in this verse, namely

---

[17] Frame, though he thinks the meaning is likely to be "to be in honour," quotes a letter written to him by Dr. Milligan in which he says he "is inclined to think the more literal idea of 'burden,' 'trouble' was certainly uppermost in the Apostle's thought and that the derived sense of 'gravitas,' 'honour' was not prominent, if it existed at all."

[18] The literature on the subject is vast. For an important advocacy of the view that the essence of ministry is to be found in the Apostolic Succession see K. E. Kirk (ed.), *The Apostolic Ministry* (London, 1946). For the opposing point of view, S. Neil (ed.), *The Ministry of the Church* (London, 1947), and T. W. Manson, *The Church's Ministry* (London, 1948). There are some valuable observations on the apostolate in A. Kuyper, *The Work of the Holy Spirit* (Grand Rapids, 1946), pp. 139 ff.

whether we should read "gentle" or "babes."[19] The two words in the Greek are very similar, there being only this difference that "babes" begins with an "n" and "gentle" does not. As the preceding word ends with this letter it would have been very easy for a scribe to have misread the text, whichever was original. All the more so would this have been the case as there were no breaks between words in early manuscripts. Transcriptional probability then, does not help us here.

The oldest and best manuscripts usually read "babes." But against this it is urged that this involves an intolerable mixing of the metaphors, for Paul would be comparing himself to a nurse and a babe in the same sentence. Moreover, Paul generally uses "babe" in a derogatory sense as indicating a failure to develop (cf. Gal. 4:3, I Cor. 13:11). The case against "babes" proceeds that this word for "gentle" is rather rare, being found in the New Testament elsewhere only in I Tim. 2:24. Remembering the tendency of scribes to replace less usual forms by more usual ones, it is conjectured that "gentle" stood in the original text.

These arguments are not decisive. Taking the last point first, we have already seen that the alteration need not have been intentional, probably was not. There is often confusion between the two words, and, for example, some manuscripts read "babes" in I Tim. 2:24, and some read "gentle" in Eph. 4:14. The mistake, in whichever direction it lay, is best understood as accidental. Again, the derogatory meaning often attaching to babes in Paul's letters proves little, for when it suited him he could use "babes" in a good sense (I Cor. 14:20). The mixture of metaphors is not very significant either, for Paul does this quite often.[20] In this very chapter he compares himself to a father (v. 11) and to an orphan (v. 17 where "being bereaved" = "being orphaned"). Then there are some grammatical points, such as the fact that a noun would be more natural after "apostles" of the previous verse. So, too, the phrase "in the midst of you" would in Greek be more natural after "babes" than after "gentle." These points do not prove much, for Paul could be impatient of grammatical niceties. But for what they are worth we cite them. Finally, there is what Westcott and Hort have put so forcefully, "the change from the bold image to the

---

[19] ἤπιοι or νήπιοι.

[20] Lightfoot cites a number of examples of this and he does not include a building growing (Eph. 2:21), and a body being built (Eph. 4:12).

tame and facile adjective" which is "characteristic of the difference between St. Paul and the Syrian revisers."[21]

When the arguments are so nicely balanced it is not possible to be absolutely sure of the original text. But the balance of probability seems to favor "babes," and we adopt this reading. The meaning of it will then be that the apostles became as simple as possible, as simple as babes as they preached. It is a strong expression for the extreme lengths to which they went to meet the needs of the hearers.[22]

Paul speaks of being "in the midst of you" and not simply "among you."[23] There may be no significance in this, but the expression used would more naturally indicate the taking of a place of equality than would the other. It is of interest that the Lord Jesus used the same expression in Luke 22:27, "I am in the midst of you as he that serveth." There also the thought is of a condescension to the level of others.

Paul compares his behavior to that of a nurse among children.[24] ARV reads "cherisheth her own children," and "own" is probably correct.[25] A nurse in such a position could be relied upon to give the children the most tender care,[26] and this Paul claims to have done for the Thessalonians. So far from trying to make gain of

---

[21] "Notes on Select Readings," p. 128 (Appendix to *The New Testament in the Original Greek*, Introduction, [London, 1907]).

[22] Findlay cites Origen's comment, λαλοῦσα λόγους ὡς παιδίον διὰ τὸ παιδίον, and that of Augustine, *delectat . . . decurtata et mutilata verba inmurmurare*. He adds, "But this is only a single trait of the picture: the nurse-*mother (θάλπει τὰ ἑαυτῆς τέκνα)* is child-like with her children—as far from selfish craft as they, and filled besides with a care for them (see *v.* 8) which they cannot feel nor reciprocate toward her" (CGT). Bicknell says, "The idea is the condescension of the true Christian pastor who is willing to put himself on the level of others, which is the essence of sympathy. It is the application of the principle of the Incarnation itself."

[23] ἐν μέσῳ ὑμῶν, and not ἐν ὑμῖν or παρ' ὑμῖν.

[24] ὡς ἐάν with the subjunctive is a fairly rare construction. It seems to be a case of the late use of ἐάν for ἄν and to be distinguished from the ordinary use of the indicative as denoting contingency. Findlay speaks of it here as implying "a standing contingency—'as it may be (may be seen) at any time.'" Milligan cites examples of this construction from the papyri.

[25] That is, understanding ἑαυτῆς to mean "her own." Sometimes this is used in a sense equivalent to αὐτῆς and then it means simply "her." In that case it would denote somebody else's children entrusted to the nurse's care. But here there seems every reason for giving ἑαυτῆς its natural sense.

[26] Cf. Calvin, "a mother in nursing her children manifests a certain rare and wonderful affection, inasmuch as she spares no labour and trouble, shuns no anxiety, is wearied out by no assiduity, and even with cheerfulness of spirit gives her own blood to be sucked."

them he had become one with them. He had lavished affectionate care upon them.

8 All this had followed naturally enough from the fact that Paul and his companions had cherished such a deep regard for the Thessalonians, and he now employs a most unusual word to express it. The verb is found only here in the New Testament, and it is very rare elsewhere. It expresses a real depth of desire. "Being affectionately desirous of you" brings out quite a lot of its significance.[27]

He does not say "we would have been well pleased to impart," but simply, "we were well pleased to impart." The turn of phrase points us to what was actually done rather than contemplated. It is part of the picture Paul is painting for us that this should be so definite. The verb is in the imperfect, a continuous tense, and the implication is that this was no passing whim of the apostles, but their habitual style. Throughout their stay at Thessalonica they had been happy continually to be giving to their hearers.

When Paul speaks of the gift they made he puts "the gospel of God" first. Although he may be putting the emphasis elsewhere. he never loses sight of the fact that it was the gospel that gave the reason for the very existence of the preachers. They were "slaves of Christ." They lived only to render God service. The particular service to which they were called was the imparting of the blessed news of the salvation that God Himself had made available to man through the atoning death of His Son. Nothing must ever obscure that great fact.

But real preaching of the gospel implies the total committal of

---

[27] The best attested reading appears to be ὁμειρόμενοι, the variant being ἱμειρόμενοι, which latter means "to desire, to long for" (ἵμερος = "longing"). Two suggestions are made about the derivation of ὁμείρομαι, the one that it comes from ὁμοῦ and εἴρειν, and so means "to be attached to," the other that it is a strengthened form of μείρομαι (= ἱμείρομαι). Objections may be urged against both. We cannot be sure of the derivation. But in either case the word must denote strong affection. Milligan notes the attractive conjecture of Wohlenberg that it is a term of endearment from the nursery. This would suit the context admirably. He also regards derivation from ὁμοῦ and εἴρειν as "philologically impossible," and proceeds to cite Moulton's idea of a root meaning "to remember." MM cite a sepulchral inscription (4th century A.D.) which speaks of the parents as "greatly desiring their son." Moulton and Howard suggest that "It may be a compound of μείρομαι *obtain*, which in the conative present could take the required meaning or we may compare directly the root *smer* 'remember'" (*Accidence*, p. 251).

the preachers to the task. If they give a message, they also give themselves. This Paul makes clear by the addition of "also our own souls." By "souls" he means their whole personalities. It is an expression which sums up the inmost being of a man.[28] Thus he is saying that in their preaching they gave themselves without stint (cf. also II Cor. 12:15, Phil. 2:17. It is clear that this meant much to Paul).

The verse ends, as it began, with an expression of tender affection. We, the preachers, have done all this, says Paul, "because[29] ye were become very dear to us." "Very dear" is the rendering of an adjective connected with *agape*, the specifically Christian quality of love (see note on 1:3). Its use brings to mind the essentially self-giving quality of Christian love. It is not a desire to possess, but a desire to give, a desire inspired by the nature of the God whom Christians worship. Paul had come to see the Thessalonians as the objects of God's love, and therefore as the objects of the love of God's servants also.

9 This is not something that rests simply on Paul's word. He invites his readers to recall the incessant toil of the preachers, toil undertaken with a view to their imposing no burden on those to whom they preached. It was a Jewish custom, emphasized in the teaching of the Rabbis, that every boy should learn a trade. This does not seem to have arisen from any conviction that a well-rounded life with interests in many directions was highly desirable, as much as from sheer economic necessity.

There were no paid teachers in Palestine.[30] It was necessary

---

[28] Findlay sees the difference from καρδία (v. 4) thus: "*καρδία* is the inner man *by contrast with* the outer, while *ψυχή* is the man himself as *feeling and acting through* the outer organs, the soul within the body" (CGT). *ψυχή* is discussed in books on the nature of man, e.g., H. Wheeler Robinson, *The Christian Doctrine of Man* (Edinburgh, 1926), pp. 108 f.; W. David Stacey, *The Pauline View of Man* (London, 1956), Ch. VIII. Robinson's view that in this passage the term means "life" seems preferable to that of Stacey that it signifies "'energy' or 'vitality'."

[29] διότι. Sanday and Headlam on Rom. 1:19 note that there are three uses of this expression: "(i) for δι' ὅ τι . . . 'wherefore,' introducing a consequence, (ii) for διὰ τοῦτο ὅτι . . . 'because,' giving a reason for what has gone before; (iii) from Herod. downwards, but esp. in later Greek = ὅτι 'that.'" However in the New Testament it always seems to mean "because."

[30] Making money out of teaching the Law is expressly discouraged in the Mishnah. Thus Rabban Gamaliel said, "Excellent is the study of the Law together with worldly occupation, for toil in them both puts sin out of mind. But all study of the Law without (worldly) labour comes to naught at the last

therefore for a Rabbi to have some other means of income than the gifts that might now and then be made to him. It was natural accordingly for teachers to stress the importance of a trade. But, whatever the motive, the fact is clear. Even boys from well-to-do homes were taught a trade as a matter of course. From Acts 18:3 we learn that Paul's particular trade was tentmaking. As tents were often made of leather, this may mean that he was a leather-worker. But as a kind of canvas was also used (Lightfoot says it was manufactured from the goats' hair of Paul's native Cilicia, which may account for the choice of this trade), we cannot be sure. What is plain is that Paul and his companions had worked, and had worked hard, to support themselves, and to see that no burden was placed on their converts.

The two words rendered "labor and travail" occur together also in II Cor. 11:27, II Thess. 3:8. The former word is derived from the verb meaning "to strike." Thus properly it means "a blow." It comes to denote the result of a blow, and thence work which produces such an effect. It denotes work which produces weariness, wearisome toil. The other word is from a root giving the idea of difficulty. It brings before us the thought of that labor which is an overcoming of difficulties. The combination of the two stresses the fact that the work which the preachers had done had not been token work, something in the nature of a public show to demonstrate their willingness. It had been laborious toil. They had had to work hard. They had also had to work constantly, "night and day." We do not know at what hours they had been able to engage in evangelism. But whenever it was they had had to fill up their other hours, whether by night or by day, with toil in order to effect their purpose.

This purpose is given as "that we might not burden any of you." Paul had no doubt as to his right to be maintained as he preached (I Cor. 9:6, 12). On occasion he received gifts (or "wages," II Cor. 11:8) from his converts. While he was in Thessalonica he was helped by his Philippian friends (Phil. 4:16). But he made a point

---

and brings sin in its train" (Ab. 2:2, Danby's translation). Similarly R. Zadok, "make them [i.e., the words of the Law] not a crown wherewith to magnify thyself or a spade wherewith to dig. And thus used Hillel to say: He that makes worldly use of the crown shall perish. Thus thou mayest learn that he that makes profit out of the words of the Law removes his life from the world" (Ab. 4:5, Danby). The saying of Hillel is reported also in Ab. 1:13.

of seeing that any such gift should be received only when it would help in the furtherance of the gospel. It was another example of the working out of his great principle: "All things are lawful for me; but not all things are expedient" (I Cor. 6:12). He would not accept anything from those to whom he was preaching if it imposed a burden on them.[31]

This section concludes with a reiteration of the divine origin of the message. The verb rendered "preached" is that which signifies the action of the herald. It is the function of a herald simply to pass on the words given to him. His is not to give a message of his own devising, nor even to elaborate what has been given to him. He simply passes on what he is told. So Paul thinks of the preacher as one who passes on "the gospel of God." This conviction that the message comes from God is fundamental to effective preaching. And the message must indeed be that which comes from God. Little moral essays will never take its place. It is easy to distort the message or to substitute something else for it. But what gives Christianity its power is the fact that the gospel *is* "of God." Any trifling with this is bound to result in loss of power.

c. The Preachers' Behavior Had Been Impeccable, 2:10–12

10 Ye are witnesses, and God *also*, how holily and righteously and unblameably we behaved ourselves toward you that believe:

11 as ye know how we *dealt with* each one of you, as a father with his own children, exhorting you, and encouraging *you*, and testifying,

12 to the end that ye should walk worthily of God, who calleth you into his own kingdom and glory.

10 A striking feature of Paul's defense of his position is the confidence with which he appeals to the Thessalonians themselves to bear witness to the truth of what he says. It is abundantly clear that the true facts of his mission were known to all. In v. 5 he called on the Thessalonians as those who knew the facts and invoked God as witness to the truth of what he said. Now he does

---

[31] In the New Testament there does not seem to be a great difference between ἐπιβαρέω, "to place a burden *upon*" (the word used here) and καταβαρέω, "to weigh *down*." Frame cites Ellicott as saying that ἐπιβαρεῖν is "nearly but not quite equivalent in meaning to καταβαρεῖν."

the same, except that the two are joined more closely, and they are more emphatic.

Three adverbs are used to indicate the upright conduct of the preaching band during their stay in the city. Attempts have been made to distinguish between "holily" and "righteously" along the lines that the former refers to conduct before God and the latter to that before man (so, for example, Lightfoot). But it is difficult to substantiate this in the New Testament, whatever may be true of the classics. In the Bible "righteous" fundamentally means "conformity to God's law."[32] This may refer to one's duty to God or one's duty to man. It is better to understand that all the Christian's conduct, be it towards God or man, springs from the fact that he is born again. The significance then of our adverbs is a piling up of the necessity for right conduct somewhat in the manner of Titus 2:12. This is put first positively, "holily and righteously," and then negatively, "unblamably."[33]

"Believers" is often a synonym for Christians in the New Testament, so fundamental is faith to Christianity (see on 1:7). Here Paul does not mean that he had behaved in one way toward believers and in another way toward them that are without. It is simply that he is reminding the Thessalonians that there was nothing to complain about in the way he and his companions had conducted themselves. There is possibly also an emphasis on the difference between the reaction of the church and that of outsiders. Whatever other people might think of the apostles, the Thessalonian church had reason for a good opinion of them. They believed the message. They must therefore trust the messengers.

11 The construction of this sentence is difficult, for there does not seem to be a main verb. ARV supplies "dealt with," which gives a very good sense. Some have thought that the verb of v. 10 should be repeated, others that the participles of this verse are used for the indicative. There are other suggestions of greater or less

---

[32] For the essentially legal basis of righteousness in the Bible, see the chapters on Justification in my *The Apostolic Preaching of the Cross* (London and Grand Rapids, 1955).

[33] Cf. Frame, "A man is ὅσιος who is in general devoted to God's service; a man is δίκαιος who comes up to a specific standard of righteousness; and a man is ἄμεμπτος who in the light of a given norm is without reproach. All three designations are common in the LXX. and denote the attitude both to God and to men, the first two being positive, the third negative."

complexity. Fortunately the meaning is fairly clear, so that not much hinges on the particular reconstruction we adopt. The suggestion of ARV seems to be as good as any, and we understand the verse accordingly.

Once again we see the appeal to the personal knowledge of the Thessalonians. On this occasion the knowledge is of the personal dealings the evangelists had had with their converts. "Each one of you" implies attention to individuals.[34] It may even signify house to house visiting as well as public preaching (cf. Acts 20:20). But it is more probable that it means giving attention to the individual needs of those converted through the public preaching. House to house visitation in a city the size of Thessalonica would have presented problems to a small group like the apostolic band, especially if the campaign were short.

The note of affection is combined with care that the right way should be chosen, both in the use of the metaphor of a father with his children and in the participles which follow. That rendered "exhorting" is from the same root as the noun "exhortation" in v. 3 (where see note). The meaning here is probably that Paul and his friends had directed the converts into suitable lines of conduct. "Encouraging" is from a verb which, in the classics, means much the same as does the preceding verb. It is used in the New Testament elsewhere only in 5:14; John 11:19, 31. In chap. 5 it is used of comforting the fainthearted, and in the Johannine passages of comforting the bereaved. Clearly the verb is well adapted to the thought of consolation. We shall not be far wrong in assuming that here it is used with special reference to those who found it difficult to live the Christian way in the face of the opposition they encountered. To them the apostles spoke words of cheer and inspiration.

The third participle, "testifying," is from a verb which properly means "to bring forward a witness" and hence "to declare solemnly" (perhaps with the idea of calling God to witness). It is used in this way in Acts 20:26, Gal. 5:3. It is thus adapted to a solemn declaration of the truth. It may refer to serious words addressed to slackers or the like.

12 If Paul could be tender and considerate, he yet never lost

---

[34] ἕνα ἕκαστον is stronger than the simple ἕκαστον and puts an emphasis on the individual aspect.

sight of the high demands Christ makes on His followers. Thus all the exhorting and encouraging and testifying were directed towards the aim of seeing that the Thessalonians should "walk worthily of God."[35] Walking is a favorite way with Paul of designating the whole of a man's life (see on 4:1). The verb has its usual sense here. The expression to which it is joined sets before men the highest standard that could possibly be conceived. While it is well that we should appreciate the wonder of God's loving-kindness to us, and the fact that His love does not grow less no matter how low we may fall, yet we should not waver in our grasp of the complementary truth that such a God must be served with all our powers. Nothing less can be offered to Him who gave His Son for us than all that we have and all that we are.

Paul rapidly turns from contemplating what men should do for God to what God does for men. He speaks of God as "calling." It is more common to use the past tense, which gives an air of finality to the call. This timeless present reminds us rather that God's call never ceases. Always He is calling us.

The kingdom of God is not a very frequent idea in the Pauline correspondence, though in Acts 20:25 the term sums up Paul's preaching at Ephesus. In the Gospels we come across references to the kingdom again and again. It is the most frequent topic in our Lord's teaching. The kingdom is in some sense present, and in some sense future. That is to say, men may enter the kingdom here and now, and experience some measure of its joys. But the full apprehension of what it involves cannot be attained until the end of the age. The kingdom is essentially dynamic. It is something that happens, not a static realm (Moffatt's translation "realm" is inadequate). It is God's righteous rule operating within men and over men. There is an idea prevalent in some modern circles that we should work to establish the kingdom of God on earth. That is a noble ideal, but it is not the Biblical idea of the kingdom. In the Scriptures it is clear that God and no other establishes the kingdom. The death of the Son is not linked with the kingdom in so many words, but throughout the New Testament the cross is viewed

---

[35] There does seem to be some idea of purpose expressed here by εἰς τό, though Moulton says, "Purpose is so remote here as to be practically evanescent" (*Proleg.* p. 219). But this is to make the exhortation purposeless, which is not Paul's meaning. Nor is he simply giving the content of the exhortation, but exhorting with a view to a certain result in the lives of the Thessalonians.

as integral to its being set up. It is in virtue of the work that
Christ has accomplished for men that their sin is put away and
that God's rule becomes operative in them.[36]

In this passage "the kingdom" is closely linked with "the glory."
In the Greek they share a common preposition and a common
article. Phillips' rendering, "the splendour of His Kingdom" may
be going just a little too far,[37] but the two are certainly thought of
as closely related. For the word rendered "glory" see on v. 20. It
stands for the manifestation of God's glory to men, the revelation
of God in His majesty.

Paul holds out this glorious future as an incentive to the Thessalonians to live worthily here and now. They have been saved by
such a wonderful God. They have been brought into His kingdom.
They face a glorious future. Let them so live here and now as to be
worthy of such a God!

d. The Message of the Preachers Was the Word of God, 2:13

13　And for this cause we also thank God without ceasing,
that, when ye received from us the word of the message, *even the word* of God, ye accepted *it* not *as* the
word of men, but, as it is in truth, the word of God,
which also[38] worketh in you that believe.

13　Fundamental to Paul's preaching was the conviction that
what he spoke was not his own message but God's (see on 2:9). He

---

[36]　There is an immense literature on the kingdom of God. It may be
sufficient to refer to the list given by Norval Geldenhuys in his *New International
Commentary on the Gospel of Luke*, p. 179. To this we should add E. Stauffer,
The Theology of the New Testament (London, 1955), Ch. 28. Perhaps the best
survey, as including both the critical scholars and the conservative evangelicals
(dispensationalist and other) is that of G. E. Ladd, *Crucial Questions About the
Kingdom of God* (Grand Rapids, 1954).

[37]　Cf. Milligan, "The two expressions must not however be united as
if = 'His own kingdom of glory,' or even 'His own kingdom culminating in
His glory,' but point rather to two manifestations of God's power, the first
of His *rule*, the second of His *glory*."

[38]　καὶ ἡμεῖς is emphatic, "we, for our part." Lake thinks the proper force
of the expression "can be given only if we assume that St. Paul means 'we
give thanks just as you say that you do'" (*Earlier Epistles*, p. 87), and finds
in it evidence that Paul was replying to a letter. The case was put strongly
by Rendel Harris (*Expositor*, 5th Series, Vol. VIII, pp. 168 ff.). He found
other evidence for such a letter in the repeated "ye know" (1:5; 2:1, 5, 10;
3:3, 4), which he argued means "as you said." Others emphasize the way

rejected human wisdom, and thought little of mere eloquence
(I Cor. 2:1 ff.). He was content to pass on, in the manner of a
herald, what God had given him. There were philosophical points
of view which were at variance with the stark simplicity of the
preaching of the cross. The pressure to accommodate his message
to the demands of the "modern thought-world" of the day must
have been great. But Paul rejected all this. His drive and force-
fulness came not from some thought that he was abreast of contemporary trends in philosophy or religion or science, but the deep-
seated conviction that he was simply God's mouthpiece, and that
what he spoke was the veritable word of God.[39]

So he thanks God, and says he never ceases to do so, for the fact
that the Thessalonians had recognized this feature of the gospel
when it was first preached to them. The word preached was "of
God." Paul finds matter for thanksgiving negatively, in that the
Thessalonians had not received it as of human origin,[40] and
positively, in that they had perceived it for what it really was,
"the word of God." He underlines this with his contrast between
"from us" and the very emphatic "of God."[41] The preachers were
the immediate source of the message. But Paul and his companions

---

new steps in the argument are brought in in 4:9, 13; 5:1. This is very like the
way correspondents in antiquity referred to points raised in letters to which
they were replying.

There is nothing unlikely in the hypothesis that the Thessalonians wrote
a letter to Paul, but the arguments adduced come short of proof. I Thessalonians is completely explicable on the view that Paul is replying to Timothy's
report on his mission to the city. See further, Introduction, pp. 20, 21.

[39] Cf. Denney, Paul "was conscious that... [his theology] rested at
bottom on the truth of God; and when he preached it—for his theology was
the sum of the divine truth he held, and he *did* preach it—he did not submit
it to men as a theme for discussion. He put it above discussion. He pronounced
a solemn and reiterated anathema on either man or angel who should put
anything else in its stead. He published it, not for criticism, as though it had
been his own device; but, as the word of God, for the obedience of faith."

[40] That is, accepting the insertion of "as" by ARV as correct. There is
no "as" in the Greek, and Bicknell says "its insertion seriously alters the drift
of the sentence. What causes St. Paul to thank God is not the attitude of the
Thessalonians to the Gospel, or their appreciation of its divine origin, but the
fact that the word that they accepted is divine and therefore charged with
divine power." While there is no doubt that Paul is stressing the divine
nature of the gospel, yet he does seem to be thankful that the Thessalonians
had recognized it for what it was. The insertion of "as" seems to be necessary.

[41] παρ' ἡμῶν is to be taken with παραλαβόντες. τοῦ Θεοῦ is in emphatic
contrast. It must be taken as a subjective genitive, "the word from God,"
"the word originating with God," and not as objective, "the word which
tells of God," "the word about God."

were no more than intermediaries in proclaiming a gospel whose ultimate source and originator was none less than God Himself.

There is an interesting and significant contrast between the receiving of the message spoken of in the two halves of the verse. In the first half the word for receiving is one which denotes an objective, outward receiving. What is heard is likewise called "the word of hearing" (mg.), a peculiar phrase[42] which also directs attention to the outward. The second word for receiving denotes rather a subjective reception, a reception which involves welcome and approval (the word is the usual one for the reception of a guest). It is followed by an expression indicating the presence of faith in the recipients, and the working of the power of God.

The verb rendered "worketh"[43] is almost always used in the New Testament of some form of supernatural activity. Mostly it is that of God (I Cor. 12:6, Phil. 2:13, and elsewhere), but sometimes, by contrast, that of Satan (Eph. 2:2). It can be used of such things as faith (Gal. 5:6), prayer (Jas. 5:16), life or death (II Cor. 4:12), in each case a force not human being involved. Here it draws attention to the fact that the power manifested in the lives of the converts is not of this world, but divine. Where the word of God is welcomed with obedient faith, there the power of God is at work.

When he speaks of believing[44] Paul uses the present tense to convey the idea of a continuous process of belief (rather than the

---

[42] λόγον ἀκοῆς. It occurs elsewhere only at Heb. 4:2 (where both nouns have articles). There also is a contrast between the merely outward reception which it denotes, and the hearing of faith. The outward reception, however, is a necessary step on the way to a genuine faith (Rom. 10:17), and Paul can even refer to an ἀκοὴ πίστεως (Gal. 3:2, 5).

[43] ἐνεργεῖται. Lightfoot maintains that Paul always uses this verb in the active of God (and by contrast of Satan), and in the middle in all other cases. Here then he takes it as middle, with the subject, ὅς, referring back to λόγον, not Θεοῦ. But Armitage Robinson contends that in the New Testament the passive is to be understood rather than the middle of this verb (Commentary on Ephesians, pp. 241–47). Milligan and Findlay accept this. Armitage Robinson's argument is difficult to accept in its entirety, but what is quite clear is that the New Testament makes a distinction between God's working and the working of intermediaries. Where God is directly spoken of the active is used. Where it is His word, or such an activity as "faith working through love" (Gal. 5:6), a more oblique form is found. Milligan would bring this out by rendering, "which is also set in operation," thus emphasizing that it is God, and not some quasi-magical power in the word itself, that works.

[44] The verb is used absolutely. Even at this early stage it was not necessary to add in whom they believed, so central is faith to Christianity. See further on 1:7.

aorist, which would single out the act of decision). It is the condition of the working of God in men that they continue to exercise faith. Or to put it another way, we cannot live today on the spiritual capital of yesterday.

e. Persecution, 2:14–16

14 For ye, brethren, became imitators of the churches of God which are in Judæa in Christ Jesus: for ye also suffered the same things of your own countrymen, even as they did of the Jews;

15 who both killed the Lord Jesus and the prophets, and drove out us, and please not God, and are contrary to all men;

16 forbidding us to speak to the Gentiles that they may be saved; to fill up their sins always: but the wrath is come upon them to the uttermost.

14 Persecution in some form is the common lot of Christians and always must be in the nature of the case. The way in which the Thessalonians had borne severe persecution Paul sees as evidence of their real Christianity. It showed that they had indeed received the gospel as divine in origin, that the gospel had produced results in them and was still working in them. The persecution came from "your own countrymen." This expression may be in part geographical and include Thessalonian Jews, but it points to a large Gentile element in the opposition.[45] We are probably not far wrong in seeing the opposition as rooted in the hostility of the Jews. But the Greeks were so stirred up by them that they took action on their own account. Incidentally the expression reveals that the church was predominantly Gentile.

In their endurance of persecution the Thessalonians had become imitators of the Palestinian churches.[46] The word rendered "church," namely *ekklesia*, is not a specifically religious word. It could be used of such assemblies as that of the rioting Ephesians in

---

[45] The basic meaning of συμφυλέτης indicates this, and so does the use of ἰδίων and the contrast with ὑπὸ τῶν 'Ιουδαίων. But the word appears to have more of a national than a racial content. As Lightfoot points out, it "would include such Jews as were free citizens of Thessalonica."

[46] 'Ιουδαία could be used in a restricted sense of the province of Judea, but it also could bear a wider sense, comprising all Palestine. The latter seems the meaning here.

Acts 19:32, 39, 41. It is true that it is sometimes used in the Septuagint of the assembly of Israel, but that assembly was just as much political as religious. The word does not seem to have been used in a religious sense in Greek literature generally. Beside this we should set the fact that the Christians passed over the many Greek words for religious brotherhoods. The force of this is that Christianity is not just another religion. It is not to be named with any of the words proper to religions in general. Its designation is unique for a religious community.[47] At the same time there were many "assemblies" both Jewish and Greek. The Christian assemblies are distinguished as being "of God," and further as "in Christ Jesus." This order of the names is almost peculiar to Paul and indicates that "Christ" is already thought of as in the nature of a personal name (see further on 1:1, 3:11). It is typical of Paul to think of the churches as being "in" Christ. In Him they live and move and have their being.

We do not know the exact force of the reference to persecution by the Jews. It may point to an allegation by the Thessalonian Jews that in taking action against the Christians they were simply doing what their compatriots in Judaea had earlier been compelled to do. Or it may be that the sufferings of the Palestinian churches were well known in Christian circles and could be used as the basis of instruction without further explanation anywhere among the believers.

15-16 This leads on to a denunciation of the Jews more severe than anything else in the Pauline writings. It is not an outburst of temper, but in Denney's words, "the vehement condemnation, by a man in thorough sympathy with the mind and spirit of God, of the principles on which the Jews as a nation had acted at every period of their history." Paul begins with the accusation that they had killed the Lord Jesus. His unusual word order emphasizes both words. They had killed the heavenly Man, the Lord, and they had killed One who was of their flesh, the human Jesus. Paul emphasizes the heinousness of this crime, and proceeds to bring out the point that it was no isolated act. "Which of the prophets

---

[47] On the church see especially K. C. Schmidt, *The Church* (London, 1938), R. Newton Flew, *Jesus and His Church* (London, 1938), and F. W. Dillistone, *The Structure of the Divine Society* (London, 1951). A useful summary of much writing on the subject is J. E. Nelson, *The Realm of Redemption* (London, 1951).

did not your fathers persecute?" asked Stephen (Acts 7:52). This is Paul's thought, too. The slaying of the Lord was the outworking of the same essential attitude as that displayed so often to the prophets.[48]

And it continued. "They drove out us." Paul's verb is a compound rare in the New Testament, and denoting the extreme in persecution. Their manner of life is such that they "please not God." The present tense marks their habitual attitude (for the meaning of the verb see on v. 4). Just as they displease God, so they are "contrary to all men." We are reminded of Tacitus' accusation that the Jews were "haters of the human race." The word "contrary" is usually referred to things, like winds (Acts 27:4, Mark 6:48), or deeds (Acts 26:9, 28:17). This is the only place in the New Testament where people are said to be contrary, and this we may take as a measure of the Apostle's feeling. Ordinary expressions will not serve.

His indignation mounts as he thinks of their trying to prevent the gospel being preached to the Gentiles, quite in the spirit of the Pharisees of Matt. 23:13. Such preaching was in order that men might be saved, which underlines the guilt of the Jews. He probably had in mind the incident recorded in Acts 17:5 ff., which in any case is an excellent example of the conduct Paul is condemning.

But this cannot go unnoticed on the part of God. Paul brings this out by using a construction expressing purpose.[49] The Jews have done this "to fill up their sins always," which we might well explain in Frame's words: "The obstinacy of the Jews is viewed as an element in the divine plan." Something of the determination of the Jews is brought out in Moffatt's translation, "So they would fill up the measure of their sins to the last drop!" They are seeing to it that nothing is left out in the catalogue of their sins. The

---

[48] Grammatically the reference to the prophets could be taken with what follows, "who killed the Lord Jesus, and drove out both the prophets and us." But the meaning adopted seems more in harmony with the natural meaning of the Greek, and with such other passages as Luke 11:47 f., 13:33, 20:9 ff., Acts 7:52, Rom. 11:3. Frame points out also that the argument would be weakened if προφήτας were attached to ἐκδιωξάντων. Some have taken the prophets to mean the New Testament prophets, but no sufficient reason has been produced for this. It is the continuing opposition of the Jews to God's messengers through the centuries which forms so powerful an argument.

[49] εἰς τό with infinitive may also indicate result (see E. de W. Burton, *Syntax*, p. 161), but purpose seems better here.

plural "sins" points to the aggregate of their separate evil acts, and not to the general abstract concept of "sin." The consequence is sure. Paul speaks of the wrath coming on them. Indeed, so sure is their punishment, that he uses the aorist tense which might be rendered "came" upon them. The use of this tense does not refer to the imminence of the punishment. It refers rather to its certainty, for Paul is thinking of wrath in an eschatological setting. It is at the last great day that his nation will receive the due reward of all its misdeeds. But though it is postponed there is no doubt about what their fate will be. "The cup of the nation's sin is now full. They can do no more to provoke the divine wrath" (Bicknell).

At the same time we should notice that Paul's anger is the anger of a man with his own nation, with his own people. He is very much part of them, and he sorrows for their fate. He is not invoking dire disasters upon them. He is grieving over the effects of their misdeeds. Phillips brings out some of this in his translation, "Alas, I fear they are completing the full tale of their sins and the wrath of God is over their heads." It is the same anguish which is so poignantly expressed in Rom. 9:1 ff.

Paul's sorrow is not mitigated by any ray of hope. The wrath is come "to the uttermost."[50] Judah's sin had been so constant and serious that Paul sees no other possible outcome.

---

[50] εἰς τέλος might also be rendered "at last" (a number of commentators accept this meaning here), or "to the end."

IV. THE RELATIONSHIP OF PAUL TO THE
THESSALONIANS, 2:17–3:13

1 PAUL'S DESIRE TO RETURN, 2:17, 18

> 17 But we, brethren, being bereaved of you for a short
> season, in presence not in heart, endeavored the more
> exceedingly to see your face with great desire:
> 18 because we would fain have come unto you, I Paul
> once and again; and Satan hindered us.

17 As Paul enters this new section of the Epistle it is not without a backward glance at the last. His "But" is an adversative conjunction contrasting him with the Jews, as is also the emphatic "we." It seems probable that one of their accusations had been that the Apostle had never intended to revisit Thessalonica. His continued absence was further proof that he had no real regard for his converts.

So Paul addresses them affectionately as "brethren," and goes on to use a very strong term to express his sense of loss at their absence from him. "Being bereaved" is really "being orphaned." While the word had developed the general sense of our translation, it seems likely that Paul is not unmindful of its original associations. He has already in this chapter likened his attitude to them to that of a mother-nurse (v. 7), and to that of a father (v. 11). The present verb, while it radically alters the imagery by making Paul the "orphan," continues the thought of the tender affection that bound the Apostle to his converts.[51] This deep sense of bereavement had arisen even though their separation had been only for a very short time, "a season of an hour." He stresses that the separation is only physical. They are still joined in heart. "Out of sight, out of mind" runs our proverb, and Moffatt brings out some of the significance of Paul's words here with his "out of sight, not out of mind." For "heart" see on v. 4.

Because of this deep feeling Paul had made a determined attempt to see them. We have no precise equivalent of the Greek

---

[51] Cf. the comment of Chrysostom: "He says not χωρισθέντες ὑμῶν, not διασπασθέντες ὑμῶν, not διαστάντες, not ἀπολειφέντες but ἀπορφαὰισθεγτες ὑμῶν. He sought for a word that might fitly indicate his mental anguish. Though standing in the relation of a father to them all, he yet utters the language of orphan children that have prematurely lost their parent" (cited by Frame).

93

word rendered "endeavored," a word which manages to combine the two ideas of haste and earnestness. It means that Paul did not delay, nor did he put forth a token effort only. Rather, he had used all his might and used it speedily in his endeavor to come to them. He reinforces this strong verb with a comparative adverb, "the more exceedingly"[52] which should leave them in no doubt as to the strength of his endeavors.

But he is not finished yet. He tells them that he had endeavored to see them "with great desire." The last word is rather surprising, for it nearly always means something like "lust" in its New Testament occurrences. It is generally mentioned only to be condemned. Here Paul uses it in its original sense of a very strong desire, almost a fierce passion (cf. Rutherford, "absence has made us anxious out of measure to see you face to face with passionate desire"). He wants his friends to be in no doubt as to the strength of his feelings for them.

18 Paul repeats that he had wished to come to them. The verb "would fain" expresses a wish. It seems to be connected with the feelings rather than the will.[53] It strengthens the emotional element which is so marked a feature of this section of the Epistle. Whatever had kept Paul away from them it had not been his personal desires.

This again underlies his emphatic "I Paul." Throughout these two Epistles, as we have noted, the plural is used much more than in most of Paul's letters. This makes the singular the more signifi-

---

[52] In late Greek the comparative tends to take over the functions of the superlative, and thus it is likely that περισσοτέρως here is to be understood as elative (so Frame). Some commentators, however, maintain that περισσοτέρως in Paul always has a strictly comparative force (e.g., Lightfoot, Milligan). But they are not at all agreed as to what is to be supplied as the other member of the comparison (see various reconstructions in Frame). It seems simpler to accept the elative sense. It is very doubtful whether the strictly comparative sense will hold in II Cor. 7:13, and this may well serve as a parallel to the elative sense here.

[53] The verb is θέλω. The distinction between this verb and βούλομαι has been understood variously, with scholars sometimes reaching diametrically opposite conclusions. Grimm–Thayer say that βούλομαι "seems to designate the will which follows deliberation" and θέλω "the will which proceeds from inclination." This does seem to be the New Testament usage. At the same time it must be borne in mind that the two verbs are close in meaning and on occasion seem to be used interchangeably. Also that θέλω was tending to encroach on the territory of βούλομαι. In the New Testament it is found about five times as often as βούλομαι.

cant when it does occur. Here the intense personal feeling breaks
through, and we have the emphatic singular reinforced by the
personal name. He had not simply made one attempt. He had
wished to come "once and again." This represents an unusual
Greek expression which seems to denote a plurality of occasions
with no attempt at giving the exact number. "More than once" is
probably our nearest equivalent.[54]

However, Paul's endeavors had been frustrated by Satan (for
Satan, see on 3:5). The verb used here means literally "to cut
into." Milligan says the idea is that of cutting up a road to make
it impassable,[55] and thence of hindering in general. A number of
suggestions have been put forward as to the particular mode
Satan's activities took. But we are completely in the dark in this
matter, and all the attempts are simply guess work. There is no
means of knowing just what Paul had in mind. Clearly the
Thessalonians were expected to catch the allusion, but we lack
their detailed knowledge of the circumstances. One thing of
importance is clear to us, though, and that is that Satan makes his
presence felt to Christian workers. He even prevents them from
doing things that they would dearly love to do. Scripture makes it
clear that his power is derivative, and always subject to God's
overruling. But within the limits allotted to him he does hinder
God's servants.

---

[54] The Greek is καὶ ἅπαξ καὶ δίς. The first καί is usually taken as part
of the expression, but this is probably incorrect. ἅπαξ καὶ δίς occurs four
times in the LXX (each time meaning "more than once," the number of
times not being specified). Other similar expressions occur without a
preliminary καί, as ἅπαξ καὶ ἅπαξ. If we can accept ἅπαξ καὶ δίς as the
idiomatic expression, then the first καί here will be ascensive and the meaning
"and that more than once." The expression occurs again in Phil. 4:16 where
the meaning appears to be "both (when I was) in Thessalonica and (καὶ)
more than once (ἅπαξ καὶ δίς) (when I was in other places) you sent . . ."
This is very near to Frame's understanding of the expression, the difference
being that he prefers the slightly stronger "repeatedly." See further my note
in *Novum Testamentum*, Vol. I, pp. 205–8.

[55] Cf. Lightfoot on Gal. 5:7, "a metaphor derived from military operations.
The word signifies 'to break up a road' (by destroying bridges, etc.) so as to
render it impassable."

2. PAUL'S JOY IN THE THESSALONIANS, 2:19, 20

19 For what is our hope, or joy, or crown of glorying?
Are not even ye, before our Lord Jesus at his coming?
20 For ye are our glory and our joy.

19-20 Paul brings all this to a climax in an excited outburst of esteem for his converts. It is probable that the two questions in ARV should be regarded as one, with a shorter little question as a parenthesis: "For what is our hope, or joy, or crown of glorying (are not you?) before our Lord Jesus . . .?" There were two words in common use in Greek for "crown." That used here commonly denoted something like a festive garland or a laurel wreath awarded to the victor at the games. It is likely that Paul has in mind thoughts of joyfulness and victory[56] as being symbolized by the crown (though we cannot be dogmatic on this point, for the word is sometimes found in the sense of a royal crown also). It is described as a "crown of glorying," the last word giving the thought of the outward expression of the feeling of joy. It denotes rather an exuberant activity, and is sometimes rendered "boasting." It is from a different root and expresses a different idea from that rendered "glory" in the next verse. Perhaps the nearest we can come in English to Paul's form of expression is to speak of the Thessalonians as his "crowning glory."

This high place assigned to the Thessalonians in Paul's esteem is further emphasized with the insistence that it is "before our Lord Jesus" (which raises it to the highest level), and "at his coming" (which sounds the eschatological note and makes it permanent).

The word rendered "coming" is *parousia*. This is the first occurrence in Christian literature of this important word. Its basic meaning is simply "presence" (as in I Cor. 16:17, II Cor. 10:10). This gives rise to the sense of "coming to be present," "arrival" (II Cor. 7:6 f.). In the ordinary language of the people the term was especially applied to the arrival of a great personage, a king or an emperor, and it was the usual word for a royal visit.[57] In

---

[56] Lightfoot, commenting on Phil. 4:1, says that the idea conveyed by the word "is not dominion, but either (1) victory, or (2) merriment, and the wreath was worn equally by the conqueror and by the holiday-maker. Without excluding the latter notion, the former seems to be prominent in this and in the parallel passage; for there, as here, the Apostle refers in the context to the Lord's coming. His converts then will be his wreath of victory."

[57] See Deissmann, LAE, pp. 368–73 for examples.

the New Testament it became a technical expression for *the* royal visit, the second coming of our Lord. From the New Testament it passed into Christian literature generally. As distinct from other words for the second coming Milligan maintains that it "lays stress on the 'presence' of the Lord with His people, which, while existing now, will only at that Return be completely realized."[58] So here Paul uses for the first time in Christian literature that term which was to be the characteristic designation of the Lord's triumphant return.[59] And even then, says Paul, the Thessalonians will be his hope and joy and crown of boasting. It may not be without significance that on the occasion of a royal *parousia* the people sometimes found themselves under the necessity of providing a crown. But at the coming of this King the crown will be His people's.

Paul rounds off this section by a further statement that the Thessalonians are "our glory and our joy." The word for "glory" is *doxa* (from which we get "doxology"). It originally signified "opinion," "view," but it is not found in this sense in the New Testament. From "opinion" it came to mean "good opinion," and so "praise" or "honor" as in Luke 14:10, Heb. 3:3, and elsewhere. In the Septuagint it was used to render the Hebrew *kabhodh*, and so took on the meaning "splendor," "magnificence." It could be used of human splendor as in Matt. 4:8, and elsewhere, but came to have its characteristic use in connection with the "glory" of God, as in Rom. 1:23. It could similarly be used of the glory of Christ (II Cor. 4:4), and even of that glory which is won for the believer (Rom. 8:18, and elsewhere). It is a word with many overtones.

Paul uses it to indicate that the Thessalonians are the cause of much rejoicing to the apostles. "Yes, you are indeed our pride and our joy!" Phillips renders it. His opening words are an attempt to bring out the emphatic "you" and "are." Paul is giving a special place to no other than the Thessalonians. And, while he looks forward to continuing to esteem them right up to the time of the Parousia, yet he insists that at the moment of writing, right now. they *are* his pride and joy.

---

[58] Additional Note F, p. 151.
[59] See also the note on this word in G. Vos, *The Pauline Eschatology* (Grand Rapids, 1953), pp. 74 ff.

COMMENTARY ON I THESSALONIANS

3. TIMOTHY'S MISSION, 3:1–5

> 1 Wherefore when we could no longer forbear, we thought it good to be left behind at Athens alone;
> 2 and sent Timothy, our brother and God's minister in the gospel of Christ, to establish you, and to comfort *you* concerning your faith;
> 3 that no man be moved by these afflictions; for yourselves know that hereunto we are appointed.
> 4 For verily, when we were with you, we told you beforehand that we are to suffer affliction; even as it came to pass, and ye know.
> 5 For this cause I also, when I could no longer forbear, sent that I might know your faith, lest by any means the tempter had tempted you, and our labor should be in vain.

1 More than one problem makes its appearance here. There is the problem of the movements of the missionaries. In Acts 17:14 Paul went on to Athens alone, leaving Timothy and Silas at Beroea. From Athens he sent for them (17:15). Then he preached to the Athenians, and proceeded to Corinth (18:1), where Silas and Timothy joined him from Macedonia (18:5). However, from this passage it is clear that Timothy at any rate was with Paul in Athens. There is no contradiction as some have supposed. The writer of Acts has omitted the journey of Timothy to Athens and back to Thessalonica, which is not surprising, for it was not important for his purpose. But it was important for Paul's purpose in writing, and he mentions it accordingly.

Then there is the problem of the meaning of "we."[1] As we saw on 1:1 the practice in this Epistle differs somewhat from that in the Pauline epistles generally. The plural is used almost throughout, whereas in most of his letters Paul prefers the singular. Some

---

[1] Milligan discusses the problem of the epistolary plural in Note B in his commentary. See also Moule, *Idiom Book*, pp. 118 f., and O. T. Allis, *Revision or New Translation* (Philadelphia, 1948), pp. 61 f.

commentators deny that Paul ever used the epistolary plural, maintaining that the plural is always meant to associate others with him. This, however, does not seem to be tenable. In the present passage even the emphatic use of the singular in v. 5 cannot outweigh the fact that one person is meant by the plural in this verse. This seems clear from the plural form of the adjective "alone," which yet can only refer to Paul. It is reinforced by the fact that the same subject is also to be understood of the verb "sent" in v. 2. We cannot think of Timothy as sending himself. It is hard to think of Silas as being included, for, in the first place, we do not know whether he was in Athens or not and, in the second, it is difficult to think of "we" as meaning two people out of three. So certain does it seem to Moffatt that one person only is meant that throughout these verses he translates "I" and not "we."

The emotional atmosphere of the preceding verses continues (the chapter division should be ignored, for this section is very closely connected with the preceding). The separation Paul has been speaking of became unendurable,[2] and thus he took action. "We thought it good" renders the same verb as "we were well pleased" in 2:8. It points here to something in the nature of a resolve, but the word has a definite emotional content. This is continued with the choice of word for "to be left behind," which means strictly "to be abandoned." It is used of leaving one's loved ones at death (Mark 12:19). In the papyri it is the technical word for leaving something in a will. Linked with the emphatic "alone" it gives us some idea of the depths of the Apostle's feelings. We must not think that it was easy for him to stay and preach in Athens. That city was the intellectual capital of the world. Many of its inhabitants were cultured people. Not a few were cynical and ready to mock at such a gospel as Paul preached. Paul was not insensitive, and he did not relish the prospect of working alone in such a place. For the good of the work he realized that it was necessary for Timothy to go, but this verse gives us a glimpse of what it cost him.[3]

---

[2] στέγω ("forbear") means first "to cover," then "to ward off by covering," and thus "to see something through," "to bear up," "to endure." This last seems to be the meaning in each of the New Testament occurrences of the verb (v. 5, I Cor. 9:12, 13:7). Another line of development from "to cover" leads to the idea of "to conceal," but, although some adopt this meaning here, the sense appears to be "to endure."

[3] Cf. Denney, "He seems to have been in many ways dependent on the

2 This cost is further emphasized in the fact that when he was facing such a grim prospect Paul sent to them one whom he valued as highly as he did Timothy. According to the most probable reading Timothy is called "God's minister in the gospel of Christ."[4] "Minister" is our rendering of *diakonos*, from which we derive the word "deacon." It is sometimes used in the New Testament of one of the orders of the Christian ministry in the technical sense, but it is very unlikely to have that meaning here. Originally the word denoted the service of a table waiter, and from that it came to signify lowly service of any kind. It was often used by the early Christians to give expression to the service that they habitually were to render both to God and to man. Where a word like "slave," which is often used of Christians, puts the emphasis on the personal relation, this word draws attention to the act of service being rendered. It is not Paul's habit to refer to Timothy in this way (he prefers to call him "our brother" or the like, but cf. I Tim. 4:6). The elaborate and high-sounding title may be meant to impress on the readers the importance he had attached to Timothy's mission.

When Timothy's service is defined as being in the gospel of Christ the gospel is referred to Him whose death is its basis. It is the gospel of what Christ has done for man. The gospel may also be spoken of as "the gospel of God" (2:2, where see note), and "our gospel" (1:5, where see note).

The purpose of the mission is twofold, but both verbs used refer to strengthening. That rendered "to establish" has the idea of putting in a buttress, a support, and in classical Greek it is used mostly in the literal sense. However, the metaphorical sense is

---

sympathy and assistance of others; and, of all places he ever visited, Athens was the most trying to his ardent temperament.... Never had he been left alone in a place so unsympathetic; never had he felt so great a gulf fixed between others' minds and his own." Bicknell also remarks that "Athens was particularly uncongenial to St. Paul's temperament."

[4] The textual questions are whether διάκονον or συνεργόν should be read, and whether to include or omit τοῦ Θεοῦ. The manuscript evidence favors διάκονον τοῦ Θεοῦ. Transcriptional probability may be held to favor συνεργόν τοῦ Θεοῦ. Although it occurs in I Cor. 3:9, it is a bold, even startling expression. A scribe would perhaps be ready to alter this by the substitution of another noun or by dropping τοῦ Θεοῦ. Yet this is not decisive, for διάκονον τοῦ Θεοῦ is neither an easy expression in itself (though it does occur three times outside this passage), nor is it a usual way of referring to Timothy. Under the circumstances it seems best to follow the better attested reading, διάκονον τοῦ Θεοῦ.

found in late Greek, and is usual in the New Testament. "To comfort" is somewhat misleading (unless we understand "comfort" in its etymological sense), for the Greek verb has the meaning of strengthening. Basically it means "to call to the side of." From this derive various ways of helping. It is used in a legal sense ("Advocate" in I John 2:1 is a noun from this root), and also in a more general sense. It is primarily help by way of exhortation, and so encouragement. Timothy's visit, then, had been for the purpose of buttressing their faith. He came to encourage them with a view to the strengthening of their faith.[5]

3 This is further explained.[6] The sense of the verb rendered "be moved" is not certain. Most of the translations accord with ARV (e.g., Moffatt, "being disturbed"; Phillips, "to lose heart"; RSV, "be moved"). However, the verb does not often (if ever) have this meaning. More usually it has something like its original meaning of a dog wagging its tail, e.g., "to fawn upon" or "to wheedle." Here Paul seems to have in mind the possibility that, while the Thessalonians were in the midst of their troubles, some of their enemies, by fair words, should turn them out of the right way.[7] Perhaps while the Gentiles were persecuting them the Jews spoke kindly to them (or Paul feared that they would) with a view to persuading them to accept Judaism, which, of course, could have as one of its effects immediate cessation of persecution.

There had appeared to be an easy way out of their troubles. But Paul insists that they knew better. "Yourselves" is emphatic,

---

[5] See further on 2:3. ὑπέρ is not well translated "concerning." The word means "on behalf of," and has the notion often of "for the advantage of," though it sometimes is used in neutral fashion (as when Christ is said to have died ὑπέρ our sins). Here the meaning is that Timothy's visit was to benefit the faith of the Thessalonians.

T. W. Manson argues that ὑπὲρ ττς πίστεως ὑμων "refers to the faithfulness of the Thessalonian Christians to their profession" (*Bull. Ryl. Lib.*, Vol. 35, p. 440, n. 2). But the word πίστις never seems to have this meaning in the New Testament when it is used of men (see further on II Thess. 3:2). I see no reason for abandoning the usual meaning of the word here.

[6] τό introduces a statement in apposition with the foregoing, or, as Lightfoot thinks, it is more or less equivalent to ὥστε, giving the result of the preceding. Moule thinks that this is an exception to the rule that the articular infinitive is preceded by a preposition (πρός, εἰς, ἕνεκεν) expressing purpose (*Idiom Book*, p. 140).

[7] This is supported by the fact that the process he speaks of takes place "in" their troubles. We should expect "by" if the verb meant "moved." For θλίψις see on 1:6.

and the sense of this part of the verse is well given by Moffatt, "Troubles are our lot, you know that well" (so long as we understand "lot" not as the action of blind fate, but as the portion God allots to us). The verb "are appointed" is a strong one. It gives the impression of something stable, something which cannot be altered. As Calvin puts it, it "is as though he had said, that we are Christians on this condition." Tribulation is not to be wondered at by Christian people as though some strange and unusual thing befell them. Under the conditions of this world, with so many opposed to the gospel, tribulation is inevitable. More, it is the means of teaching us many lessons. Human nature being what it is, there are some things that we will only learn the hard way. If we are in trouble and need help and advice we do not run over our list of friends and say: "Ah, there's so-and-so. Just the person. Never had a day's trouble in his life, he'll be just the one to help!" Rather, we know that there are qualities of character that are only brought out by affliction. In our hour of need, someone who has these qualities is invaluable (cf. II Cor. 1:4). Suffering, then, is part of the very process of living out the Christian life, and we should not regard it as something strange and alien. The God who is over all watches over His children, and the affliction that comes to them is only such as He permits. There is always some lesson to be learned from it. It is always part of our being shaped into what God would have us be. It is inevitable. We are appointed unto it.[8]

4 Paul had asserted that the Thessalonians knew this basic truth. He now reminds them that he had foretold their sufferings when he was in their city, and foretold them repeatedly, for such is the force of the continuous tense he employs (cf. Rutherford, "the warning was often on our lips"). The certainty of persecution loomed large in the Apostle's mind, as well it might, both from the nature of things and from his own experience. So he often spoke of it.

He goes on, "we are to suffer affliction." This emphasizes the certainty of the affliction and hints at its divine appointment. This same expression is used in a number of places in the New Testament (e.g., Rom. 8:13, 18; Gal. 3:23) to give greater certainty than

---

[8] An excellent popular treatment of the whole question of suffering is C. S. Lewis, *The Problem of Pain* (London, 1940).

the use of the simple future, and to hint at the fact that God is in the particular act being foretold. Cf. also Acts 14:22 for coincidences both of thought and language. So Paul reiterates what he had said in the previous verse, that trouble, for the Christian, is not to be dismissed as totally evil. The hand of God is in it. He has appointed His people thereto.

Once more Paul appeals to the knowledge of the Thessalonians. He is not telling them something strange and novel. He does not need to produce proof at every step. He had repeatedly foretold suffering. This was not just so much empty sound, for the prediction had been fulfilled.[9] The Thessalonians themselves had knowledge that this was so.

5 There is a good deal of repetition in these verses. Paul was very stirred as he wrote. He was anxious to leave his correspondents in no doubt as to his essential meaning, so he does not scruple to go over his points. In this verse he repeats what he has said in vv. 1, 2, about sending Timothy when he could no longer endure the separation. He is very emphatic as to his personal feeling and action and adopts the unusual course in this Epistle of using the singular, and that with the emphatic pronoun.[10]

In the earlier verses he had referred to Timothy's being sent to strengthen the faith of the Thessalonians. Now we have the other side of it, namely that he had been sent also in order that the Apostle might be reassured. Paul was anxious to hear that their faith had not failed in the time of testing.

The concluding part of the verse employs a change of construction, from indicative to subjunctive, which it is impossible to reproduce in English. The effect of the indicative is to give the impression that the writer feels it probable that the tempter has

---

[9] Rather curiously, E. G. Selwyn sees in vv. 3, 4 evidence of "the close connection between persecution and the approaching final judgment" (W. D. Davies and D. Daube, ed., *The Background of the New Testament and Its Eschatology* [Cambridge, 1956], p. 399). While there is much eschatology in the Thessalonian Epistles, these verses do not seem to form part of it. Paul is talking about persecutions which have already come to pass, not some which would herald the End.

[10] Also with καί, the form being κἀγώ. The force of this is "I also," "I for my part." Frame thinks it means "I too as well as Silvanus," but this seems to be reading rather much into the expression. We do not know that Silvanus was with Paul in those days. In any case the Greek expression seems simply to emphasize the "I." Moule thinks the force of καί here is "I actually sent," "that is in fact why I sent" (*op. cit.*, p. 167).

indeed tempted them. But the subjunctive throws doubt on the idea that the preachers' labor had been in vain. In other words, Paul manages to convey his confidence that they had resisted the temptation that he knew they would have encountered.[11]

The reference to the activity of the tempter should not be overlooked. Satan is referred to in every major division of the New Testament. He is supreme in the realm of evil spirits (Eph. 2:2, II Thess. 2:9). His activities are always opposed to God and to man's best interests.[12] Afflictions like sickness are often spoken of as due to the activity of his minions, and Paul's "stake in the flesh" is described as "a messenger of Satan to buffet me" (II Cor. 12:7). His activities in the realm of the spirit are seen in the taking away the good seed from the heart of men (Mark 4:15), and "sowing" evil people in the world (Matt. 13:39). As "the god of this world" he blinds the minds of the unbelieving (II Cor. 4:4). He tempted our Lord (Matt. 4, Luke 4) and he tempts His followers (Luke 22:3, I Cor. 7:5). He hindered Paul's missionary work (I Thess. 2:18). He sought to gain advantage over the faithful (II Cor. 2:11). Had he been successful in his fell work among the Thessalonians Paul's hard work (the word he uses means toil to the point of weariness; it is that rendered "labor" in 2:9) would have been rendered futile. Yet he is not conceived of dualistically, as commensurate with God. He is surely the chief among the enemies to be subjugated at the end (I Cor. 15:25). Yea, he has been defeated already (Col. 2:15). Christians here and now may defeat his purposes (Eph. 6:16).[13]

---

[11] It is possible also that the subjunctive clause looks to the future. Paul is sure of the temptation of Satan and nothing can be done about it. But it was possible to do something to prevent his toil being in vain, and so he sent Timothy.

[12] It is often said that Satan is not invariably opposed to man in the Old Testament. This is hard to establish. He is opposed to man in Job 1–2, and the only other places where Satan is referred to by name in the Old Testament are I Chron. 21:1; Ps. 109:6; Zech. 3:1, 2, in each of which the same seems true. Cf. also the "serpent" in Gen. 3.

[13] H. P. Liddon has a forceful passage on the existence of Satan: "We are told that men no longer believe in Satan; that for our generation the invisible house of bondage, with its fallen monarch, no longer exists! If this be so, a great deal more is or will be presently disbelieved in as well; but a Christian who submits to and accepts the teaching of the New Testament cannot but be struck with this fresh proof of the finished ingenuity of our great spiritual enemy. Like those masters of the art of earthly war who conquer less frequently by an ostentatious display of force on the battle field than by carefully concealed surprises which turn the position of an antagonist,

4. TIMOTHY'S REPORT, 3:6-8

6 But when Timothy came even now unto us from you, and brought us glad tidings of your faith and love, and that ye have good remembrance of us always, longing to see us, even as we also *to see* you;

7 for this cause, brethren, we were comforted over you in all our distress and affliction through your faith:

8 for now we live, if ye stand fast in the Lord.

6 A new section begins at this point and there is a real break in the sense. Paul has been speaking of what took place in the past, but here he comes practically right up to the present moment. It is evident that he was writing very soon after Timothy's arrival which he can speak of as taking place "even now." We have seen how all the indications are that Paul had been rather depressed at the turn of events. But the coming of Timothy with news of the way in which the Thessalonian converts had not only stood firm, but had gone on in the faith, had acted on him like a tonic. He wrote immediately with a full heart.

Something of his joy comes out in his description of Timothy's news with the term "brought us glad tidings." The verb he employs is the one which is usually translated "preach the gospel." Indeed, this is the only place in the whole of Paul's writings where it is used in any other sense than that. Some have felt that the news that the Thessalonians were making progress in Christian things was itself part of the gospel. But this seems far fetched. It is more likely that the term is used as being the most expressive open to Paul. For Christians generally there is no good news that can compare with the tidings that God has given to men life through the death of His Son. One word became the technical term to denote this best of good news. That Paul just this once uses it for other good news is the measure of the joy it had brought him.

There are three points that he enumerates. The first is the news about the faith of the Thessalonians. His deep concern for their

---

so Satan, it seems, has persuaded a frivolous and shallow generation that he no longer exists but as a discredited phantom of the past, as an extinct terror, as a popular joke! Ah! he has not been at work upon the human heart for nothing during these many thousands of years; he knows how to lull us to sleep to the best advantage, that he may take our thoughts and affections, and, above all, our passions, well into his keeping" (*Sermons on Old Testament Subjects* [London, 1904], pp. 29 f.).

faith has been noted already (vv. 2, 5). He expresses his relief now that they have not wavered in maintaining a right attitude to God.

The second point is that they had continued in love. Just as faith is the characteristic attitude of the Christian toward God, so is love his characteristic attitude toward man. It stands for his complete readiness to give himself in wholehearted service for others (see on 1:3). Timothy had gladdened Paul with the news that the Thessalonians were exercising this virtue. The combination of faith and love is no mean summary of the whole duty of the Christian man. As Paul says elsewhere, "neither circumcision availeth anything, nor uncircumcision; but faith working through love" (Gal. 5:6). Calvin comments: "in these two words he comprehends briefly the entire sum of true piety. Hence all that aim at this twofold mark during their whole life are beyond all risk of erring: all others, however much they may torture themselves, wander miserably."

The third point is their attitude to Paul. He had evidently wondered how far the propaganda of his enemies had been effective. He had feared that his converts might now hold him in small esteem. But he was delighted to find that, "you cherish happy memories of us" (Phillips). The Thessalonians had not allowed hostile propaganda to distort their recollections of the visit of the great Apostle. They still looked back on it with joy. They did more. They looked forward with eager longing[14] to a reunion, and were just as anxious to see Paul again as he was to see them.

7 Paul was comforted "for this cause." He uses the singular, so that he is gathering up the faith and the love and the good remembrance and the eager desire to see him into one whole. This represented one great fact. It was the total impression left by these various facets of the attitude of the Thessalonians which meant so much.

The verb "comforted" is that used in v. 2 (where see note). It does not mean that he was soothed, but that he was given new strength. The tidings brought by Timothy had reinvigorated him. "Over" is an unusual preposition in such a connection, and its

---

[14] ἐπιποθέω, which is the verb used, looks like a stronger expression than the simple ποθέω, though this cannot be pressed in view of the well-known fondness of later Greek writers for compound forms. More decisive is the fact that the verb does seem to have a marked emotional content in passages like II Cor. 5:2, Phil. 1:8, 2:26, and, we conclude, here also.

significance is that Paul's new strength was securely based "on" the Thessalonians. The same preposition is used in the next phrase (ARV "in"), and, while it is very difficult to find one English word which will do justice to the Greek, it is not hard to see the force of the word. The idea is still something like "over," "upon," and the impression it leaves is that the new strength given Paul enabled him to rise above the difficulties in which he found himself.[15]

That Paul was in no easy situation when Timothy reached him is brought out in his reference to "distress and affliction." The former of these words basically denotes "necessity." It is that which constrains one into a certain position. From this it gets the derived notion of compulsion, and so straits, distress (cf. Luke 21:23). "Affliction" is the word used in 1:6 (where see note). The combination denotes that the Apostle was carrying on his work under grave difficulties and against much opposition. Rutherford renders, "We were altogether miserable and crushed; but your faith has recovered us."

This is the fourth time in this chapter that Paul has mentioned the faith of the Thessalonians. It was this that strengthened him. Again and again he comes back to it. There is more to Christianity than faith, but faith is the primary thing.

8 This is brought out in another way in the reference to standing fast in the Lord.[16] Elsewhere Paul speaks of standing by faith (Rom. 11:20, II Cor. 1:24). We need not think that this was out of his mind here. The thing that really rejoiced him, the thing that really strengthened him, the thing that gave him life, was the fact so clearly demonstrated by Timothy's mission, that the Thessalonians did indeed believe. Their lives were characterized by faith. This meant that they had a place in God's kingdom, and this in turn that Paul's work among them had not been in vain.

Elsewhere Paul writes, "to me to live is Christ" (Phil. 1:21). The present passage gives another facet of the same truth. The service

---

15 "The first ἐπί denotes the basis of the encouragement; the second ἐπί the purpose for which it was welcome; and the διά the means by which it was conveyed, 'through this faith of yours' (ὑμῶν being emphatic . . .)" (Frame).

16 There is a division of opinion among the commentators as to whether νῦν should be taken as temporal or logical. The truth appears to be, as Lightfoot says, "in a case like this it is almost impossible to distinguish the temporal sense of νῦν ('now') from the ethical ('under these circumstances'). The one meaning shades off imperceptibly into the other."

of Christ was for Paul no halfhearted thing, but that which
mattered most in life. This service did not mean an idle contemplation of the excellencies of the Savior. It was an active, fruitful
work of preaching Him and His atonement among the Gentiles.
Thus Paul could equally say that Christ was his life, and that it
meant life to him to know that his converts were standing. It was
his service of Christ to win men for Him ("that I may by all means
save some," I Cor. 9:22). Thus it was life indeed to know that this
had happened. "Ye" is emphatic, which indicates some of the
importance Paul attached to the conduct of the Thessalonians. At
the time of which he was writing it was they and no other who
were to prove the vindication of the gospel that he preached.
Similarly, the verb he uses for "stand fast" is important. It is not
the ordinary word for standing. By the use of the less usual term
Paul manages to convey the idea of a firmness, a steadfastness in
the stand taken up.[17]

5. PAUL'S SATISFACTION, 3:9, 10

9 For what thanksgiving can we render again unto God
for you, for all the joy wherewith we joy for your
sakes before our God;
10 night and day praying exceedingly that we may see
your face, and may perfect that which is lacking in
your faith?

9 The turn of events might have been understood by some as
affording good reason for the founders of the church at Thessalonica indulging in some self-congratulation. They had built
well, and their handiwork had survived a severe test. But Paul's
is a satisfaction at what God has wrought, and not in any way a
self-satisfaction. He knew—none better—that it is not of men to
do a spiritual work. That is only done by the grace of God. Now
that he has had such a signal manifestation of this grace he asks
what thanksgiving (not "thanks," but the expression of thanks is
meant) can be rendered[18] to God for all that He has done (cf.
II Cor. 4:15).

---

[17] The verb στήκω is a late form deriving from ἕστηκα. Grimm–Thayer
give its meaning as "to stand ... with an emphasis, to stand firm."
[18] ἀνταποδοῦναι conveys the idea of a recompense which is both due and
adequate. Lightfoot translates, "What sufficient thanks can we repay?"

Similarly, at the end of the verse Paul rejoices mightily at what has happened. But it is a joy before God. That is to say, his joy is a spiritual state, and not a fleshly satisfaction. He recognizes that the joy wherewith he rejoices is something that comes from God.

If it is true that his thoughts are God-centred, it is also true that he finds a large place for the Thessalonians. Findlay points out that in verses 6–10 he has used the Greek pronoun for "you" in one or other of its cases no less than ten times (CGT). He dwells on them with frank delight.

10 In harmony with this he is always praying for them. "Night and day" does not denote prayer at two set times, but rather continued prayer. And if it is continual it is also fervent, an unusual adverb being employed to bring this out. Paul uses it elsewhere only in 5:13 and Eph. 3:20, and nobody else in the New Testament employs it at all. There are various ways of expressing the thought of abundance, and this double compound is probably the most emphatic of all. There is nothing perfunctory or merely formal about Paul's prayers. They come from his heart and his passionate yearning to see his friends once more. It is in line with this that he uses here a word for "praying" which basically signifies "a want," "a lack," rather than the more common word expressive of devotion. His prayer springs from a sense of deprivation. He feels that he needs them and prays accordingly.

His prayer is, firstly, that he might see them. This follows on much that he has said earlier, and which has left no doubt of his deep desire for reunion with his friends. But when he joins them again he does not wish simply to talk about the weather. So he goes on that he wishes to "perfect that which is lacking in your faith" (cf. Rom. 1:11). Notice this further reference to the faith of his converts. Throughout this chapter he has come back to their faith again and again. Yet in his joy at the faith that they undoubtedly possessed he was not oblivious to the sterner realities of the situation. His desire to be with them was accompanied[19] by the desire to be useful by remedying the defects there were in that faith. This comes out both in the verb he employs for "perfect" and the noun rendered "what is lacking."

The former means basically "to render complete" and of itself

---

[19] The closeness of the connection between the two ideas is shown by the fact that the two infinitives are linked under a single article.

indicates that its object is not complete. It is used in the material
sphere of such an activity as mending nets (Matt. 4:21), and in
spiritual things the cognate noun is employed of the process of
bringing the saints to perfection (Eph. 4:12). It is such a sense as
this last which is in mind here. "What is lacking" is our rendering
of a plural noun from a root meaning "to come behind." It may be
used of material lack (II Cor. 8:14, 9:12, etc.), but also, as here, of
deficiencies in spiritual things. The plural points us to the fact that
more than one thing needed rectification. Paul has dwelt with
obvious delight on the state of the Thessalonians, but that did not
mean that he was blind to their failings. As a true pastor he knew
that there was much that had to be done for them. It was his aim
to play some part in seeing that they were set forward on the
right road.

6. PAUL'S PRAYER, 3:11-13

> 11 Now may our God and Father himself, and our Lord
> Jesus, direct our way unto you:
> 12 and the Lord make you to increase and abound in love
> one toward another, and toward all men, even as we
> also *do* toward you;
> 13 to the end he may establish your hearts unblamable
> in holiness before our God and Father, at the coming
> of our Lord Jesus with all his saints.

11 It is characteristic of Paul's letters that he frequently slips
into some short prayer. Thus at this point, where he is so concerned
with his friends at Thessalonica and has given such evidence of his
desire to be with them, he breaks out into a prayer that God would
bring them together. It is typical that he should speak of God as
directing him to them, and not simply of his paying a visit or the
like. Paul does not forget that God rules in the affairs of men.
Even his incidental expressions reveal how much the sovereignty
of God means to him. He speaks of God as "our God and Father,"
a manner of address which brings out the characteristic Christian
insight into the nature of God. The possessive "our" directs attention to the personal relationship that has been established. It is
God's nature to be a Father. But it is not the teaching of Scripture
that He is indiscriminately a Father to all men. Rather, He makes
provision for men to become sons by adoption (cf. Rom. 8:15,

Gal. 4:5, etc.). But both Paul and his friends had entered the heavenly family by faith. Thus he can make use of "our" when he speaks of the Father.[20]

It is significant for his understanding of the nature of the Godhead that he joins so closely his references to the Father and to the Son. Here he links the two by making them the joint subject of a verb which is in the singular. This is not a formal Trinitarian definition, but it is the kind of understanding of the nature of the Godhead which led inevitably to the formulation of the dogma of the Trinity. This is all the more impressive in that it is done incidentally. Paul is not giving a theoretical discourse on the nature of deity, but engaging in prayer. Out of his understanding of God there proceeds naturally this form of expression in which we see the highest place given to Jesus. Full deity is ascribed to Him. In that Paul feels no necessity to produce arguments to demonstrate this we may feel that the point was accepted just as fully by the Thessalonians as by the Apostle. And in view of the early date of this writing this is important for the development of Christian doctrine. The deity of Christ was held from a very early date. It is not to be regarded as the culmination of a process of slow growth and reflection.

Paul prays that his God will "direct" his way to them. The verb has the idea of "making straight," perhaps even "making level." The thought appears to be that of preparing a road so that all unevenness is removed, and travel facilitated. Paul looks to God to remove the obstacles which up till this time had prevented him from paying the longed-for visit to the Thessalonians.

12 "And" at the beginning of this verse should be "but." The Greek conjunction is adversative, and the sense of it is "whatever be the case with me and my companions, as for you, may God . . . ." Paul could desire earnestly to be with his friends and impart unto them some spiritual gift. But he recognizes that their spiritual growth was in the Lord's hands, not in his. So his prayer moves on from his own desire to see them again to the more important

---

20 Some have felt that the αὐτός is emphatic, and that, taken in conjunction with the adversative δέ, there is a strong contrast between God and, either men praying (v. 10), or Satan. This seems unlikely. δέ introduces a new section of the letter, and does not seem to be strongly adversative. The emphatic αὐτός is sufficiently accounted for by Paul's stress on God's active rule in the affairs of men (cf. 5:23, II Thess. 2:16, etc.).

matter of their growth in the faith. Theoretically "the Lord" could refer to either of the Persons just mentioned, the Father or the Son, but it is Paul's habit to refer to Jesus by this title. The probability is that it is the Lord Jesus that he has in mind here. It is also probable that he made no great distinction between them. There are several passages in these Epistles where the Father and the Son are linked very closely (see the passages listed in the note on 1:1). It is evident that Paul did not separate them very decisively in his thought.

Paul prays that his friends may increase in love. Some have sought to make a distinction between the two verbs he uses, but they seem to be more or less synonymous. The use of both of them rather than one is a device for giving emphasis to what he is saying.[21] The latter verb is the more emphatic, and it is used by Paul much more frequently than the former, which in this transitive sense is found only here in the New Testament. The latter is used often of the divine grace abounding. Paul looked for Christians to abound in love just as the grace of God abounds to them.

Christians should have a special regard for one another within the brotherhood. They should also look on those outside the brotherhood as God does, with love. Paul brings both these thoughts into his prayer, and he makes petition that they may increase in love. For the specifically Christian idea of love see the note on *agape* in 1:3. It is love for men quite apart from their worthiness or otherwise, a love which proceeds in the first place from the loving heart of God. When the miracle takes place and a man passes from death to life, when he becomes a new creature in Christ Jesus, then he comes to see men in a measure as God sees them. He loves them selflessly.[22] Paul has already recognized that the Thessalonians exercise this quality, and his prayer at this point is that they may increase in this divine activity. Characteristically he appeals to the example he had set them (see on 1:6). Paul knew full well that no preacher can call on men to do what he himself is not prepared to do. He did not hesitate on more than one occasion to point out that he practiced what he preached. It may

---

[21] Cf. Chrysostom, "Do you see the unchecked madness of love which is indicated by the words? He says πλεονάσαι and περισσεύσαι instead of αὐξήσει" (cited by Frame).

[22] Moffatt comments, "no form of ἁγιωσύνη which sits loose to the endless obligations of this ἀγάπη will stand the strain of this life or the scrutiny of God's tribunal at the end."

be that under modern conditions the preacher is not wise to direct attention to himself. But it is still as true as ever it was that if a man's message is to carry conviction it must first be found true in his own life.

13 While Paul was interested in the here and now he was not preoccupied with this present life. His prayer looks forward to the second coming of the Lord. The abounding for which he prays is in order that the Thessalonians may be unshaken even at the second coming.

The verb "establish" we have met in v. 2 (where see note). The prayer here is that God will so supply the needed buttress that the Thessalonians will remain firm and unmoved whatever the future may hold. The heart, as in 2:4 (where see note), stands for the whole of the inner life, and not simply for the seat of the emotions as with us. It is easy enough for men to become a prey to fears and alarms, to take up every new doctrine, to accept the unreasoning hope that leads inevitably to irresolution, disillusionment, and disaster. Paul longs to see his converts delivered from all such instability. He prays that they may have such a sure basis in love that they will be delivered from all this sort of thing. If God gives them this good gift He will establish their whole personality.

Yet we must not think of this as nothing more than a prayer for personal calm and confidence. There is in Paul's complex thought for them a pronounced ethical and spiritual element. This comes out in the succeeding expressions. He prays for them to be "unblamable." Nothing less than the very highest standard will do for the Christian. Even before he became a Christian Paul felt that this word could be applied to his conduct (Phil. 3:6). The Christian certainly can have no lower standard before him. Indeed the word has a fuller meaning here. In Philippians Paul had claimed blamelessness only as regards "the righteousness which is in the law," but there is no such limitation here. Rather, the thought is of blamelessness before God. We should be in no doubt as to the high standard that is set before us.

But the thought is not simply ethical. The Apostle goes on to bring in the notion of holiness, in which the basic idea is that of being set apart for God. The word that Paul uses signifies the state rather than the process. In the Greek Old Testament the

113

word is used only of God Himself. In the New Testament it is applied to men only here and in II Cor. 7:1. Paul leaves no doubt as to the wholeheartedness with which the Christian is given over to his Lord. The most usual designation of Christians in the New Testament is simply "the holy ones," "the saints," the word being from this same root. The believer does not simply live uprightly. He belongs to God; he is set apart entirely for God's service. Paul's prayer is that this may be fully realized among the Thessalonians.

He makes this ultimate by bringing in the thought of the second coming (see note on *parousia* in 2:19). He prays that right through, until this event which will usher in the end of this age, the Thessalonians may realize the glorious destiny he has been speaking of. It is that aspect of the *parousia* which means the end of this present form of existence that is in mind.

There is something of a difficulty in the final expression, rendered "with all his saints." The last word means "holy ones." As we have just seen, this is the way in which Christians are most commonly described in the New Testament, but the word can scarcely have this meaning here. These "holy ones" will be coming with Jesus, and Paul is praying that *believers on earth* may have their hearts established at that coming. He is distinguishing between believers on earth, and the "holy ones" who will come with the Lord.

But "holy ones" is an expression which lends itself to other meanings. In particular, angels may be meant, or the saints who have departed this life. Good but not decisive arguments can be ranged in support of either view. Thus angels are designated "holy ones" in the Greek Old Testament, the Bible of the early church (Ps. 89:5, Dan. 4:13 [Th.], 8:13, Zech. 14:5). Angels are also associated with the second coming in the New Testament (Matt. 13:41, 25:31, Mark 8:38, Luke 9:26, II Thess. 1:7). In view of the fact that the Dead Sea Scrolls bring us examples of Jewish literature of the immediate pre-Christian era it may not be without significance that they use the term "holy ones" of angels. Millar Burrows tells us that the "Manual of Discipline" usually uses "angel" of evil spirits. For good spirits it prefers "holy ones" or "sons of heaven." Similarly the "Thanksgiving Psalms" refer to "the army of the holy ones," and "the assembly of thy holy ones."[23]

---

[23] See *The Dead Sea Scrolls* (London, 1956), pp. 261 f.

It is clear that in the Judaism of the post-Old Testament period "holy ones" was an accepted designation of angels.

Against this identification is the fact that angels never seem to be called simply "holy ones" in the New Testament. As used by the early Christians this expression seems always elsewhere to refer to men.

In this particular case there seems no reason for holding that Paul's thought is limited to the one class or the other. It is clear from the New Testament that both angels and the departed saints will be associated with the Lord when He returns. There seems no reason at all why Paul should be intending to eliminate one or other of these classes at this point. It is best to understand the "holy ones" as all those bright beings who will make up His train, be they angels or the saints who have gone before.[24]

---

[24] This interpretation is adopted by O. Allis, *Prophecy in the Church* (Philadelphia, 1945), pp. 185 ff.

COMMENTARY ON I THESSALONIANS

CHAPTER IV

V. EXHORTATION TO CHRISTIAN LIVING, 4:1-12

1. GENERAL EXHORTATIONS, 4:1, 2
   1 Finally then, brethren, we beseech and exhort you in the Lord Jesus, that, as ye received of us how ye ought to walk and to please God, even as ye do walk,—that ye abound more and more.
   2 For ye know what charge we gave you through the Lord Jesus.

1 It is Paul's habit to treat of doctrinal matters, answers to correspondents, and the like, in the earlier part of his epistles. Then at the end he deals with the practical implications for the living of the Christian life. In this Epistle "Finally then" is the expression which marks the transition. It does not mean, as the English might suggest, that he is in process of ending the Epistle. It does signify that the main section of the Epistle is concluded, but the subsidiary section which it introduces may be rather lengthy and it may be very important.[1]

Paul's exhortation to the Thessalonians is meant very seriously. He underlines it with the double injunction, "we beseech and exhort you." The two verbs have their own proper meanings, but in this context the difference is not important. They simply reinforce one another, and the combination gives emphasis to the Apostle's request.[2] The affectionate "brethren" fits into this pattern, for Paul is putting the right way before people who were dear friends of his. Indeed, it is this which makes his exhortation so very important to him. He exhorts them "in the Lord Jesus."

---

[1] The expression is λοιπὸν οὖν, a combination found nowhere else in the New Testament, though Milligan says it occurs in the papyri. λοιπόν or τὸ λοιπόν, however, is reasonably common (λοιπόν is read here by some manuscripts). It means "for the rest" and may introduce an additional item (as in I Cor. 1:16) as well as a section of an epistle. Milligan thinks that in late Greek "it is practically equivalent to an emphatic οὖν."

[2] On the use of ἐρωτάω Findlay remarks, "'Ερωτάω conceives the request in a question form ('Will you do so and so?') . . . thus gives a personal urgency to it, challenging the answer as αἰτέω does not" (CGT).

That is to say, he is not taking up any position of superiority, nor, on the other hand, is his attitude one of hesitant timidity. He speaks as one who has authority committed to him by the Lord. He speaks as one who has "the mind of Christ" (I Cor. 2:16). He speaks to men who themselves are in Christ.[3] He speaks of the conduct that befits men in Christ.

In these first two verses he is not concerned with specific problems of behavior, but with the whole of the Christian life. Accordingly he uses general terms like "walk" and "abound." The former is commonly employed, especially by Paul and John, as a way of referring to the whole of a man's manner of living. So common is that that Grimm–Thayer can give as one of the meanings of the verb, "Hebraistically, *to live*." This may connect with the fact that a favorite designation of Christianity in the earliest days was "the Way" (Acts 9:2, 19:23, 24:22). Or it may be that the metaphor suggested itself from the idea of continual, if unspectacular, advance, which should, of course, characterize the Christian.

Walking is connected with pleasing God (for "please," see on 2:4). The whole Christian life is God-centered. The Christian does not "walk" with a view to obtaining the maximum amount of satisfaction for himself, but in order to please his Lord. Paul does not specify any particular matter in which they should "please" God; he is concerned with the whole bent of the life.

There is nothing new in all this, as Paul is at pains to make clear. He had told them to live in this way at the time of his mission among them ("as ye received[4] of us"), and he is not now introducing some novelty. He had told them that they "ought" to behave in the fashion outlined, and the word is a strong one. It is usually translated "must," and it brings before us the compelling necessity under which Christians lie. When a man is saved by the

---

[3] The position of ἐν Κυρίῳ ᾽Ιησοῦ at the end, with ὑμᾶς between the two verbs, probably means that "in the Lord Jesus" is to be taken with "we," the subject, rather than with ὑμᾶς. However, the connection is not so strong that a side glance at ὑμᾶς may not be included, especially since Paul elsewhere insists that the Thessalonians, too, were in Christ. The main point, though, is the authority with which Paul speaks, an authority proceeding from the fact that he is "in the Lord Jesus."

[4] παραλαμβάνω is the verb usually used to denote the receiving of the message by converts, e.g., I Cor. 15:3. It has reference rather to the formal external act of reception, than to the subjective act of welcoming (δέχομαι), cf. 2:13 (where see note).

work of Christ for him it does not lie open before him as a matter for his completely free decision whether he will serve God or not. He has been bought with a price (I Cor. 6:20). He has become the slave of Christ. Christian service is not an optional extra for those who like that kind of thing. It is a compelling obligation which lies upon each one of the redeemed.

It is Paul's habit to blend his exhortations and reproofs with a judicious mixture of praise where that can in good conscience be done. It does not surprise us accordingly to find him interjecting, "even as ye do walk." He is not complaining that they had not been living out the Christian life. They had heeded the exhortation when it was originally given. Timothy's report showed that they were still putting it into practice. Paul lets them know that he is not unmindful of their achievement. But the Christian can never rest satisfied. So Paul urges them to further endeavor.

The substance of his exhortation is that they should "abound more and more." This is an unusual way to employ this verb, for it is much more common to have the quality which is to abound specified. This is the case, for example, in 3:12, where Paul speaks of abounding in love (cf. Phil. 1:9). The absence of any such specific virtue in this place is in keeping with the fact that this is the general introduction, and Paul is dealing with the whole of life. Specific instructions are to follow, but here he is concerned with the thought that the Christian is to grow continually. His life is far from static. Paradoxically it can be said of him that he is the slave of Christ, and that he is the freest of men (John 8:36).[5] The Thessalonians were under the necessity of living to please God, but far from leading them into a narrow and cramped existence, this opened the door for them to live the abundant life (cf. John 10:10).

2 Again Paul looks back to the days of his visit to assure them that he is doing no more than lead them along the way he had then showed them. "Ye know," he says, calling them to witness that this was so.

The word rendered "charge" is plural, and better taken as mg.

---

[5] Cf. the remark of Martin Luther, "A Christian man is a perfectly free lord of all, subject to none. A Christian man is a perfectly dutiful servant of all, subject to all" (*The Works of Martin Luther* [Philadelphia, 1915–32], Vol. II, p. 312.

"charges." Paul and his companions had given instructions on several matters, possibly in the form of rules. The word is an unusual one in a Christian context. It is found elsewhere in the New Testament of commands to believers only in I Tim. 1:5, 18. It is more at home in a military environment, being a usual word for the commands given by the officer to his men (cf. its use in Acts 5:28, 16:24).[6] It is thus a word with a ring of authority. It is this which makes it suitable for this context where Paul is stressing the authoritative nature of the injunctions in question.

These, though given by Paul, did not originate with him. He makes the point that they were given "through the Lord Jesus." "Through" is not the preposition that we might have expected. It may be a shorthand way of saying that the commandments referred to came from the Father, and that therefore they came with all the authority that was possible. Or it may mean that Paul spoke only on the authority of the Lord Jesus.[7] Either way he is disclaiming personal responsibility and ascribing the highest possible authority to the injunctions to which he refers.[8]

2. SEXUAL PURITY, 4:3-8

3 For this is the will of God, *even* your sanctification, that ye abstain from fornication;
4 that each one of you know how to possess himself of his own vessel in sanctification and honor,
5 not in the passion of lust, even as the Gentiles who know not God;
6 that no man transgress, and wrong his brother in the matter: because the Lord is an avenger in all these things, as also we forewarned you and testified.
7 For God called us not for uncleanness, but in sanctification.
8 Therefore he that rejecteth, rejecteth not man, but God, who giveth his Holy Spirit unto you.

---

[6] παραγγελία is probably a command passed along (παρά) a line of soldiers. From this it comes to signify any authoritative order. Though this noun is rare in the New Testament the cognate verb is used quite often.

[7] Moule gives the meaning as: "in the name of the Lord Jesus," though he proceeds to ask whether it may not signify: "as those who are in contact with the Lord Jesus" (*Idiom Book*, pp. 57 f.). Plainly the expression indicates that the words to which it refers are authoritative.

[8] Either way also he is connecting the Father and the Son in the closest possible fashion. Denney cites this as one of the passages in which we see "this co-ordination of Christ with the Father, this elevation into the sphere

3 It comes as something of a surprise to modern men to find an exhortation to sexual purity in the forefront of practical directions to a Christian church. This, however, was very much in place in writing to the inhabitants of a first-century Greek city, for by the Greeks sexual sin was but lightly condemned.[9] Continence was regarded as an unreasonable demand on a man. In society at large it was taken for granted that men would naturally seek the satisfaction of their sexual desires outside the marriage bond. The pressure to conform to the easy standards accepted throughout society must have been strong on the early church.[10] Especially so since so large a proportion of her membership consisted of men and women of limited ability and circumscribed outlook, men and women, moreover, who of necessity were imperfectly instructed in the Christian faith. Yet the leaders of the church did not compromise for one moment. They knew that God required of them the highest standard, and they had no authority to lower that standard. Thus they refused to allow the practice of the Christian church to be determined by the ideas of contemporary society.

In the light of modern surveys of the sexual behavior of the community we may take liberty to doubt whether such exhortations as the one before us are yet out of date. Just as much in the twentieth century as in the first it must be insisted that Christian standards are to be taken from God and not from the low ideals of contemporary society. This is true of all of life, but we must not overlook its relevance in the sphere of sexual morality.

Paul does not mention any specific sin of this kind as having taken place among the Thessalonians (contrast I Cor. 5:1 ff.). There is no reason for thinking that the Thessalonians had actually given way to the temptation. The strong warning is probably to be understood in the light of the prevalence of low standards. It is

---

of the divine in which Christ and the Father work harmoniously the salvation of men." Denney proceeds, "Every function of the Christian life is determined by it" (*Jesus and the Gospel* [London, 1908], pp. 31 f.). See also the notes on 3:11.

[9] This was not the case among the Jews. S–BK, for example, can cite Rabbinic statements which regard unchastity as incompatible with holiness.

[10] This would be all the more so at Thessalonica if, as Lightfoot thought, the cult of the Kabeiroi there promoted "gross immorality . . . under the name of religion," and gave rise to "foul orgies" (*Biblical Essays* [London, 1893], p. 258). Such practices were common in many forms of worship, and there is nothing improbable in Lightfoot's suggestion. However, positive evidence of the nature of the worship at Thessalonica seems to be lacking.

meant to prevent rather than to rebuke sin. Had a definite case occurred we must think that Paul would have been much more direct. But he takes no risks with his beloved Thessalonians, and so he warns them.

He puts chastity before them as "the will of God." "Will" is without the article in the Greek. The force of this is that Paul is not attempting to tell them everything that is included in God's will for them. This includes many things.[11] Among them is the one of which he speaks. Paul's direction, then, is on the very highest plane. He does not speak on the level of ethics or prudence or ecclesiastical regulations. This is what God wants them to do, and there could be no higher sanction.

This is his point also in referring to "sanctification." We have already noticed the consistent New Testament doctrine that every one who believes is holy, i.e., set apart for God (see on 3:13). We come to Christ in all our sin, and we receive cleansing by His atoning death. Then day by day we become more and more what God would have us to be. We increasingly experience the reality of being set apart for Him. Sanctification is the name given to this process as holiness to the final state. When Paul speaks at this point of sanctification as being God's will for the Thessalonian converts, he is reminding them of the implications of their having been purchased by the blood of Christ. Henceforth they belong to Him. Their lives must reflect this.

But Paul is not now concerned with a general dissertation on the dedicated Christian life, but with the particular aspect of sexual purity. So he proceeds to the point, "that ye abstain from fornication." His verb is a strong one, and it is reinforced by a preposition which emphasizes the separation. The Christian must have no truck with this evil thing. The noun covers all forms of illicit sexual intercourse.[12] These are incompatible with the sanctification required of a Christian. The whole question of sex relationships has to be viewed in the light of the fact that the body of the Christian belongs to God (cf. I Cor. 6:19 f.).

---

[11] Lightfoot and Frame cite Bengel *multae sunt voluntates*.

[12] A. J. Mason, however, writes: "The word is often used in late Greek for any kind of impurity . . . but here it must be understood in its strict sense. To the Gentile mind, while the wickedness of adultery or incest was fully recognized, it was a novelty to be told that fornication was a 'deadly sin'" (*ad. loc.*).

4 Having said negatively that one should abstain from certain forms of conduct Paul now puts the positive side of the same truth, namely, that men should live continently. The big problem in this verse is to know exactly what he had in mind when he exhorted each man "to possess himself of his own vessel." Usually "vessel" has been understood to mean "body," but there are some ancient and many modern commentators who maintain that in this passage it signifies "wife."

In favor of the former are the facts that the early Greek commentators usually understood it in this way. There does not seem to be any other instance of "vessel," without qualification, as meaning "body."[13] But there are partial parallels, as in the reference to treasure "in earthern vessels" (II Cor. 4:7). Moreover, in Greek writers generally, the body is often thought of as the instrument or vessel of the soul. The big difficulty in the way of accepting "body" as the meaning is the verb, which really means "to acquire," and it is not easy to see how a man can "acquire" his own body. However, there is evidence from the papyri that it could be used in the sense "possess,"[14] so that this difficulty is not insuperable.[15]

A few early commentators like Theodore of Mopsuestia and Augustine held that the word means "wife," and a good number of modern writers follow them. The strongest argument for this view appears to be that there are a few passages (Grimm–Thayer cite two in the Septuagint and one in Xenophon) where the combination of this noun and verb means "to marry." This is said to be supported by the reference to the wife as "the weaker vessel"

---

[13] In *The Epistle of Barnabas* 7:3, 11:9, we have the expression "the vessel of His Spirit," τὸ σκεῦος τοῦ πνεύματος αὐτοῦ, which refers to the body of our Lord. Again, in Hermas, *Mandate* 5:2 σκεῦος is the vessel in which the Holy Spirit dwells.

[14] MM cite a papyrus dated A.D. 23 where κτάομαι is used with the meaning "have": "I swear that I have thirty days in which to restore to you the man whom I bailed out of the public prison." A meaning like "acquire" is impossible here. (It should, however, be added that their own opinion of the verb in I Thess. 4:4 is that it means "gradually obtain the complete mastery of the body"). The perfect of the verb is, of course, used regularly in the sense "to have acquired," "to possess." The importance of the papyrus cited is that it shows that the present took on this meaning also. Liddell and Scott cite Luke 18:12 as another example of this use.

[15] Some see difficulty also in the use of ἑαυτοῦ, feeling that it is inapplicable to the body. However, the word is often used in a non-emphatic way in late Greek, and this is to be taken as an example of such. Mason thinks it means "the vessel or instrument which consists of himself" (*ad loc.*).

THE FIRST EPISTLE TO THE THESSALONIANS

in I Pet. 3:7. This latter point must, however, be discounted, for
the wife is not spoken of as the husband's "vessel" at all. Both are
"vessels" of the Holy Ghost, the wife being the weaker. Thus the
passage does not really bear on our problem. Among the Rabbis
the Hebrew equivalent of the Greek word here is used of the
wife,[16] and this may have influenced Paul.

It is not easy to decide the point, but it does seem to me that it
would not be very natural for a Greek writer to speak of a wife as
a "vessel." And in this case it would be the less likely since Paul
is inculcating a high view of marriage, and it is a very low view
that thinks of the wife as no more than a vessel for gratifying the
husband's sexual desires. This, taken in conjunction with the
positive evidence above, inclines me to the view that "body" is
meant. Paul then is exhorting his Thessalonian friends to keep
their bodies pure.

He does not use the term "pure," but prefers to use the idea of
sanctification again, and with it he joins honor. There is a right
use for a body which is set apart for the service of God. Sanctification excludes impurity. Again, impurity dishonors the body, so
that Paul's linking of honor with sanctification is much in point.[17]
Lightfoot well remarks: "The honour due to the body as such is
one of the great contrasts which Christianity offers to the loftiest
systems of heathen philosophy (e.g., Platonism and Stoicism)."[18]

5 The positive state of sanctification and honor is further
defined, the absence of a connecting particle showing that the same
idea carries on. The God-empowered man rules his body. He is
not caught in the grip of lustful passions he is quite unable to
control. The word "passion" is always used by Paul in a bad sense.

---

[16] See the passages in S–BK, *ad loc.*

[17] ἁγιασμῷ and τιμῇ are linked by one preposition, ἐν, and Findlay
comments, "the 'honour' of the human person has a religious basis in the
devotion of the body and its functions to God" (CGT).

[18] Cf. the comment of Chr. Wordsworth: "The deadly sin here reprobated . . . was excused by parents (*Terent.* Adelph. I. ii. 21), *commended* by
moralists (*Horat.* I Sat. ii. 32; cp. *Cicero* pro Coelio 48), and consecrated by
the Religion of Heathenism, especially in Greece, and particularly at *Corinth*,
where St. Paul now was" (*ad loc.*). Similarly W. E. H. Lecky says, "In Greece
monogamy, though not without exceptions, had been enforced, but a con-
currence of influences very unfavourable to chastity prevented any high
standard being attained among the men, and almost every form of sensual
indulgence beyond the limits of marriage was permitted" (*History of European
Morals* [London, 1869], pp. 106 f.).

It denotes not so much the violent desire, which the English "passion" suggests, as an overmastering desire. The root connects with the thought of suffering, and this noun expresses the feeling which a man suffers. It expresses the passive side of the vice. "Lust" on the other hand is the active, aggressive word.[19] It is used of strong desire of any kind. Occasionally it is used of some good desire, as in 2:17 (where see note), but more characteristically it denotes an evil desire, and that a very strong one. Paul is picturing the man who gives himself over to his lusts.

This conduct, he says, is typical of "the Gentiles." The word is a very general one, and means "the nations." Its usual use is by the Jews to denote the entire non-Jewish world, and we become used to the word as signifying non-Jews. It is not usual to find it in the sense "non-Christians," but that is evidently the meaning here. This does not mean that Paul is including the Jews among those who succumbed to impurity, for their high moral standards were well known. Rather, he is thinking of Christians (who at Thessalonica were predominantly non-Jewish in origin as we see from 1:9) as non-Gentiles. He is dividing the world into Christians and Gentiles. It is an eloquent commentary on the lax standards of sexual morality which were prevalent that Paul can speak of sexual vice as so entirely characteristic of the world of his day.

He puts it all down to their ignorance of God. They are "Gentiles who know not God." His thought on this matter is more fully developed in Rom. 1:18 ff., where he makes the point that they rejected the knowledge of God that was afforded them: "they refused to have God in their knowledge" (Rom. 1:28). Because of this they were delivered up to unnatural lusts (Rom. 1:24, 26, 28). It is a solemn thought that those who reject the knowledge of God which has been afforded them thereby make it inevitable that they

---

[19] Grimm–Thayer give the difference between the two words πάθος and ἐπιθυμία, thus: "π. presents the passive, ἐπ. the active side of a vice; ἐπ. is more comprehensive in meaning than π.; ἐπ. is (evil) desire, π. ungovernable desire" (sub. πάθος). Similarly Lightfoot, on Col. 3:5, says, "While πάθος includes all ungovernable affections, ἐπιθυμία κακή reaches to all evil longings." Trench affirms that ἐπιθυμία "in Scripture is the larger word, including the whole world of active lusts and desires, all to which the σάρξ, as the seat of desire and of the natural appetites, impels; while the πάθος is rather the 'morosa delectatio,' not so much the soul's disease in its more active operations, as the diseased condition out of which these spring . . . the 'lustfulness' ('Leidenschaft') as distinguished from the 'lust'" (Synonyms of the New Testament [London, 1880], p. 324).

will be given over to evil passions. Though his thought here is condensed there is no doubt that Paul has in mind the sort of thing he has expressed more fully in Rom. 1.

6 There are many ways of viewing sexual license. The way Paul chooses here is that it is a matter of defrauding another of his rights.[20] "You cannot break this rule without in some way cheating your fellow-men" (Phillips). The verb rendered "transgress" in ARV means "to go beyond," and thus "transgress." But where it has an object it means something like "to overreach." If we are to understand it here as being closely joined with the following verb and governing "brother,"[21] the meaning will be something like "defraud" (so Moffatt).[22] Joined with "wrong" it reminds us that all sexual looseness represents an act of injustice to someone other than the two parties concerned. Adultery is an obvious violation of the rights of another. But promiscuity before marriage represents the robbing of the other of that virginity which ought to be brought to a marriage. The future partner of such a one has been defrauded.[23]

Paul now gives reasons why this sort of conduct should be eschewed. His first point is that God will take action against these sins, as he had already warned them. It is noteworthy how often he comes back to the point that he had told them of this matter or that. It is clear that his instruction of the converts had been thorough, and had embraced the important matters that he felt called upon to emphasize in his letter.

---

[20] Cf. Moffatt, "The metaphors are drawn from trade, perhaps as appropriate to a trading community."

[21] While "brother" in the New Testament commonly denotes another member of the Christian brotherhood, here the meaning is wider, "brother man." If, however, we understand it as "fellow Christian," the meaning of the passage will be, in Bicknell's words: "This does not imply that it is allowable to wrong a non-Christian, but that it is doubly wicked to wrong a brother in Christ."

[22] It is, of course, quite possible to take ὑπερβαίνω here as intransitive (as ARV), in which case the thought of defrauding another is to be discerned in πλεονεκτέω only.

[23] Some have thought that this verse does not refer to sexual morality at all, taking "the matter" to refer to conduct generally, e.g., AV, "that no man go beyond and defraud his brother in any matter." However, the article with πράγματι points to the matter under discussion, and the fact that impurity is mentioned again in the next verse indicates that the thought is being continued throughout the whole passage.

ἐν τῷ πράγματι has sometimes been held to signify "in business." But while the plural τὰ πράγματα may have this meaning it does not seem to be attested for the singular.

The form in which this particular warning is cast is the reminder that God is "an avenger." This is a thought which is frequent in the Old Testament (e.g., Deut. 32:35), and, with somewhat different terminology, in the New also. We must not understand vengeance in the sense of the settling of private scores, but rather of the administration of an evenhanded justice. It is required of men that they live in accordance with moral law. If they do not, unpleasant consequences follow. These consequences are inevitable, for the hand of God is in them. As He is the Avenger, no man can reckon on escaping the consequences of his ill deeds. There is a sense in which that happens here and now, for the sinner is less a man because of his sin (cf. also the process described so solemnly in Rom. 1:18 ff.). In another sense the full requital for wrong will not be exacted until the last day. It is likely that Paul is glancing at the great Assize.

7 A second reason for purity is the whole character of the Christian life. In v. 4 Paul has spoken of "sanctification and honor," and it is this sort of thing he has in mind now. Indeed, he uses the same term "sanctification," and he adds to it the thought of the divine call, a call which involves the rejection of uncleanness. This last word can theoretically be used in various senses. In Matt. 23:27 it refers to the uncleanness within a tomb. But everywhere else in the New Testament it seems to refer to moral impurity, as is the case here.

Paul bases his demand for the renunciation of all uncleanness on the priority of the divine in the Christian way of life. God has called believers, and called them "in sanctification." The priority of God's call is a big point in Pauline theology. Everywhere he insists that man's salvation is brought about not because man has taken action, but because God has. He goes further. When the natural man learns that he cannot remove the burden of his sins, but must rely on Christ's atoning work for that, he tries to save some shreds of self-respect by claiming at least the credit for turning from his sin to God. But that, too, is ruled out. Men only come to God because of His effectual call. In this place it is not so much the fact that God called the Thessalonians initially that is in mind, as the kind of living to which He has called them. He has called them to be set apart for Him, that is, to live in sanctification (see on v. 3).

The change of preposition from "for" with uncleanness to "in" with sanctification is interesting. The former expresses purpose (cf. its use in Gal. 5:13, Eph. 2:10). When God called the Thessalonians it was not an aimless procedure. He had a very definite purpose, and that purpose was not uncleanness. "In" gives us rather the thought of atmosphere, of the settled condition in which He required them to live out their lives. This atmosphere for the believer is sanctification. It is the very air he breathes.

8 We come to a third reason for chastity, namely, that impurity represents a sin against the Holy Spirit. This arises out of what has just been said, and the "therefore" which introduces the verse should not be overlooked. Impurity must be seen in the light of the fact that God has called men to live in sanctification. A failure to observe it is thus more than simply a failure to keep some man-made rule. It is a sin against the living presence of God.

This last point is brought out by referring to God as Him "who giveth his Holy Spirit."[24] The verb is in the present, which is unusual for Paul. He usually thinks of the Spirit as given once for all. But in this present passage there is a profound truth in the use of the present. The man who carries on an act of impurity is not simply breaking a human code, nor even sinning against the God who at some time in the past gave him the gift of the Spirit. He is sinning against the God who is present at that moment, against One who continually gives the Spirit. The impure act is an act of despite against God's good gift at the very moment it is being proffered.[25]

The heinousness of such a sin is further emphasized by an unusual word order which has the effect of emphasizing "holy." The conduct in question outrages a Spirit who is not only mighty, but holy. This sin is seen in its true light only when it is seen as a preference for impurity rather than a Spirit who is holy.

The heinousness is also brought out with the contrast between rejecting man and rejecting God[26] in the first part of the verse.

---

[24] The Spirit is spoken of as given εἰς ὑμᾶς, "into you," and not simply ὑμῖν "to you." The Spirit is given so as to be within the believer, strengthening his innermost being. Cf. Rutherford, "God, who offers his Holy Spirit to dwell in you."

[25] If I Cor. 3:16 applies to the individual, and is not simply a reference to believers as a whole (i.e. to the church), it will form a close parallel to the present passage. Cf. also I Cor. 6:19 f.

[26] The use of the article with Θεόν and its absence from ἄνθρωπον is noteworthy: "rejects not a man, but the one God."

The verb is not an easy one to translate, and it is rendered in various ways in its different occurrences in the New Testament. Basically it means something like "to hold as null and void." From this various meanings arise. Here the significance is that the man who holds sexual sin as a thing indifferent thereby treats God (not simply man) as of no account. He thinks of God as One who can be neglected with impunity, this God who has just been spoken of as the "Avenger" (v. 6), and is about to be described as the continual Giver of His Holy Spirit.

3. BROTHERLY LOVE, 4:9, 10

9 But concerning love of the brethren ye have no need that one write unto you: for ye yourselves are taught of God to love one another;

10 for indeed ye do it toward all the brethren that are in all Macedonia. But we exhort you, brethren, that ye abound more and more;

9 Something which should give modern Christians much food for thought is the way in which the early church was characterized by love. "Behold how these Christians love one another"[27] is hardly the comment which springs spontaneously to the lips of the detached observer nowadays. But if our manner of life was based on the New Testament picture something like it would be inevitable. The characteristic Christian attitude as we see it there is a profound faith in God, a faith which spills out into all of life in the form of self-denying, self-giving love.

Paul has had occasion to remark on the way the Thessalonians displayed this virtue (1:3, 3:6). They showed that steadfast love to others which can only come about in a man when he has been transformed by the power of the divine *agape*, and has come to see men in a measure as God sees them. But there is something else than this. When this miracle occurs in a man he finds himself in company with others of like mind, and he will naturally be drawn to them. His soul will be knit to theirs. Thus, in addition to *agape*, that self-denying love toward all men, he should practice *philadelphia*, the love of the brethren.[28] This is often insisted

---

27 See Tertullian's *Apology*, Ch. 39.

28 φιλαδελφία outside the New Testament almost invariably denotes affection for the brother by birth. In the New Testament, however, it always

upon, and it has always been a hallmark of vital Christianity that love of those within the brotherhood has abounded. John, indeed, gives this as the criterion whereby a man may know that he really has "passed out of death into life" (I John 3:14, cf. 3:10). It is this that is in mind when Paul praises his friends. He gladly acknowledges that there is no real need for him to write on such a subject to people so well taught as they. Yet, in the spirit of v. 1, he does write. He is never satisfied. While he is mindful of their very real achievement, he yet knows that the Christian must look ever onward. So he urges them to "abound more and more" (v. 10). He makes their well-known love for one another the basis of an appeal that they would go on to ever new heights of love. When he later wrote II Corinthians he praised the practical expression of their love in making a substantial gift for the poor saints in Jerusalem (II Cor. 8:1 ff.). It is this kind of thing he has in mind here also. The passage in II Corinthians may indicate how well his remarks were heeded.

Paul gives as his reason that he need not write to them the fact that they were "taught of God." He uses a very uncommon word. It occurs here only in the New Testament (though a very similar expression is found in John 6:45).[29] In I Cor. 2:13 there is a reference to being taught of the Spirit. This is relevant to our present passage because Paul has just been speaking of the Holy Spirit given "into" the Thessalonians. So his thought is that God within them shows them the right way.

10 Not only does God show them, but they act upon what He shows them. Paul rejoices that they practice this God-taught love toward all the Christians in Macedonia.[30] Some have felt that this is something in the nature of an extravagant statement, for there

---

denotes love within the Christian brotherhood. It is not that Christianity sits loose to natural ties. On the contrary, it insists that they should be conceded their due importance, and it castigates those without natural affection (Rom. 1:31, II Tim. 3:3). But it catches up natural ties into the wider circle. The really significant thing is membership of the heavenly family (Luke 8:21). φιλαδελφία is distinguished from ἀγάπη in II Pet. 1:7.

[29] His word is θεοδίδακτοι. In John 6:45 we have διδακτοὶ Θεοῦ.

[30] The καί in καὶ γάρ, as Lightfoot says, "marks this statement as an advance upon the preceding one. 'You are not only taught the lesson, but you also practice it, and that, to every one of the brethren throughout Macedonia, i.e., all the brethren with whom you can possibly come in contact.'"

were Macedonian churches only in Philippi and Beroea besides
that at Thessalonica. But to this we must add the qualification,
"of which we know." There may well have been many churches
of which we have no record. Our knowledge of the details of
church life in New Testament times is very meager. We know that
missionaries like Silvanus, Timothy, and Luke had worked in
Macedonia, and we know that the early Christian communities
were evangelistically minded. Consequently there is nothing improbable in the idea that a number of groups of Christians had
sprung up (cf. 1:7 ff., and the notes there). However, be the
number large or small, Paul's point is that his friends of Thessalonica had acted with a commendable Christian love towards
them all. His use of the continuous present tense indicates their
habitual attitude.

The fact that they practice such love toward the wider circle is
proof of the reality of their brotherly love. As Calvin says, it is
"an argument from the greater to the less; for as their love diffuses
itself through the whole of Macedonia, he infers that it is not to be
doubted that they *love one another*."

But tenderly (note the affectionate "brethren") Paul urges them
to "abound more and more." Christians must never be weary in
welldoing. To sit back satisfied with what one has done is to
sound the knell of effective Christian service. For the verb
"exhort" see on 3:2 (where it is rendered "comfort"). It fits the
note of tenderness, while yet leaving no doubt as to the urgency of
the course of action being recommended. "Abound" is the verb we
have already met in 3:12 of abounding in love, and in 4:1 of the
Christian life in general. While the verb here has no object, yet
it is implied that the Thessalonians should abound in love of the
brethren. That is the quality which is in Paul's thoughts. He wants
his friends to excel in its practice. It is interesting that three times
within such a short space Paul should have thought of the Christian
life in terms of abounding. It illustrates something of the exuberant quality of a right Christian faith. Far from acting as a
brake on men's enjoyment of life, as so many wrongly think, it
opens up the door into real living (cf. John 10:10).

4. EARNING ONE'S LIVING, 4:11, 12

> 11 and that ye study to be quiet, and to do your own
> business, and to work with your hands, even as we
> charged you;
> 12 that ye may walk becomingly toward them that are
> without, and may have need of nothing.

11 This is the first indication that we have had in this Epistle
that there were some who were so excited by all the wonderful
things in the Christian faith that they were not bothering to earn
their living. But there are a number of indications in the Thessalonian correspondence that this was so (cf. especially II Thess.
3:11). It is most likely that this arose out of second-advent speculations.[31] They had learned very well that the Lord would be
returning in mighty power, and evidently they felt that it would
be very soon. Accordingly there was no point in continuing in
some steady job. It was much more realistic, they evidently
thought, to be about the business of proclaiming the near end of the
world. If they had need of this world's goods in the meantime,
why, there were others, Christian brethren, who could be relied
upon to come to their rescue. This kind of thing can be done from
a sense of serious purpose. But, human nature being what it is, it
can easily degenerate into downright laziness and idleness. Men
can be so taken up with the spectacular, with excitements over the
near approach of the Lord, that they pass over the important things
of everyday life. So Paul gives his attention to such matters, and
counsels these brethren to mend their ways.[32]

"Study to be quiet" is a striking paradox. The verb rendered
"study" is a compound with the basic meaning "to love honor,"
hence "to be ambitious." Some think that this is the significance of
the verb in this verse, when Paul's remark is something like "be
ambitious to be unambitious." But the verb develops another
meaning "to fix one's aim on," "to strive earnestly for." If this is
the meaning here (as it is in Rom. 15:20, II Cor. 5:9, the only other
New Testament passages where the verb is found), then the

---

[31] It may not be without significance that in the very next section of this
Epistle Paul deals with problems arising out of the second advent.

[32] Cf. Luke 12:35–38 for a very different way of preparing for the coming
of the Lord. On this Lukan passage Creed comments, "The expectation of
the Lord's return does not paralyse energy. The imperatives call up a fine
picture of preparedness" (*ad loc.*).

paradox will be "seek strenuously to be still." The verb "to be quiet" is used of silence after speech (Luke 14:4), cessation of argument (Acts 21:14), rest from labor (Luke 23:56). It denotes tranquillity of life. It is clear that some of the Thessalonians were far from living the simple life, and Paul is very anxious to recall them to a balanced outlook. If the Lord were coming soon, then the best way for them to be found was doing their ordinary work, but this they had not learned.[33]

Paul joins to the general injunction to be quiet the specific one to "attend to your own business" (Moffatt). The expression is found only here in the New Testament, though it is not uncommon in non-Biblical Greek. It perhaps points to a tendency to interfere in the running of the church on the part of those who were not church officers. It does not seem extravagant to suggest that, meeting trouble in their endeavor to be kept by the earnings of their brethren, some had attempted to have the church officially support their demands. Or it may be that it is simply taking an undue interest in the concerns of one's neighbors that is condemned. At any rate, it is clear that Paul wants each to put his attention where it belongs.

Closely joined to this is the command to work with their hands. This unashamed advocacy of manual labor in a letter to a community in a Greek city must be remarked. The typical Greek attitude was that slaves did this sort of work, but that free men would not stoop to it. It was degrading. Here, as in so many other ways, the Christians refused to take their standards from the community in the midst of which they lived. Rather, they held that all things they did should be done as service to Christ (Col. 3:17), and they specifically held that manual labor was good (Eph. 4:28). Doubtless they remembered that Jesus Himself had been a carpenter (Mark 6:3). How could the followers of the Carpenter do other than welcome manual work?[34]

---

[33] Neil quotes from Paterson Smyth a story from New England "of a day during one of those times of excited expectancy of the end of the world when a sudden darkness at noon interrupted the session of the Assembly. Some cried fearfully: 'It is the coming of Christ: it is the end of the world.' But the old President ordered lights to be produced: 'Bring in candles,' he said, 'and get on with your work. If the Lord is coming, how better can He find us than quietly doing our duty?'"

[34] There is another inference which Denney draws from this section of Thessalonians. With reference to the earning of our daily bread he says: "The bulk of most men's strength, by an ordinance of God that we cannot

This reference probably points us to the status of the Thessalonians. While, of course, manual work may be skilled as well as unskilled we are probably right in thinking that the majority of the believers came from the lower social classes, and were poor.

Once again we find Paul insisting that he was not bringing some new teaching, but simply repeating what he had said when he was among them. It is remarkable that he had been able to provide so well for the future needs of his band of converts. The pity of it is that they had not learned as well as he had taught.[35]

12 Paul gives two reasons for earning their living in this way. The first is the effect of their behavior on those who are not Christians. The believer must always bear in mind the impact of his line of conduct on those who are without faith.[36] What he does may be done from a good motive, but yet appear to the outsider in quite a different light. Under these circumstances it is impossible for the faithful follower of the Lord to go ahead without regard to appearances. He must reflect that he is his Lord's ambassador, and his conduct must commend his Lord to others. If that may be so in the case of things which are innocent in themselves, much more is it the case in matters like the one before Paul at this moment. When some of the believers did no work at all, but lived on the charity of others, so that they spent their time in what must have looked like idle gossip, what could outsiders think? It would be a sure way of bringing the church into disrepute. Paul urges upon the Thessalonians a consideration of the implications of all this. He suggests that they should walk (see on 4:1) "becomingly," his adverb directing their attention to the fitness of things (cf. Col. 4:5).

There is a slight doubt as to the exact meaning of Paul's second reason for working. The word rendered "nothing" could equally be translated "no man." The gender is indeterminate. In actual

---

interfere with, is given to that humble but inevitable task. If we cannot be holy at our work, it is not worth taking any trouble to be holy at other times."

[35] The verb rendered "charged" is παραγγέλω. This indicates authoritative commands. For example, it is used of commands given by military officers. Although not as exclusively military as the corresponding noun (see on 4:2), it yet gives the idea of a command with authority.

It seems likely that "even as we charged you" is to be taken with the last infinitive ("work with your hands"), and not the whole three (so, e.g., Frame).

[36] On πρὸς τοὺς ἔξω cf. Frame, "πρός = 'with an eye to,' as in Col. 4:5; not coram, 'in the eyes of.'"

practice, though, it comes to much the same whichever interpretation we adopt. The situation clearly was that those who were not working were depending on their more industrious brethren for their means of livelihood, and Paul is counseling them to work so that this undesirable state of affairs may be ended. He may mean, "work, and then all your needs will be supplied. You will be in need of nothing." Or he may mean, "work, and then you will have need of no man to help you. You will be quite independent." Either way he is making the point that the Christian cannot be a parasite.[37]

This whole section on earning one's living is closely connected with the previous one on brotherly love, and that not only in syntax. Those who imposed on the generosity of their fellows were not living in love. Or, to put the same thing the other way round, the exhortation to brotherly love carries with it the necessity for providing for one's own needs, that undue strain be not placed on the brother (though Paul does not specifically mention this point).

VI. PROBLEMS ASSOCIATED WITH THE PAROUSIA, 4:13–5:11

1. BELIEVERS WHO DIE BEFORE THE PAROUSIA, 4:13–18

13 But we would not have you ignorant, brethren, concerning them that fall asleep; that ye sorrow not, even as the rest, who have no hope.

14 For if we believe that Jesus died and rose again, even so them also that are fallen asleep in Jesus will God bring with him.

15 For this we say unto you by the word of the Lord, that we that are alive, that are left unto the coming of the Lord, shall in no wise precede them that are fallen asleep.

16 For the Lord himself shall descend from heaven, with a shout, with the voice of the archangel, and with the trump of God: and the dead in Christ shall rise first;

17 then we that are alive, that are left, shall together with them be caught up in the clouds, to meet the Lord in the air: and so shall we ever be with the Lord.

18 Wherefore comfort one another with these words.

---

[37] The issue may be decided in favor of "nothing" by the grammatical point that χρείαν ἔχω is more usually followed by a thing than a person. But this cannot be absolutely conclusive because in the nature of things one is more likely to speak of needing things than people.

13 The Parousia (see on 2:19) is a difficult topic. Within the short space of the mission it would have been impossible for the apostolic band to have given anything like complete instruction about it. Clearly they had spoken much of it, for the Thessalonian correspondence gives evidence of a lively interest in the whole subject. It is worth asking ourselves whether the comparative neglect of the doctrine in much modern Christianity has not resulted in great loss.

The Thessalonians had welcomed the teaching they had received. But with the passage of time and the march of events questions arose in their minds. The one which occupies our attention at this point is, "What becomes of believers who die before the second coming?" This question must have arisen quite early in the history of the church (which, incidentally, is evidence for the early date of this Epistle). We get the impression that the Thessalonians had understood Paul to mean that the Parousia would take place within their lifetime. They had become perplexed when some of their number died. Did this mean that they had lost their share in the events associated with that great day? What a calamity to be robbed of that great triumph by failing to live out the few years intervening, and this after having passed out of the darkness of heathendom into the light of the gospel! In the light of I Cor. 11:30 it is possible that some of them thought of the deaths as indicating that the deceased were under the wrath of God. If they were being punished for some sin it would be natural enough that they should miss the Parousia. The converse, that missing the Parousia meant that they were being punished for some sin, may well have seemed true also.

Paul introduces what he has to say with the formula "we would not have you ignorant." He employs this formula elsewhere,[38] and it usually seems to introduce something which is new to his readers, and on which he wants to fasten their attention. It is invariably accompanied with the address "brethren," an affectionate touch which should not be overlooked.

He does not refer to the dead, but to "them that fall asleep."[39]

---

[38] The passages are Rom. 1:13, 11:25, I Cor. 10:1, 12:1, II Cor. 1:8. Milligan says that the corresponding formula γινώσκειν σε θέλω is very common in the papyri (it occurs also in I Cor. 11:3, Col. 2:1, though with the verb εἰδέναι).
[39] The present participle κοιμωμένων is used, though the perfect is more

In many religions death is spoken of in this way (cf. the frequent
Old Testament statement that such-and-such a person "slept with
his fathers"), but it is a metaphor which is much more at home in a
Christian context than elsewhere. For Christians death is no longer
that adversary whom no man can resist, that tyrant who brings all
worthwhile existence to a horribly final end. Death has been overcome by the risen Lord, and that has transformed the whole
situation for those who are in Him.

So Paul goes on to the thought that they should not sorrow[40] like
"the rest[41] who have no hope." When the non-Christian world is
characterized in this way it is probably not an absence of hope of
an after life that is meant primarily, but an absence of the knowledge of God, in the spirit of Eph. 2:12, "having no hope and
without God in the world." But this shows itself strikingly in the
attitude towards death. Few things are more impressive in the
contrast between early Christianity and the surrounding pagan
systems than their attitudes in the face of death. There are some
fine statements on immortality here and there in pagan literature.
There seems no doubt that some of the philosophers had an idea
of a life beyond the grave. But they did not glory in it. And, in
any case, it was the lofty view of the few. Nowhere did it penetrate
to the beliefs of the common man. The same might be said about
the mystery religions. Sometimes they speak of a life beyond the
grave for the initiates. But they did not have the ringing certainty
of the Christians, nor did such views influence very many. The
typical attitude of the ancient world to death was one of utter
hopelessness. Deissmann cites a letter of the second century
written to a friend who had been bereaved, and we may quote it
as typical.

> Irene to Taonnophris and Philo, good comfort. I am as sorry
> and weep over the departed one as I wept for Didymas. And
> all things, whatsoever were fitting, I have done, and all mine,

---

usual. The use of the present points us to a continuing activity. Also, and
perhaps more significant in the present connection, its use points forward
to the future awakening more definitely than would the perfect. Frame notes
the possibility that the present denotes the class, "the sleepers."

40 The tense is the present subjunctive ($\lambda \upsilon \pi \tilde{\eta} \sigma \vartheta \varepsilon$), and signifies a continuing sorrow.

41 $o\dot{\iota} \lambda o\iota \pi o\dot{\iota}$, "the rest," means much the same as $\tau o\dot{\upsilon}\varsigma \, \dot{\varepsilon}\xi\omega$, "them that
are without" of v. 12. The difference is, in Findlay's words, "that expression
implies *exclusion*, this implies *deprivation*" (CGT).

Epaphroditus and Thermuthion and Philion and Apollonius and Plantas. But, nevertheless, against such things one can do nothing. Therefore comfort ye one another.[42]

It is clear that Irene feels for her friends, but her "comfort ye one another" is a pathetic little conclusion to a letter which reveals all too clearly that she has no comfort to give. "Against such things one can do nothing."

Over against that we might set Paul's triumphant "O death, where is thy victory? O death, where is thy sting?" (I Cor. 15:55). Or his calm contemplation of his own decease, "For to me to live is Christ, and to die is gain . . . having the desire to depart and be with Christ; for it is very far better" (Phil. 1:21-23).[43]

When Paul counsels the Thessalonians not to sorrow[44] as the pagans do he is not urging them to endure with a deep Stoic calm the buffetings of fortune which they cannot avoid. Nor is he counselling a callous indifference. Rather, he is rejoicing in the complete victory which Christ has won. Those who have died have simply fallen asleep in Christ, and they will awake with Him. Clearly, in the face of this prospect there is no reason for despair.[45]

14 The Christian confidence is not the result of some philosophical speculation, nor the elaboration of a religious myth. Rather, it rests on a sure historical foundation. Paul proceeds to draw his readers' attention to this fact and to the deductions which

---

[42] LAE p. 176. Deissmann comments, "Irene, who knows how to write a business letter quickly and surely, experiences the difficulty of those whose business it is to console and who have no consolation to offer . . . . Who could help feeling for the helplessness of this woman . . .?" Milligan remarks, "The general hopelessness of the pagan world in the presence of death is almost too well known to require illustration," but he cites a few passages like Theocr. *Id.* iv. 42, ἐλπίδες ἐν ζωοῖσιν, ἀνέλπιστοι δὲ θανόντες.

[43] Lightfoot is of the opinion that even more striking is the difference between the inscriptions on the magnificent tombs of the heathen and those on the poor graves in the catacombs. "On the one hand there is the dreary wail of despair, the effect of which is only heightened by the pomp of outward splendour from which it issues. On the other the exulting psalm of hope, shining the more brightly in all ill-written, ill-spelt records amidst the darkness of subterranean caverns."

[44] The word for sorrow, λυπῆσθε, denotes primarily an inward grief, whereas words like πενθέω, κλαίω, etc., indicate the outward expression of grief.

[45] This, of course, does not exclude the natural feeling of sadness at parting. Paul is not giving a full account here, but simply drawing the attention of his friends to what it was important for them to know.

are to be drawn from it. "If we believe" is not to be taken as indicating any uncertainty. The implication of this type of conditional clause is that the condition has been fulfilled. Paul thinks his statement is so far beyond dispute that he can safely throw it into the form of a conditional. Again, the reference to believing is not to permit of doubts, but to indicate the certainty of faith.

He speaks of Christ not as sleeping, but as dying. In the New Testament there are two distinct strands of teaching about death. On the one hand it is the most natural of all things, and is an inevitable part of the conditions of our earthly existence. On the other hand it is completely unnatural, a horror, the result of sin.[46] Christ in His death bore the wages of sin. He endured the worst that death can possibly be. Thereby He transformed the whole position for those who are in Him. It is because there was no mitigation of the horror of death for Him that there is no horror in death for His people. For them it is but sleep.

Jesus not only died, but also "rose again." The resurrection was the great event which demonstrated that death really was conquered. Elsewhere Paul could say, "If Christ hath not been raised, your faith is vain; ye are yet in your sins. Then they also that are fallen asleep in Christ have perished" (I Cor. 15:17 f.). The resurrection is the great triumphant act wherein the divine quality of the Christian gospel is conclusively demonstrated. In the light of the resurrection there can be no doubt that God was in Christ, and if God was in Christ, then, just as He raised His Son, so in due time He will raise those who are in Christ. The resurrection is the guarantee of the Christian hope.

Paul draws this conclusion, though the form in which he puts it leaves us in some doubt as to his exact meaning. The difficulty is that "in Jesus" is literally "through Jesus," and it is not certain whether it should be taken with "fallen asleep" (as ARV) or with "will bring" (so RSV, Moffatt). This second view is probably taken because of the difficulty of seeing what "falling asleep through Jesus" can mean. But it raises many difficulties of its own. For example, the balance of the sentence is against it, and so is the fact that if we adopt it we are left with the thought that *all* the dead (and not simply the Christian dead) will be brought through Jesus. Moreover it is not easy to think that Paul means "God will bring

---

[46] On the subject of death see further my Tyndale Lecture, *The Wages of Sin* (London, 1955), and the literature there cited.

through Jesus with Jesus. . . ." This is tautology, and such a tame ending is not what we associate with Paul's vigorous mind.

It is likely, then, that we should understand the passage as ARV.[47] The meaning of it probably is that it is through what Jesus has done,[48] through Jesus, that Christians "sleep" only, and do not undergo the horrors of death.[49]

Outside this verse the designation of our Lord simply as "Jesus" is found in these Epistles once only (1:10). It is the name which brings before us the Man of Nazareth, the human Jesus. In this context we are reminded of the historical facts of the death and resurrection. These things really happened, and they happened to Jesus. Moreover, the term reminds us that Jesus is "the firstfruits of them that are asleep" (I Cor. 15:20). The first fruits imply later fruits.[50] As Jesus has risen we are sure that one day we, too, will rise (cf. I Cor. 15:22 f., Col. 1:18).

One more point remains to be determined in this verse, and that is the bearing of "bring with him." Some understand this to mean that Jesus will take these people with Him into the glory, but this does not seem to be justified. Paul is talking about the Parousia. It is their share in the events of that great day that is in view. It is best to understand the words to mean that Jesus will bring the faithful departed with Him when He comes back. Their death does not mean that they will miss their share in the Parousia. Notice the definiteness of Paul's statement. After "if we believe . . ." it would be natural to find "we should also believe. . . ." By avoiding the conditional form Paul conveys the certainty of the event he describes.

---

[47] On the grammatical reasons for favoring this interpretation Frame quotes Ellicott, "The two contrasted subjects Ἰησοῦς and κοιμηθέντας διὰ τοῦ Ἰησοῦ thus stand in clear and illustrative antithesis, and the fundamental declaration of the sentence ἄξει σὺν αὐτῷ remains distinct and prominent, undiluted by any addititious clause."

[48] Milligan speaks of διά as "pointing to Jesus as the mediating link between His people's sleep and their resurrection at the hands of God" so that the argument runs: "those who fell asleep through Jesus, and in consequence were raised by God through Him, will God bring with Him." Moule understands the expression to mean, "those who have fallen asleep (i.e. died) as Christians (perhaps in contact with Jesus)" (Idiom Book, p. 57), but this seems inadequate.

[49] Some have felt that the expression points to martyrdom, but it does not seem definite enough for that.

[50] Cf. the chapter on "The Resurrection of the Church" in L. S. Thornton, The Common Life in the Body of Christ (London, 1942).

15 Paul does not speak of the resurrection of the faithful departed, and we are probably right in assuming that that was taken for granted. What worried the Thessalonians was not whether their friends would rise, but whether they would have any share in the great events associated with the Parousia. Now comes another expression indicating certainty, namely a statement given on the authority of the Lord Himself. "By the word of the Lord" is literally, "in the word of the Lord,"[51] and it would be very natural to understand this of a saying of Jesus. The difficulty urged against this is that there is no saying anywhere in the Gospels which closely resembles this one, or from which we might think this to have been adapted.[52] This makes it likely that Paul is referring to a saying of Christ which is not mentioned by any of the four evangelists. There must have been many such sayings, and, for example, one is recorded for us in Acts 20:35. Moffatt's translation runs, "as the Lord has told us," which seems to point to a revelation made to Paul himself.[53] This is not impossible, but there is no other evidence, and the Greek does not seem to mean so much. Some have felt that we should understand the words to represent the result of the Apostle's thinking the problem through under the guidance of the Spirit (cf. I Cor. 2:16).[54] Others that it represents some saying of Christ's which has been expanded with traditional Jewish imagery. But all such explanations seem needless when we have the simple one, that it is a saying of Jesus unrecorded in the Gospels. If we had reason for thinking that all He said is recorded matters would be different. But as it is we are expressly told that many things are not mentioned in the Gospels (John 21:25). We must feel that this is one of them.[55]

The saying raises the question of whether Paul expected that he himself would still be alive when the Lord would come back. Many exegetes think that he did, but the Greek here does not affirm this. The expression he uses may mean no more than "those

---

[51] ἐν here probably has the force of "by means of."

[52] Matt. 24:31 seems to be the closest parallel.

[53] Or, if the plural be pressed, it may point to a common Christian tradition. But this raises the question, Where did such a tradition originate?

[54] In support of this might be urged Old Testament references to prophets speaking in the word of the Lord, בִּדְבַר יהוה (I Kings 13:2, etc.).

[55] O. Cullmann includes this among "the relatively small number of words of Jesus quoted by Paul" (*The Early Church* [London, 1956], p. 65).

Christians who will be alive at that day,"[56] and as Paul in this very context speaks of the time as unknown (5:2, 3) it would be unwise to read more into his words. While there is nothing at all improbable in the idea that Paul, or any other first-century Christian, thought of the Parousia as to take place in his own lifetime (some seem to have thought that in every age of the Christian church, and some think it now), yet it must be borne in mind that he does not say so. It must be borne in mind also that in I Cor. 6:14 he classes himself with those who will be raised.

Those surviving to that day will have no advantage over the faithful departed, and Paul uses an emphatic expression, "in no wise,"[57] to underline his point. His concern is that there should be no doubt at all on the point that believers who die will be at no disadvantage when the Parousia comes.

16 This verse makes us reflect on the very little that the New Testament has to say about the manner of the Parousia. Nowhere else have we as full a description of what is to happen as here, but the details are few, and do not paint for us a very full picture. The point of it all is that the Scriptures are intensely practical in this matter, as in others. There are many things that our curiosity would like to know, but the Bible is not there to gratify our curiosity. Rather, it is to help our Christian lives, and for that the important thing is that we should be ready whenever the Lord comes. Thus it is that we are often warned to prepare, and told that the coming will be unexpected.

---

[56] Lightfoot gives as his paraphrase of οἱ ζῶντες, οἱ περιλειπόμενοι, "When I say 'we,' I mean those who are living, those who survive to that day." Denney thinks the natural impression is that Paul expected to be alive, but adds a note, "It is easy to state the inference too strongly. Paul tells us expressly that he did not know when Christ would come; he could not therefore know that he himself would have died long before the Advent; and it was inevitable, therefore, that he should include himself here in the category of such as might live to see it."

[57] οὐ μή is often used in the Gospels where there seems no particular emphasis. Close examination, however, reveals that it is used in this way only in quotations from the Septuagint, or in the words of our Lord. When these last were translated from the Aramaic it would seem that the emphatic οὐ μή was commonly used as congruous with the style of deity. Moulton speaks of "a feeling that inspired language was fitly rendered by words of a decisive tone not needed generally elsewhere" (*Proleg.* p. 192, and see pp. 39, 187 ff.). The important point is that this gives a natural explanation of the frequent use of the expression in the Gospels, and disposes of the idea that in the New Testament it has lost its force. Paul uses it four times only (outside quotations from the Septuagint), and each time it has its proper emphasis.

In this verse Paul makes three points. The first of them is that the One who will come at the end of this age is no less than "the Lord himself." It will be no angel or other created being to whom will be committed the task of bringing this age to an end. The Thessalonians are assured that they look forward to nothing less than a Divine intervention.

This is underlined by Paul's second point. The Lord's second coming will be one of majesty and honor, and he lists various accompaniments which demonstrate this. It is not certain whether the "shout," the "voice of the archangel," and the "trump of God" are three ways of speaking about the same triumphant noise, or whether they are three different sounds.[58] Rev. 1:10 speaks of "a great voice, as of a trumpet" (cf. Rev. 4:1, 5:2, etc.). Some have felt that something of the sort is meant here. This may be so, but the impression left by this present passage is that there are three distinct sounds. The "shout" denotes an authoritative utterance. The word is found quite often. It is the cry made by the ship's master to his rowers,[59] or by a military officer to his soldiers, or by a hunter to his hounds, or by a charioteer to his horses. When used to military or naval personnel it was a battle cry. In most places, then, it denotes a loud authoritative cry, often one uttered in the thick of a great excitement. All these associations make it an apt word for the great day to which Paul looked forward. It is not said by whom the shout will be uttered, but the probability is that it is the Lord (cf. John 5:28 f., "the hour cometh, in which all that are in the tombs shall hear his voice, and shall come forth").

The alternative is that the shout is to be identified with "the voice of the archangel." Neither of these nouns has the article (the

---

[58] Frame thinks that the fact that the second and third clauses are joined by καί indicates that they are "in some sense an epexegesis of the first." He gives the meaning as "At a command, namely, at an archangel's voice and at a trumpet of God." This view would be supported by the consideration that κελεύσματι has no qualifying genitive, so that the following expressions would naturally be held to explain it. Hendriksen thinks of two different sounds, the "shout" being the voice of the Lord, while in addition there is the archangel sounding the trumpet of God.

[59] The meaning of the cognate word κελευστής is given by Liddell and Scott as, "boatswain, who gives the time to the rowers." O. Cullmann thinks of the κέλευσμα as pointing to God's sovereignty. He speaks of the time "when God, as in the first creation, will decide in his sovereign act (κέλευσμα, I Thess. 4:16) to constitute the *new creation* by means of the spirit of life" (*op. cit.*, p. 143).

Greek reads "a voice of an archangel"), which makes it unlikely that Paul is thinking of any particular archangel.[60] It is even possible that he does not mean that an archangel will actually say something, but simply that the voice that will be uttered will be a very great voice, an archangel type of voice. But more probably the meaning is that some archangel will add his voice to the call which wakes the dead.

Then there will be "the trump of God." Trumpets are often mentioned in the Old Testament in connection with times of festivity and triumph. They were a frequent accompaniment of great religious occasions. Paul speaks of the trumpet elsewhere as associated with the Parousia (I Cor. 15:52). It fits in as part of the pageantry, stressing the majesty of the Lord, and the greatness of the day.[61]

The third point which Paul makes in this verse is that the faithful departed will rise first. The Thessalonians had been agitated by the possibility that they would not have a place in the events of the great day. Far from that, Paul assures them, they will be very prominent. Indeed, they will rise before those who live on earth until that great day arrives.[62]

17 It is only after the faithful departed have taken their place with the Lord that the saints on earth are caught up to be with Him, or more strictly, to be with them and meet Him. The reunion with those who have died is sometimes overlooked in the exposition of this passage, but to Paul it was clearly important. He stresses

---

[60] Those who try to identify the archangel usually think of Michael, the only archangel named in the New Testament (Jude 9). Gabriel is mentioned in Luke 1, but he is called simply an angel (Luke 1:19, 26). Michael, Gabriel and Raphael are mentioned in "The War of the Sons of Light with the Sons of Darkness", see Millar Burrows, *The Dead Sea Scrolls* (London, 1956), p. 261.

[61] Jesus likewise mentioned the trumpet in connection with the gathering of the elect (Matt. 24:31). The sounding of the trumpet is associated with the activity of the Lord in Old Testament passages like Exod. 19:16, Isa. 27:13, Joel 2:1, Zech. 9:14. Klausner attests the idea for first-century Judaism, *From Jesus to Paul* (London, 1946), pp. 538 f. The trumpet is very frequently mentioned in the descriptions of battles in "The War of the Sons of Light with the Sons of Darkness" (see Millar Burrows, *op. cit.*, pp. 390 ff.).

[62] "First" must be taken here as first in relation to the events mentioned, i.e., before the rapture spoken of in the next verse. It cannot be pressed to mean first in relation to non-believers, as though the first and second resurrections of Rev. 20 (however these are understood) were being described. That is not the thought of this passage.

the fact that they will be together,[63] and mentions it before saying they will be caught up. It is a very precious thought, especially to those who have been bereaved, as had some of the Thessalonians.

The verb he uses of being "caught up" is one which means, according to Grimm–Thayer, "to seize, carry off by force." There is often the notion of a sudden swoop, and usually that of a force which cannot be resisted. The applicability of such a verb to the snatching away (the "rapture") of the saints is obvious. Some have seen in this a secret action which suddenly removes the saints from the world preparatory to the great tribulation (Rev. 7:14). To this two things must be said. The one, that this is the only place in the New Testament which speaks unambiguously of the rapture (there are other places which may justly be held to refer to it when it is established by this passage, but none which is sufficient to establish it). Therefore we must not be unduly dogmatic about it. Had we an abundance of detail recorded we could say a great deal. But we have no more than a few simple facts, and we must not read our pet theories into them.

The other is that it is very hard to fit this into a secret rapture. In v. 16 Paul speaks of the Lord descending "with a shout, with the voice of the archangel, and with the trump of God." It may be that from this he intends us to understand that the rapture will take place secretly, and that no one except the saints themselves will know what is going on. But one would hardly gather this from his words. It is difficult to see how he could more plainly describe something that is open and public.[64] I do not doubt that, if He so wished, God would make the voice of the archangel, the shout, and the trumpet call to be inaudible to unbelievers. But I do greatly doubt whether that is what Paul is saying.

It should be stressed that the precise words Paul uses here do not take us far in our understanding of the details of that day. It is legitimate for students to ponder what he says and to draw their

---

[63] He does not say simply σὺν αὐτοῖς, but ἅμα σὺν αὐτοῖς and he places the expression early before the verb. ἅμα is usually taken as an adverb giving a separate idea, "simultaneously, together with them." This may be so, but Lightfoot maintains that the combination ἅμα σύν is too common to allow the words to be separated.

[64] Cf. Calvin, "As a field marshal gathers his armies to battle by the sound of the trumpet, so Christ will summon all the dead with a voice that rings and resounds throughout the whole world," on I Cor. 15, (cited by H. Quistorp, *Calvin's Doctrine of the Last Things* [London, 1955], p. 142).

inferences therefrom. But that does not give license to them to condemn others who do not draw the same inferences. There must be room for legitimate differences of opinion among those who respect the revelation made in the Bible.[65]

There may be significance in the meeting place being in the air. In the first century the air was often thought of as the abode of demons (in Eph. 2:2 Satan is described as "the prince of the powers of the air").[66] The fact that the Lord chooses to meet His saints there, on the demons' home ground so to speak, shows something of His complete mastery over them.

The expression for "to meet" may be used of commonplace meetings. But it has also a more formal use, and, for example, Milligan is able to cite examples of its denoting "the formal reception of a newly arriving magistrate." It implies "welcome of a great person on his arrival" (Moffatt). It may well be that there is a touch of the formal here, with the thought of a royal reception. They were to be presented to the King.

Paul brings his account of these glorious happenings to a close with the assurance, "so shall we ever be with the Lord." Everything leads up to this, and after this there is nothing more to add.[67] Nothing could more adequately indicate the Christian's bliss.

18 In the light of this glorious prospect Paul calls on them to strengthen one another's hands (for "comfort" see on 3:2). It is interesting that he does not urge them simply to faint not. These tidings, he thinks, should impel them to be active in seeking one another out and strengthening one another. And well they might, for it is an inspiring thought that death makes no difference to our relationship to the Lord. All things and all men are in His hands. When it is His will to bring in the end of this age, those who have died in Him and those who still survive will be united in His presence. The thought gives meaning to existence, and suggests the certainty of ultimate triumph. Neil asks whether Paul's words are any encouragement to us,

---

[65] This point is very well made by G. E. Ladd, *The Blessed Hope* (Grand Rapids, 1956), *passim*.

[66] Cf. the passages cited by S–BK, iv, I, p. 516 for the idea in Judaism.

[67] It is possible that nothing more is added because the sequel is so well known. Heb. 6:2 includes the teaching of "eternal judgment" among "the first principles of Christ." Paul may have it in mind that the Thessalonians were in no doubt on that score.

and he proceeds, "If we seek information as to the actual procedure to be gone through by believers after death, or the events that will accompany the end of time and history, our own guess is as good as Paul's or the apocalyptists'." He proceeds to argue that we can look beneath "the traditional superstructure of eschatological imagery" and reach the conviction that "those who die in Christ live in Christ." We might reach a more satisfactory position by another route. Phillips translates, "God has given me this message on the matter, so by all means use it to encourage one another." While we may feel that this is more of a paraphrase than a transla-

---

Note from following page.

68 It is this which makes C. H. Dodd's view of "realized eschatology" unsatisfactory to very many. It is a view which is not easy to state shortly, but the essence of it appears to be: "The *eschaton* has moved from the future to the present, from the sphere of expectation into that of realized experience" (*The Parables of the Kingdom* [London, 1938], p. 50). He speaks of "the ministry of Jesus as 'realized eschatology,' that is to say, as the impact upon this world of the 'powers of the world to come' in a series of events, unprecedented and unrepeatable, now in actual process" (*op. cit.*, p. 51). It is possible to welcome this emphasis on the unique powers exercised by Jesus during His earthly ministry without agreeing that this does away with His future return. Passages giving clear expression to the idea of the Parousia occur with great frequency in the New Testament. It is hard to see any valid reason for denying that the Parousia is part of the authentic revelation.

The whole idea of realized eschatology has been decisively rejected by many modern scholars. Thus J. E. Fison says, "realized eschatology . . . is frankly and flatly heretical by the standards of a considerable portion of the New Testament evidence" (*The Christian Hope* [London, 1954], p. 63). Even Emil Brunner, whose views are far from conservative, says, "It is clear that this thought of the future coming is anything but a piece of mythology which can be dispensed with. Whatever the form of this event may be, the whole point lies in the fact that it will happen. To try to boggle at it means to try to boggle at the foundation of the faith; to smash the corner-stone by which all coheres and apart from which all falls to pieces. Faith in Jesus Christ without the expectation of His Parousia is a voucher that is never redeemed, a promise that is not seriously meant. A Christian faith without expectation of the Parousia is like a ladder which leads nowhere but ends in the void" (*Eternal Hope* [London, 1954], pp. 138 f.).

Theo Preiss condemns Bultmann's demythologizing and Dodd's realized eschatology in one breath. "Let us then demythologize the spatial ideas: the above, the below, the seven heavens, the underworld . . . but we must be careful not to touch the temporal framework. In ignoring this essential distinction Bultmann lapses into a sort of existential gnosis where history loses its meaning except in its reduced anthropological terms, while C. H. Dodd dissolves eschatology in a sort of Platonizing idealism; D-day would really have been enough for the first Christians, the V-day of the Parousia and of the new creation would be only a myth symbolizing God's mastery of all the periods of history" (*Life in Christ* [London, 1954], pp. 65 f.).

tion, yet it faithfully reproduces the thought of the Apostle. He is not suggesting that he has made a guess, which he believes to be a good one, and of which they may care to make some use. He speaks "by the word of the Lord" (v. 15; cf. Phillips, "Here we have a definite message from the Lord"). It is because God has been pleased to reveal this part of His purpose that the Thessalonians (and we) may comfort one another. It is not on Paul's guesses or our own that our strength rests. It is on what God has revealed.[68]

[68] Footnote 68 appears on the preceding page.

COMMENTARY ON I THESSALONIANS

CHAPTER V

2. THE TIME OF THE PAROUSIA, 5:1-3

> 1 But concerning the times and the seasons, brethren, ye have no need that aught be written unto you.
> 2 For yourselves know perfectly that the day of the Lord so cometh as a thief in the night.
> 3 When they are saying, Peace and safety, then sudden destruction cometh upon them, as travail upon a woman with child; and they shall in no wise escape.

Having begun to speak about the Parousia, Paul uses the certainty of the Lord's coming as a means of urging the Thessalonians to greater efforts in Christian living. But before he actually gets into this exhortation he has a few words to say on the subject of the time of the Parousia.

1 The distinction between the two words "times" and "seasons"[1] is not very easy to reproduce in English, for we habitually regard time simply as a matter of duration. Our idea of time is very nearly identical with that conveyed by the first of the two words. Indeed, we derive our word "chronology" from it. It denotes time simply as sequence.

It is the word rendered "seasons" that is difficult. This word has about it the thought of time in its qualitative rather than its quantitative aspect. It often indicates the suitableness of the time for the purpose in mind, and thus comes to mean something rather like "opportunity." It is the kind of time we have in mind when we think of "one crowded hour of glorious life." Chronologically, an hour of this type is exactly the same length as another when we are bored stiff. But while the one seems to pass in a flash, the other stretches endlessly. Our second word, then, has reference rather to the kind of events that are taking place than simply to the duration that is being measured.[2]

---

[1] The words are χρόνος and καιρός.
[2] There is quite an amount of interest in the understanding of time in recent theological literature, and the two words we are considering are

The combination of the two is a way of bringing before the mind both the duration of the time that must elapse before the coming of the Lord, and also the nature of the events that will characterize the end time.

Paul maintains that there is no real need for anyone to write to the Thessalonians about the times. This is not to be taken as the language of complimentary exaggeration. Paul did not hesitate to castigate his converts where they fell down on the job, nor to put them right when they were in error. There is abundant evidence from the two letters that he had spoken a good deal about the Parousia during his initial preaching.[3] An expression such as the one we are considering means that Paul was quite happy with the way the converts had learned this part of their lesson. It is not beyond the bounds of possibility that there were some who had been disturbed when they saw some of the believers die, not only as to what would be the fate of such when the Lord comes again, but also as to whether they themselves would live through to see the great Day. Yet this did not mean that they were unsound on the matter of "the times and the seasons." They knew quite well that there was no way of predicting when the great event would take place, but they had been reminded of their own mortality. They feared lest they lose their place in the Parousia. Paul's answer to the previous difficulty should have cleared up the position for such people. But he leaves nothing to chance. He reminds them of what they already knew on this subject, and helps them to relate this knowledge to their current problem.

2 What has been said negatively in v. 1 is repeated in another form. Paul puts the same truth positively when he says that they

---

frequently discussed. See especially John Marsh, *The Fulness of Time* (London, 1952), O. Cullmann, *Christ and Time* (London, 1951), and the chapter on "Time and Times" in E. Stauffer, *New Testament Theology* (London, 1955). Marsh cites S. H. Butcher as saying that the Greeks tried to depict καιρός in sculpture as a "youth pressing forward with wings in his feet and back, holding a pair of scales, which he inclines with a slight touch of the right hand to one side. His hair is long in front and bald behind; he must be grasped, if at all, by the fore-lock." Marsh adds, "Thus while *kairos* presents an opportunity, it does not do so indefinitely" (*op. cit.*, pp. 117 f.).

[3] It is being increasingly recognized in modern theology that early-Christian teaching was thoroughly eschatological. Interesting evidence of this will be found in the volume of essays presented to C. H. Dodd, *The Background of the New Testament and Its Eschatology* (London, 1956). The contributors make it clear that eschatology is everywhere to be seen in the New Testament.

"know perfectly." "Yourselves" is emphatic. They have no need
of an instructor in the matter. So also with "perfectly." Their
knowledge in this matter is complete, and needs no supplement.
There is a touch of irony about this way of putting it: you know
perfectly that no one can know at all when this will be! Some have
felt that the term implies that their knowledge rested ultimately
on some saying of the Lord. That would mean that it was solidly
based and that no addition or modification need be looked for.
Such a saying might be Matt. 24:43 (Luke 12:39), or that reported
in Acts 1:7, which is noteworthy in that it makes use of the same
expression "times or seasons" as here.[4] But we cannot be sure that
this is really implied.

The coming day is spoken of as "the day of the Lord."[5] This is
a very ancient expression, for it was already well known in the
time of Amos. That prophet mentioned it for the express purpose
of refuting erroneous ideas about it that were current (Amos
5:18 ff.). The idea was thus older than his day, and perhaps
considerably older. The point that Amos made was that the day
would be one of judgment upon all men. The Israelites could
expect to be punished then for their sins, just as they expected that
other people would be punished. This thought of final judgment
carries over into the New Testament understanding of the Day,
and one way of referring to it is "the day of judgment" (II Pet.
2:9). In line with this is its designation as "the day of wrath and
revelation of the righteous judgment of God" (Rom. 2:5). By
contrast it may be thought of as "the day of redemption" (Eph.
4:30). Again, its connection with the Deity may be stressed, for
on that day God's action will be manifested as never before. Thus
we find "the day of God" (II Pet. 3:12), "the day of Jesus Christ"
(Phil 1:6), "the day of the Lord Jesus" (I Cor. 5:5), "the day of
our Lord Jesus Christ" (I Cor. 1:8). It may be simply "that day"
(II Thess. 1:10), or "the last day" (John 6:39 f.), or "the great
day" (Jude 6). It is clear that the men of the New Testament

---

[4] Except that in Acts 1:7 neither word has the article.

[5] Neither noun has the article, which indicates that the expression was a
stereotyped one, almost a proper noun. Milligan thinks that in addition there
is "emphasis laid on the character of the day, a day *of the Lord*." He cites
Davidson: it "belongs to Him, is His time for working, for manifesting
Himself, for displaying His character, for performing His work—His strange
work upon the earth." For the concept of "the day of the Lord" in the Old
Testament see H. H. Rowley, *The Faith of Israel* (London, 1956), pp. 177–201.
Rowley gives full references to the literature on the subject.

found a large place for the events of that Day, and that it was a major concept for them.

The event is vividly before Paul's mind and he makes use of the present tense rather than the future ("cometh"). Yet for all that it is so vivid to his mental vision, he knows full well that its coming will be totally unexpected. In this we see the combination of two strands of teaching which are common throughout the New Testament. On the one hand the day is certain, and believers must be continually expecting it. The Lord comes "quickly" (Rev. 22:20). Yet none can know when it will be (Mark 13:32).[6] It will come upon men unexpectedly. It will come like "a thief in the night." The comparison to the coming of a thief is found elsewhere, but this is the only place where "in the night" is added.[7] The addition completes the picture of a completely unheralded approach, devastating in its unexpectedness. This does away with all date fixing.

What he says bears upon another matter which is a source of dispute among evangelicals, namely as to whether believers will be left on earth to pass through the great tribulation of the last days. The language of this chapter could be understood either way. It seems to me that the probability is that it should be taken as meaning that believers will pass through the day spoken of. Paul speaks of them as being ready (v. 4), not as being taken out of the trouble in question.[8] But I fully recognize that other interpretations are possible, and suggest that it is not wise for any of us to condemn those who see such passages differently.

---

[6] This is one of the many points in which Paul's understanding of the End is derived from that of Jesus. G. R. Beasley–Murray has convincingly demonstrated that Paul's eschatology, as shown in these Epistles, is dependent on that of the Lord Jesus (*Jesus and the Future* [London, 1954], pp. 232–34).

[7] The addition is found in some manuscripts of II Pet. 3:10, and it occurs, for example, in AV. But it is absent from the better manuscripts, and is no part of the true text.

J. Jeremias points out that the symbol of the thief "is foreign to the eschatological imagery of late Jewish literature" (*The Parables of Jesus* [London, 1954], p. 40). He infers that it is derived from the saying of Jesus recorded in Matt. 24:43 f., Luke 12:39 f. For the relationship of Pauline to Jewish eschatology see G. Vos, *The Pauline Eschatology* (Grand Rapids, 1953), pp. 27 f., n. 36.

[8] For the question of whether Paul expected believers to undergo the events of that day or escape them may I refer once more to the very sane and able discussion in G. E. Ladd, *The Blessed Hope* (Grand Rapids, 1956). Ladd argues for a pre-millenarian, post-tribulationist coming of the Lord. Although his subject is so very controversial his discussion is in a thoroughly irenic spirit, and is on a high plane throughout.

3 The unexpectedness of the coming of that Day is illustrated by the behavior of the unbelievers at the time when it comes.[9] The subject of the verb is not given, but there is no real doubt as to who are meant.[10] Unlike the Christians, the unredeemed world will have no thought of a cataclysmic end to the universe, and they will be rejoicing in a fancied security right up to the very moment of the disaster.[11] (Moffatt brings this out by rendering, "when 'all's well' and 'all is safe' are on the lips of men"). "Peace," as we saw on 1:1, usually in the New Testament denotes the prosperity of the whole man, but in this context the emphasis is rather on the absence of alarms. It is a complete failure to reckon with the realities of the situation. So also with the word "safety." It is an unusual word with a basic meaning like "that cannot be shaken."[12] Under the circumstances this is the height of folly and misapprehension

The startling nature of the disaster is further emphasized by the use of the unusual adjective rendered "sudden" (elsewhere in the New Testament it is found only in Luke 21:34). This word is placed in an emphatic position, right in the forefront of the clause. Again, the verb is in the present for greater vividness, and it is a verb which is often used of sudden appearances (though the verb itself does not necessarily include the idea of suddenness).

The disaster itself is described as "destruction." It is not completely clear what this means, but we are probably right in refusing to see in it anything approaching annihilation. Rather, the term is to be understood as denoting loss of fellowship with God, the loss of that life which is really life. Like the term "death" when applied to ultimate reality, it is the opposite of life and not simply

---

[9] There is no connecting particle (the need for it is indicated by the fact that the poorer manuscripts insert "For"), so that the thought of the previous verse is continued.

[10] When believers are mentioned in v. 4 it is with the words ὑμεῖς δέ, ἀδελφοί. This indicates a marked contrast with the preceding, who must assuredly be unbelievers. But we hardly need this grammatical point. The sense is clear enough.

[11] The present, λέγωσιν, indicates that they will still be saying these words at the very moment when the "sudden destruction" comes. On the construction see E. A. Abbott, *Johannine Grammar* (London, 1906), p. 385.

[12] ἀσφάλεια = ἀ privative + σφάλλω "to make to totter." MM inform us that in the papyri "the noun occurs innumerable times in the commercial sense, 'a security'." Frame thinks the two words to be "virtually synonymous," but he notes Ellicott's distinction: "εἰρήνη betokens an inward repose and security; ἀσφάλεια a sureness and safety that is not interfered with or compromised by outward obstacles."

the cessation of existence. The word is used again in II Thess. 1:9, and there it clearly means banishment from the living presence of the Lord. This is its meaning here also.

If the destruction in question is to be sudden, it is also inevitable. This is the point of the last words of the verse. Sometimes the figure of childbirth is used to bring out the thought of the pain of birth (Isa. 13:8, Jer. 4:31, Matt. 24:8, Gal. 4:19). But here the thought is different. When the time has come, what is in the womb must come forth. The travail cannot be avoided, and so with the destruction of which the Apostle writes. It is written into the nature of things, and must inevitably come to pass.[13]

It will be completely impossible for men to escape, and Paul does not leave this to be inferred, but states it categorically. He employs the emphatic form of the negative (which, outside quotations, he uses four times only in all his epistles; see note on 4:15), and the compound form of the verb. It still needs emphasis that there are no other alternatives than life with the Lord or eternal loss. One or the other is inevitable.

3. CHILDREN OF THE DAY, 5:4-11

4 But ye, brethren, are not in darkness, that that day should overtake you as a thief:
5 for ye are all sons of light, and sons of the day: we are not of the night, nor of darkness;
6 so then let us not sleep, as do the rest, but let us watch and be sober.
7 For they that sleep sleep in the night; and they that are drunken are drunken in the night.
8 But let us, since we are of the day, be sober, putting on the breastplate of faith and love; and for a helmet, the hope of salvation.
9 For God appointed us not unto wrath, but unto the obtaining of salvation through our Lord Jesus Christ,
10 who died for us, that, whether we wake or sleep, we should live together with him.
11 Wherefore exhort one another, and build each other up, even as also ye do.

---

[13] Some hold that the figure of childbirth is another way of indicating unexpectedness. But the mother-to-be is aware from the beginning of approximately when the childbirth will take place. The idea of inevitability seems much more clearly indicated than unexpectedness.

Paul is led from a consideration of the day of the Lord to the thought that the Thessalonians have nothing to fear from the coming of that Day. This leads to the further thought that their lives should be in harmony with all that that day stands for. It is not a difficult step from the idea of the Day of the Lord to that of walking in the light, from that of the coming of Christ to that of the character of Christian people as "sons of light." The coming of the Day must inspire God's people to live lives appropriate to their calling.

4 The Thessalonians are emphatically contrasted with the unbelievers of whom he has been speaking. "But ye" sets them over against the others as men who decidedly will not come into the condemnation he has been describing. "Darkness" is a common metaphor to describe those who are unsaved, just as light is a natural designation of the sphere of the saved. "In" darkness points us to darkness as the habitual atmosphere in which such men live and move. People immersed in such an atmosphere may well be surprised by the coming of the Day,[14] but not the Thessalonians.

That Day will come with all the suddenness and unexpectedness of a thief. The mention of "darkness" leads Paul to repeat his metaphor of v. 2. Perhaps, though, we should notice that there is a variant reading, "thieves," which yields a somewhat different sense. The meaning then would be not that the Day will come as unheralded as a thief, but that it will surprise people, just as thieves are surprised by the coming of dawn. Those who are not ready will be surprised by daybreak on "the day of the Lord." But both the attestation and the sense of "as a thief" are better, and we accept this reading accordingly.[15]

---

[14] The construction ἵνα ... καταλάβῃ is what E. de W. Burton calls "Clauses of Conceived Result." In such clauses "the action of the principal clause is regarded as the necessary condition of that of the subordinate clause, the action of the subordinate clause as the result which is to be expected to follow from that of the principal clause" (*Syntax*, p. 92).

[15] Nevertheless it should be noted that many scholars accept the variant. The principal reason is that scribes would not be likely to alter κλέπτης to κλέπτας, whereas the reverse procedure is readily intelligible. This is, of course, true, but deliberate alteration is not the only explanation of this variant. If κλέπτης were original, κλέπτας could easily arise by a process of mechanical corruption, the ending being assimilated to that of the nearby ὑμᾶς. The reading we have adopted is favored also by the possibility that there is a reminiscence of the words of our Lord reported in Matt. 24:43, Luke 12:39. Furthermore, in this context the sons of darkness who are surprised are not awake and watchful, like thieves, but asleep or drunken.

155

5 Having given the reason why they should not be overtaken in the calamity that would befall the unbelievers Paul proceeds to consider more attentively what is involved in their character as believers. "Ye are all sons of light," he says, which means that "light" is their distinguishing feature. In the Semitic languages generally to be a "son" of something means to be characterized by that thing.[16] It is this manner of thinking that underlies the Apostle's expression at this point. He does not say only that they walk in the light or live in the light, but that they are "sons of light," i.e., they are characterized by light. It points us to the complete transformation which takes place when a man believes.

To this he adds the further expression "sons of the day." In this context we must understand "day" to refer to the day of the Lord. While no doubt the term is suggested by the reference to light, it goes further. Believers find in the day of the Lord a situation in which they are perfectly at home. Just as light is their characteristic, so also is participation in all the glorious events of the day of the Lord.

It should not be overlooked that Paul says this of them "all." There are some members of the church whom he must castigate, but even those he includes in this great description. He proceeds to change the subject from "ye" to "we," making his expression more comprehensive still. As he is about to engage in exhortation to right conduct the change to the first person is tactful. It indicates not the laying down of some hard regulations for the Thessalonians only, but the setting forth of the plain duty of all Christian people. We are not of the night, nor of darkness" he says, setting "night" over against "day," and "darkness" over against "light." Those of the "night" have no share in the day of the Lord, while "darkness" properly describes their spiritual condition.

6 Since Christians are not bound in the darkness of unbelief certain consequences follow.[17] They must not be characterized by the kind of conduct which is proper to the night. Paul calls on

---

[16] For this idiom in Semitic or in Greek see the note in A. Deissmann, *Bible Studies* (Edinburgh, 1901), pp. 161–66. It is not without interest that one of the Dead Sea Scrolls is called "The War of the Sons of Light with the Sons of Darkness."

[17] ἄρα οὖν is a strong expression, and it indicates that what follows is a necessary conclusion. It is found only in the Pauline writings in the New Testament.

them not to sleep as do "the rest." When he used this expression in 4:13, he spoke of such people as being without hope. This is very much in point here, too, where he is thinking of the glorious hope of the Christian at the coming of his Lord. Unbelievers may well "sleep"[18]; they are spiritually insensitive. But the believer should not take his standards from them. They are of the world and therefore they so behave. We who are not of the world should not conform our conduct to theirs. Sleep is natural enough for the sons of night, but it is entirely out of place in the sons of light.

So Paul urges to wakefulness and sobriety. The word "watch" is a natural antithesis to "sleep," but we should not overlook the fact that this very verb is used a number of times of watching for the second coming (e.g., Matt. 24:42 f., 25:13, Mark 13:34 ff.). It denotes watchfulness with some effort.[19] Joined to it is an injunction to be sober, which should probably not be thought of as a warning against drunkenness[20] (there is no indication anywhere in either Epistle that such a warning was necessary at Thessalonica) but an exhortation to temperateness and balance.[21] The word has its affinities with the preceding one and, indeed, Grimm-Thayer treat them as near synonyms. They give the particular meaning of this present verb as: "a state untouched by any slumberous or beclouding influences ... it becomes a term for wariness against spiritual dangers."

7 The thought that there are certain kinds of conduct which are appropriate enough in the sons of night, but quite unbefitting to Christians, as we have already seen, underlies this whole section. This thought now comes to the surface. Paul lists in particular sleep and drunkenness as activities of the night. The verb for

---

[18] The verb for "sleep" here is καθεύδω and not κοιμάω as in 4:13 ff. It is probably not without significance that καθεύδω is sometimes used of carelessness in moral issues, e.g., Eph. 5:14.

[19] γρηγορέω is a verb formed from the perfect ἐγρήγορα (from ἐγείρω), "to have been roused." Whereas ἀγρυπνέω indicates simply the absence of sleep, γρηγορέω has also the idea of a determination to keep awake.

[20] Nevertheless it should be noted that a warning against drunkenness is joined with an appeal to be watchful for the coming in two other passages, Luke 21:34 and Rom. 13:12 f.

[21] Since drunkenness "may suggest either stupid unconsciousness or abnormal exultation" Frame suggests that the exhortation may be "either to perfect control of the senses without which vigilance is impossible or to quietness of mind (4:11) without which the peaceable fruits of righteousness essential to future salvation are unattainable."

"sleep" is that employed in the previous verse. While it may well be that there is a side glance at the fact that moral indifference well suits those who belong to the night, yet the main force of the verb simply seems to be that there are some activities which are appropriate to the night, and sleep is pre-eminently one of them. Similarly drunkenness is not usually carried on by the light of day (cf. Acts 2:15).[22] Those who are drunken revel by night.[23]

8 Once more Paul sets believers over against worldly men with his emphatic "But we."[24] Conduct of the sort he has been outlining has no place in believers, for they are "of the day." This expression probably has a double reference, pointing us both to the light and to the day of the Lord. We Christians are characterized by light. Therefore we can have nothing to do with the deeds of darkness. We look for the day of the Lord. Therefore we must not be caught up in this world's night. "Be sober" is the same verb as that used in v. 6, and it has a similar meaning of general temperateness, with the avoidance of all kinds of excess. It is given point here by the reference to drunkenness in the intervening verse.

All this reminds Paul that the Christian is a soldier,[25] and he changes his imagery to that of the armor with which the warrior is clad. This is a favorite device of the Apostle. He employs it in a number of passages, the most notable being Eph. 6:13 ff. But it is found also in Rom. 13:12, II Cor. 6:7, 10:4.[26] A comparison of these various passages will show that Paul is not consistent in the significance he attaches to the various pieces of armor. It is the general idea which attracts him, and not the particular details. Thus in Romans he thinks of "the armor of light" and does not go into details. In II Cor. 6 it is "the armor of righteousness on the right hand and on the left." In II Cor. 10 the reference is a general

---

[22] It is counted as especially blameworthy when men "revel in the daytime" (II Pet. 2:13).

[23] The two "are drunken's" in this verse represent two different Greek verbs. The first is μεθύσκω, which in the active means "to make drunk," and in the passive "to get drunk," "to become intoxicated." The second, μεθύω, denotes "to be drunk." But in this passage it does not seem as though the difference is to be pressed. The two words are being used as synonyms. RSV, however, renders, "those who get drunk are drunk at night."

[24] ἡμεῖς δέ.

[25] Just what the connection is between the day, and the armor of the soldier is not easy to see, but Paul makes the same transition in Rom. 13:12 f.

[26] Cf. Isa. 59:17 with its description of Jehovah as a warrior armed. See also Wisdom 5:17 ff.

one, to "the weapons of our warfare." In Eph. 6 there are various differences from the armor mentioned here, notably that neither hope nor love is there mentioned. Clearly Paul found the analogy helpful, but just as clearly he regarded the details as unimportant. They could be omitted altogether, or varied to suit the occasion.

He refers again to the great triad of faith, hope, and love, as in 1:3 (where see note). These three virtues are of paramount importance to the Christian, and may well be insisted upon again and again. Something of the centrality of these virtues to the Christian life may be indicated by the particular pieces of armor which symbolize them. The breastplate and the helmet are probably the most important items in a suit of armor, and Paul may intend us to infer that nothing in the Christian's equipment surpasses faith, love, and hope.[27] He mentions only defensive armor, for his interest here is in defense, namely defense against surprise. It may also be relevant to notice that here, as in 1:3, hope comes last, as a sort of climax. This is especially appropriate in this place where so much attention is being given to the second coming with all that that means to the Christian in terms of hope's fulfillment. We should not overlook the fact hat the verb "putting on" is an aorist participle. It may well be that it is meant to convey the idea of a decisive act.[28]

The last phrase in the verse puts before us the inclusive concept of salvation. The term reminds us of the peril in which man is placed by his sin, for otherwise he would be in no need of being saved. It reminds us that the fundamental question to be faced is that of the Philippian jailor, "What must I do to be saved?" (Acts 16:30). It reminds us, too, of the adequate provision for man's salvation that has been made in Christ, and of which the great New Testament ideas like redemption, justification, and the rest are aspects. In one sense this salvation is a very present reality, but in another it is yet to be brought to its consummation, and it is this forward-looking aspect that is before us when we read of "the hope" of salvation . At the same time we must remind ourselves

---

[27] Calvin comments, "He omits nothing of what belongs to spiritual armour, for the man that is provided with *faith*, *love*, and *hope* will be found in no department unarmed."

[28] Though Frame thinks it the participle "of identical action," Findlay considers that it forms "a part of the exhortation: νήφωμεν enjoins a state; ἐνδυσάμενοι an act belonging to the state, and that goes to determine and characterize it" (CGT).

that the use of the term "hope" does not imply any uncertainty. The New Testament idea of hope is something which is certain, for it is grounded in the divine action. But it is not realized as yet, and thus it is still hope, not sight.

9 Being launched on the subject of salvation, Paul follows it up. His first point is that salvation proceeds from God's appointment. This is a point of some considerable importance to him, as we see from the prominence it has throughout his writings. We have already noticed his emphasis on the divine call (2:12, 4:7), and the way he speaks of Jesus as delivering us from the wrath (1:10). In one way or another this great truth is always coming out, for it is central to the gospel. All other religions, in the last analysis, present men with something that they must do if they would be saved. It is Christianity alone which tells us that all has been done. This is true of the manner of our salvation, for our sins were taken away through the blood of the cross. It is also true of the fact that we are saved at all. That is a matter of the divine appointment, of the fact that God calls us into this state. It is not to be understood as though we simply decided to belong to God. The word "appointed"[29] is not as specific as words like "called," or "predestinated," but here it amounts to much the same. It rests our salvation on the divine initiative.

Paul proceeds to speak of salvation negatively and positively. God's purpose for us is not wrath. We have dealt with this term in the note on 1:10. Here it is enough to add that, although the modern world likes neither the term nor the idea it connotes, we can scarcely do without either. There is an implacable divine hostility to everything that is evil, and it is sheer folly to overlook it or try to explain it away. Salvation includes the fact that God did not destine His own to experience His wrath.

On the contrary, He purposed that they should obtain salvation (with all that that means) through the Lord Jesus Christ. There is a little difficulty about the word rendered "the obtaining." Some feel that this sounds too much as though we ourselves are doing

---

[29] ἔθετο. Cf. the use of the term in John 15:16, I Tim. 2:7, II Tim. 1:11, I Pet. 2:8. Hort, discussing the use of this verb in the last-mentioned passage says it is "a somewhat vague word in itself." He adds, it "expresses simply the ordinance of God, perhaps with the idea of place added, that is place in a far-reaching order of things" (*ad loc.*).

what is necessary to acquire our heavenly possessions. It is suggested instead that the word has rather a negative meaning, and that it signifies something like "adoption" (i.e., a being adopted). It has a passive sense in Eph. 1:14, I Pet. 2:9, in both places being translated "possession." But while it can have such a meaning, it is hard to see how this fits into the present passage. Moreover, "acquiring" seems nearer the intrinsic meaning of the word (cf. its use in II Thess. 2:14, "obtaining," and Heb. 10:39, "saving"). To adopt this understanding of it is not to maintain that man is saved by works, but simply that the Christian is to make his salvation his own by entering fully into his possession. That nothing in the way of human merit or initiative is meant is made very clear by the following "through our Lord Jesus Christ." The full title is impressive, and the expression shows that the salvation being spoken about is one which comes through Christ's work for men, and not through anything that men do.

10 This is underlined by drawing attention to the basis of all salvation, the atoning death of the Lord. This is the one place in the two Epistles to the Thessalonians where Paul positively says that Christ died for us. It may fairly be held to be implicit in a number of other places, but this is the only place where it becomes explicit. It is impossible to argue that the failure to mention the cross more often means that Paul had as yet no theology of the atonement. In the first place it might be urged that the Thessalonian letters are not doctrinal treatises, but occasional letters to meet specific needs. It is all the more significant that the cross should be mentioned at all in such letters. Then there is the fact that at the very time he was writing these words he was preaching in Corinth, where his gospel included a full place for the cross as we see from I Cor. 2:1 ff., 15:3 ff. Moreover, where in the Thessalonian correspondence he does refer to the work of Christ for man the full Pauline doctrine seems to be implied. See 1:10, for example, and the passage on the transformation of death through what Jesus has done, 4:14. There is also the point that the very casual manner of the reference here argues that the significance of the death was well known to the Thessalonians. Otherwise it would have had to be demonstrated for them. The references to the *kerugma* throughout the New Testament show that the cross was the central element in the proclamation of the gospel to those outside. There is not the

161

slightest reason for thinking that things were at all different in Thessalonica, and, indeed, Acts 17:3 shows that the cross *was* preached in that city.

The purpose of Christ's death is that believers should live[30] with Him whether[31] they live or die. The verb "wake" is the same one as we have seen in v. 6, where it is translated "watch" (see note). In that verse it has reference to an attitude of general watchfulness in the light of the coming of the Lord. Here, however, it simply means "live." Moffatt renders "waking in life" to make this meaning clear. A similar comment must be passed on the verb "sleep." It is that used with reference to the conduct of the sons of night in vv. 6, 7, but here it means death (Moffatt, "sleeping in death"). From 4:14 on, Paul has been insisting that death has no victory over the Christian, and this is his thought here, too. The believer is in Christ, and death cannot affect that relationship.

It should be stressed that all this implies a very full theology. Paul is maintaining that the death of Jesus has brought about a new relationship between God and man. Those who are Christ's live with Him.[32] There is the thought of that close union that elsewhere is expressed in the pregnant phrase "in Christ." And this relationship is not disturbed by even such a final and decisive happening as death. Death is only final and decisive when we speak in worldly terms. For the believer the whole concept has been transformed. For him it holds no terrors. In life or in death he is in Christ.

11 Paul rounds off this section, as he had a previous one (4:18), with an exhortation to cheering one another. Phillips renders, "So go on cheering and strengthening each other with thoughts like these." The tense of the imperatives is the present continuous, and it conveys the thought that this is something that they should do habitually. The verb translated "exhort" (mg. "comfort") in

---

[30] Milligan thinks that the use of the aorist ζήσωμεν points us "to this 'life' as a definite fact secured to us by the equally definite death (τ. ἀποθανόντος) of our Lord."

[31] It is difficult to see any real difference in meaning between εἴτε with the subjunctive, and ἐάν with that mood (used, for example, in Rom. 14:8). Burton accounts for the construction here as due to a preference for εἴτε . . . εἴτε over the "somewhat unusual" ἐάντε . . . ἐάντε "in spite of the fact that the meaning called for a subjunctive" (*Syntax*, p. 105).

[32] "With" is ἅμα σύν, on which see note on 4:17.

ARV is difficult to render exactly in English. It has the idea of
strengthening by one's words, and thus means a little more than
"exhort" (see further on 3:2).

The second imperative brings before us the thought that these
great truths about the Parousia are not simply to enable us to hold
our ground. The Christian faith is never static, and the New
Testament envisages the Christian way as a continual growth.
Those who are in Christ are men who are growing in spiritual
stature, and in the knowledge and love of God. Paul envisages
the use of the great truths about the second coming, the day of the
Lord, the character of Christians as sons of that Day and sons of
the light, the necessity for watching, for understanding that God
has called us, not unto wrath, but unto salvation, and this at the
cost of the death of His Son, and the other matters to which he has
been referring, all as a means of promoting growth. The Thessalonians are to build each other up. It should, perhaps, be added
that Paul is very fond of this idea of the building up of Christians.
The word he uses is properly applicable to such matters as building
houses, but Paul habitually uses it metaphorically, of the building
up of Christians in the faith.

He looks to the Thessalonians to accomplish this themselves,
under the guidance of the Spirit. He uses two different expressions
"one another" and "each other."[33] These differ but little. Together they emphasize the mutual responsibility of believers for
one another and the kind of service they can render one another.
His concluding expression, "even as also ye do," shows us that
what he enjoins is no airy idealism. He knows the way in which
the Thessalonians were assisting one another and he commends
them for it. But he urges them to go forward on this way. The
Christian may never relax, thinking he has made sufficient progress.

---

[33] The latter phrase, εἰς τὸν ἕνα, is very unusual, but it does not seem to
differ greatly in meaning from the preceding ἀλλήλους. Lightfoot thinks it is
"somewhat stronger" than ἀλλήλους.

VII.   GENERAL EXHORTATIONS, 5:12–22

12   But we beseech you, brethren, to know them that labor among you, and are over you in the Lord, and admonish you;

13   and to esteem them exceeding highly in love for their work's sake. Be at peace among yourselves.

14   And we exhort you, brethren, admonish the disorderly, encourage the fainthearted, support the weak, be longsuffering toward all.

15   See that none render unto any one evil for evil; but always follow after that which is good, one toward another, and toward all.

16   Rejoice always;

17   pray without ceasing;

18   in everything give thanks: for this is the will of God in Christ Jesus to you-ward.

19   Quench not the Spirit;

20   despise not prophesyings;

21   prove all things; hold fast that which is good;

22   abstain from every form of evil.

There were evidently some problems in personal relationships among the Thessalonians, and in the concluding moments of his Epistle Paul gives attention to them. There is some difference of opinion as to whether office-bearers are being particularly addressed, and some have settled the point by reasoning that there probably were no office-bearers at this early period in the church's history. This seems very difficult to accept. The first groups of Christians seem to have been organized on the model of the synagogue (an assembly of Christians is even called a synagogue in Jas. 2:2), and thus would have had a group of elders exercising oversight. This seems implied in the numerous references to elders from the earliest times. Thus Paul, as early as his first missionary journey, is pictured as appointing elders "in every church" (Acts 14:23). We have no reason for thinking that any local church continued for long without its elders. Granted that there were elders in the Thessalonian church, the likelihood is that they were not men of experience in any position of authority. All our information seems to show that the church in this city was drawn predominantly from the lower strata of society. There is nothing improbable in the idea that inexperienced leaders exercised their authority in a rather tactless fashion. Some of the believers were misbehaving. They were refraining from working for their living, and so forth. The leaders of the church attempted to put things right, but their manner of doing so aroused opposition. It was not serious, as in the case of the Corinthian church, which was rent by the disputes that took place. But Paul felt it wise to say a few words which might clear the matter up. These words have reference primarily, but not exclusively, to the leaders of the church. Since they have relevance to all, they are addressed to the church at large.

12 The occasion is one for appeal rather than authoritative commands, and Paul's address is gentle. There is nothing peremptory about his verb "beseech." It is often used of making request.[34] In keeping is the affectionate "brethren," so common in these Epistles.

He asks them to "know" certain men. The word has the idea of knowing fully, appreciating at their true worth. It indicates that they had not realized as they should the rightful position of the people in question, and they are called upon to learn the true situation.

Those who have not been receiving their due are described as "them that labor among you, and are over you in the Lord, and admonish you." The Greek construction here is three participles following a single article. The point of this is that it is one group of people who discharge all three functions, and not three different groups. It is this as much as anything which inclines us to think that the elders of the church are being addressed. Who else would be thought of as discharging such a triple function?

The verb for "labor" is cognate with the noun "labor" in 1:3 (where see note). It indicates that these people had toiled till they were weary in the service of the church.[35] Though the term in itself is not an ecclesiastical word,[36] and could be used of weari-

---

[34] For the verb ἐρωτάω see the comment of Findlay quoted in the note on 4:1.

[35] Calvin pungently deduces from the term "labor," "that all idle bellies are excluded from the number of pastors."

[36] Deissmann argues that the word springs from the life of the manual laborer. "With regard to all that Paul the tentmaker has to say about *labour*, we ought to place ourselves as it were within St. Paul's own class, the artisan class of the Imperial age, and then feel the force of his words" (LAE, p. 313).

some labor in general, it is noteworthy how often it is used of the labor of Christian preachers. If not a technical term at least it was well adapted to expressing what is involved in ministering in Christian things.

It is possible that the two following participles represent two different and coordinate activities, but most likely they are to be understood as explanatory of the preceding one. The labor in question is that of exercising leadership and admonition, though this should not be understood as defining it exhaustively. The labor is of various kinds, but especially is it oversight and admonition.[37] Them that "are over you in the Lord" is not an official description of a technical order of ministry, but it is difficult to see who could be meant other than office-bearers in the church. The verb may be used of informal leadership, but it is also an official word, describing the function of those who are officers.[38] The addition of "in the Lord" also seems to point us to office-bearing in the church, while, at the same time, it adds the idea of the spiritual fitness of things. This is not a cold, external authority, but one exercised in the warmth of Christian bonds. Being "in the Lord" it is an authority to be exercised for the spiritual good of believers (II Cor. 10:8), and not to give the office-bearers opportunity for lording it over them (Luke 22:25 ff.).

The third function of these people is admonishing. The verb is Pauline,[39] and while its tone is brotherly, it is big-brotherly. There is often the notion of some tie between the admonisher and the admonished, and there is the thought of blame attaching to some wrongdoing which is being rebuked. "I write not these things to shame you, but to admonish you as my beloved children" (I Cor. 4:14) is a passage which brings out both thoughts: the tenderness which is unwilling to shame, and the blame for failure to do the right.

13 Paul adds the further request that the Thessalonians should

---

[37] Cf. Frame, "the correlative καὶ ... καί suggests that of the various activities involved in τοὺς κοπιῶντας ἐν ὑμῖν, two are purposely emphasized, leadership in practical affairs, and the function of spiritual admonition."

[38] MM cite a number of examples to show that the term is used in the papyri of the activities of many kinds of officials.

[39] It is found in the New Testament only in the Pauline epistles, and in Acts 20:31 in Paul's speech to the elders of Ephesus.

hold them in high esteem.[40] There is some discussion as to whether what he says should be understood with the primary emphasis on high esteem (with love added loosely), or on esteem in love (with "exceedingly highly" inserted to show that this should be done without stint). On the whole it seems most likely that the former is to be preferred. What is beyond dispute is that Paul is urging them to both attitudes (cf. Moffatt, "hold them in special esteem and affection"). He wants the officials to be highly regarded, and not dismissed as of no account. His adverb "exceeding highly" is a very expressive and emphatic compound, found in this precise form here only in the New Testament.[41] He wants them to be loved, and not thought of simply as the cold voice of authority. Love is the characteristic Christian attitude to man, and this should be shown within the church. Especially is this so in relationships like those between the rulers and the ruled, which in other groups of men are apt to be formal and distant. Christian love, *agape*, is not a matter of personal liking (see on 1:3), and it is in keeping with this that Paul expressly says that they are to esteem their rulers in love "for their work's sake." It is not a matter of personalities. It is the good of the church that is the important thing. The church cannot be expected to do its work effectively if the leaders are not being loyally supported by their fellows. It is a matter of fact that we are often slow to realize to this day that effective leadership in the church of Christ demands effective following. If we are continually critical of them that are set over us, small wonder if they are unable to perform the miracles that we demand of them. If we bear in mind "the work's sake" we may be more inclined to esteem them very highly in love.

Some exegetes have felt that the exhortation to be at peace brings us to a different subject. It is true that the verb is quite general in its meaning. Injunctions to be at peace are to be found elsewhere where there is no disciplinary problem. Yet in this place it seems rather that Paul is continuing to deal with the situation that is in mind in the earlier part of the verse. The failure of the

---

[40] ἡγέομαι usually means "to deem." The meaning "to esteem" is found very rarely, if at all, outside this passage. This has led to other suggestions (see Frame's note). These, however, are unconvincing, and the context makes it clear that "esteem" is right.

[41] The word is ὑπερεκπερισσῶς. ὑπερεκπερισσοῦ is found in Eph. 3:20, I Thess. 3:10 (and in some manuscripts in the present passage).

rank and file to be on proper terms with their leaders is serious. Therefore the Apostle includes an injunction (notice the change from "we beseech you, brethren" to the imperative, "be at peace") to set these things right. The form of the imperative indicates that Paul himself is trying to keep the peace. He does not say "be at peace with them," which would savor of calling on the church members to subject themselves to their leaders, but "among yourselves," which makes the injunction equally binding on leaders and followers. Both are to keep the peace.

14 Some see in this verse further evidence for the contention that it is not office-bearers that are addressed but ordinary church members. It is not easy to see how this can be sustained. In v. 12 the "brethren" seem to be distinguished from "them that ... are over you in the Lord." Now we have a further exhortation to the "brethren," but this gives no more reason for identifying them with those over them than did the previous one. The content of this charge is to see to the needs of certain people in the church. While this would be in especial measure the responsibility of those holding office, it was also something that lay on the shoulders of all. It is still true that all the brotherhood is charged with responsibility for all. We cannot leave it to any special class.

For "admonish" see note on v. 12. The "disorderly" are probably the "idle." The word is really a military word, and originally referred to the soldier who is out of step or out of rank, or to the army moving in disarray. It then came to mean what is out of order generally. Milligan's long note[42] shows that the term was used in Hellenistic Greek of idleness. Frame adds the point that it is not idleness in the sense of legitimate leisure[43] that is meant, but loafing. The use of this word makes it quite clear that there were some at Thessalonica who had ceased to work and were imposing on the generosity of others. Paul counsels them all to take steps to end this state of affairs.

If the first point has to do with pulling up the slackers, the second is concerned rather with exercising tenderness towards the discouraged. For "encourage" see on 2:11. The word is well adapted

---

[42] Additional Note G.
[43] Which is σχολάζω (I Cor. 7:5), cf. the use of σχολή "a school." Yet it should be borne in mind that σχολάζω can have the idea of culpable idleness as we see from the LXX of Exod. 5:8, 17.

to expressing a tender concern, quite in the spirit of "a bruised reed will he not break" (Isa. 42:3). There are those who are not naturally bold, or who are temporarily overwhelmed by the stress of things. Such should not be condemned by their more robust brethren, but consoled and encouraged, so that they may be fitted for the battle once more. A similar sympathetic attitude is inculcated by the next phrase, "support the weak."[44] The imagery is not that of holding up what is ready to fall down as the English might suggest. Rather the verb is one which is often used of holding to someone (e.g., Luke 16:13). The thought is that it is good for weak souls to know that there are others who are with them, who will cleave to them in the difficult moment, who will not forsake them. In various places Paul has a good deal to say about the weak, notably in Rom. 14 and I Cor. 8. He leaves us in no doubt that there is a place for such in the church, and that the strong have a particular duty towards them. So here the weak are not to be simply abandoned, but made to feel that they belong, that they have strong comrades in Christ.

Paul rounds off the exhortation with "be longsuffering toward all." This should be taken as putting in general terms and with some amplification what he has just been saying in particular cases. The Christian should not be putting his own interests first, and taking a strong line with those who do not agree with him. Rather, he must be patient with all men, bearing their manners, and patiently seeking to lead them in the way of the Lord. It is more important for him that he be able to render them some service than that his ego should be satisfied. To this end he will bide his time, refusing to be affronted, walking in the steps of his Lord.

15 This leads naturally to the thought that the Christian is not to be provoked into acts of retaliation.[45] Rather his ruling attitude must be one of benevolence toward all men, even those who act towards him in hostile fashion. Indeed especially towards those

---

[44] τῶν ἀσθενῶν here refers to the weak spiritually, as all commentators seem to agree. The word can mean weak physically, but the sense of this passage is not "look after those who are unable to work." Rather, the thought is "look after those who are weak in the faith."

[45] The combination of second and third persons, ὁρᾶτε μή τις, conveys the idea that the whole group is being held responsible for the conduct of each individual. They are not only to abstain from retaliation, but to see that none of their number retaliates. "Blessed are the peacemakers" (Matt. 5:9).

who are hostile to him.[46] It is easy enough to be well disposed toward those who treat us well, but it is of the essence of the Christian attitude that *agape*, self-giving love, be practiced toward all, even the unkind and vindictive. Our Master, for our salvation, endured patiently the insults and the injuries of wicked men. He, the Just, died for the unjust. In both these ways His example is important for His people. As the servant is not greater than his Lord we must expect the same kind of treatment, and therefore we must expect to be called upon to show the same kind of patience under provocation. And since He came to die for sinful men, we must expect that our meekness is to be by way of ministering to the needs of sinful men also.

Thus it is that the New Testament often calls on believers to forgive injuries. This is expressed in the Lord's Prayer, and Jesus insisted on the point more than once (Matt. 5:38 ff., 18:21 ff., Luke 6:35 ff., and elsewhere). There are very close parallels to the present passage in Rom. 12:17 and I Pet. 3:9, which indicates that it was something in the nature of a standard injunction in the early church. It may even go back to some saying of Christ. That such a precept was so widely accepted in a body subject to such constant ill-treatment as the early church is remarkable enough. That it was put into practice to such a large extent is even more so. It may be that this was responsible in some measure for the impact the early Christians made on the men of their day. At any rate, it is worth our while reflecting when we are tempted to think of the clash of hostile forces today, and of how difficult it is for us to put such precepts into practice, that the Thessalonians to whom these words were addressed were themselves in no easy situation. Subject to constant harassing from both Jew and Gentile it would have been easy for them to become embittered. But it was just in this situation that they were called upon to render to no man evil for evil. The great precepts of the Christian faith are not addressed only to those who find them easy to keep, but to all. And they can be kept, because with the command God provides the power.

---

[46] Calvin wisely observes, "For particular excuses are wont to be brought forward in some cases. 'What! why should it be unlawful for me to avenge myself on one that is so worthless, so wicked, and so cruel?' But as vengeance is forbidden us in every case, without exception, however wicked the man that has injured us may be, we must refrain from inflicting injury." Denney brings out the difficulty we experience in restraining ourselves by reminding us that "revenge is the most natural and instinctive of vices."

The positive exhortation, "always follow after that which is good," must, in this context, refer to acts of love in the face of hostility rather than to ethical goodness in general. At the same time it should be noted that the term is a wide one. Paul is not simply saying, "Do little deeds of love when you might be expected to retaliate." He is laying down goodness in the face of provocation to evil as a great general principle which must underlie the conduct of the Christian at all times. It is one of his springs of action. The verb is in the continuous present, so that a habitual attitude is inculcated, and this is reinforced by the adverb "always." The verb is "pursue," which means follow with some eagerness. The line of conduct in question is to be exercised towards members of the brotherhood and outsiders alike. As we saw on 4:9, there is a brotherly love that Christians should practice among themselves, but this pursuit of goodness in the face of provocation is something that they should not restrict. No matter where nor how they are provoked the obligation lies upon them to follow the good unswervingly.

16 Perhaps the command to continue to rejoice fits into this picture. The refusal to nurse grudges and to retaliate when provoked is not something that is to be attempted in a spirit of suffering resignation. It is possible ostensibly to forgive, but to make it quite clear that the forgiver is deserving of great credit for his restraint, and that he is very conscious of the magnitude of the wrong that has been done to him. Jesus did not give that impression, nor should His followers. Forgiveness ought to be a joyous affair, with genuine Christian zest for life bubbling through. The Christian is one who has been born all over gain (John 3:3, 7), he has been created anew (II Cor. 5:17). He does not see things as the earthling sees them, but, as a child of the heavenly Father, he goes rejoicing through his Father's world. It is not that he is always screwing himself up to the point of doing unpleasant things in the service of his God but, rather, that he is glad to live out the implications of his faith. There is a serious purpose to life, and that is not overlooked. Sometimes it will lead to stern and serious action. But by and large the Christian's way is a happy way. His spiritual resources are so great that earthly things cannot disturb his composure, and he goes on his way with a song in his heart (Col. 3:16). It is natural for men to rejoice when things go well

171

with them. But it is not this natural joy, dependent on circumstances, that is characteristic of the Christian. It is the joy that comes from being "in Christ." Thus it is that the New Testament is full of exhortations to joyful living—startlingly so, if we fix our attention on the outward circumstances of the Christian community. Persecution was always threatening and often actual. The believers were usually in straitened circumstances and compelled to work hard for their living. Their lot can rarely have been other than hard. But if we fasten our attention on these things we put our emphasis in the wrong place. They thought more of their Lord

than of their difficulties; more of their spiritual riches in Christ than of their poverty on earth; more of the glorious future when their Lord should come again than of their unhappy past. So the note of joy rings through the New Testament, and so Paul, who himself knew what it was to rejoice in difficult circumstances (Acts 16:25), can say, "Rejoice always."[47]

17 The injunction to continual prayer springs out of the same great idea as that to continual rejoicing. Christianity is a religion which turns men's thoughts away from themselves and their puny deeds to the great God who has wrought a stupendous salvation for them in Christ our Savior. It is of the very essence of the faith that it insists upon man's inability to bring about his salvation, either in the sense of the initial act whereby he enters on a state of salvation, or in the sense of the day-by-day living out of the Christian life. For the putting away of his sins the atonement wrought by the Son of God is necessary. For living the dedicated life the power of the indwelling Spirit alone suffices. All along the way man is made to feel his own insufficiency. But alongside that is the power and the love of Almighty God. God will not leave man. He comes to him

---

[47] Lightfoot points out that "on the other hand, it may be said no less truly that sorrow is especially the Christian's heritage. For with a fuller sense of the exceeding sinfulness of sin, of the fearful significance of death, he has more abundant matter for sorrow in the scenes amidst which he moves, than those whose convictions are less deep. Yet the two attitudes are not antagonistic. They may, and do, coexist." Cf. also W. A. Visser 't Hooft, "It is one of the impressive aspects of the life of the Church in history that the churches under pressure or under persecution know so much more about the secret of Christian joy than the churches which live in circumstances of tranquillity" (*The Renewal of the Church* [London, 1956], p. 73). He goes on to point to New Testament passages where "suffering is understood as the merciful act of God by which he tests the faith of his people" (*ibid.*).

at Calvary and at Pentecost. He provides for the deepest needs of man's soul.

In the light of all this the Christian man is ever conscious of his dependence on God. He realizes that he is always surrounded by God's love, and that, therefore, although he is not able to achieve anything worthwhile in his own strength, he has all that he needs. This knowledge will keep him always rejoicing. Why should he be otherwise? And it will keep him always in the spirit of prayer. Prayer and rejoicing are closely related, for often the believer finds in prayer the means of removing that which was the barrier to his joy. Prayer is not to be thought of only as the offering of petitions in set words. Prayer is fellowship with God. Prayer is the realization of the presence of our Father. Though it is quite impossible for us always to be uttering the words of prayer it is possible and necessary that we should always be living in the spirit of prayer.[48]

If we live in this way, conscious continually of our dependence on God, conscious of His presence with us always, conscious of His will to bless, then our general spirit of prayerfulness will in the most natural way overflow into uttered prayer. It is instructive to read again and again in Paul's letters the many prayers that he interjects. Prayer was as natural to Paul as breathing. At any time he was likely to break off his argument or to sum it up by some prayer of greater or less length. In the same way our lives can be lived in such an attitude of dependence on God that we will easily and naturally move into the words of prayer on all sorts of occasions, great and small, grave and gay. Prayer is to be constant.

18 The trio of injunctions is completed with the thought of continual thanksgiving. Like the preceding two, this one springs from the great central truth of the gospel. As the worldly man goes on his way he meets with some things which make him happy, and some about which he complains bitterly. He conceives of life as a matter more or less of chance. Accordingly he welcomes those workings of chance which favor his purposes, and objects to those which do not. But when a man comes to see that God in Christ has

---

[48] The word Paul uses here is προσεύχεσθε, which expresses devotion, the God-ward look, rather than δέομαι which would fasten attention rather on one's need. See on 3:10. προσεύχομαι is the more comprehensive term, and can include the other words for prayer.

173

saved him, everything is altered. He now realizes that God's purpose is being worked out. He sees the evidence in his own life and in the lives of those about him. This leads to the thought that the same loving purpose is being worked out even in those events which he is inclined not to welcome at all. When he comes to see God's hand in all things he learns to give thanks for all things. Tribulation is unpleasant. Yet who in the midst of tribulation would not give thanks when he knows that the Father who loves him so greatly has permitted that tribulation only in order that His wise and merciful purpose might be worked out? So out of this great central truth of Christianity Paul calls on his friends to practice the continual giving of thanks.[49]

As he has already done in another connection (see 4:3) the Apostle proceeds to give what he has said the highest possible authority by rooting it in the will of God. "This" is singular, but it is very probable that it applies to all three of the preceding injunctions. As we have seen, they all proceed from one root, and may fittingly be regarded as a unity. They do not represent three different attitudes to life, but three aspects of one attitude.

As he has already done in 4:3 (where see note) Paul uses the word "will" without the article. The significance of this is that he is making no attempt to deal with the whole will of God. That will includes many things, and many things of importance to the Thessalonians. But among them is this of which he now speaks. On this occasion there is the interesting addition "in Christ Jesus." The centrality of Christ to Christianity cannot be too strongly emphasized. We do not know God of our own selves, but only as He has pleased to reveal Himself to us. Pre-eminently has He revealed Himself in Christ, and pre-eminently has He revealed His will in Christ. The use of the compound name "Christ Jesus" reminds us of both the deity and the humanity of our Lord, and in this way heightens the solemnity of the injunction. Not only is it in Christ that the will of God is revealed. It is in Him that there is given power to men to enable them to live according to that will (see on 3:11 for the close connection between the Father and the Son).

---

[49] The expression here, ἐν παντί, does not mean "at every time," and, indeed, it seems to be differentiated from πάντοτε in II Cor. 9:8. Rather it means "in every thing," i.e., "under all circumstances" (cf. Phillips, "whatever the circumstances may be").

19 It is unusual to find such an exhortation as "Quench not the Spirit," though in Eph. 4:30 we have "grieve not the Holy Spirit of God." "Quench" properly applies to the putting out of a flame of some sort, as that of a fire (Mark 9:48), or a lamp (Matt. 25:8). This is the only place in the New Testament where it is used in a metaphorical sense, though we do find this in the Septuagint. It is used of quenching love (Song 8:7), anger (Jer. 4:4, 21:12),[50] a hot mind (Sir. 23:16), and passions (IV Macc. 16:4). It has particular relevance when used of the Spirit, for His presence is aptly symbolized by fire (Acts 2:3).

Exactly what is meant in this case is not clear. Many passages in the New Testament indicate that the manifestations of the Spirit occupied a large place in the life of the early church. Where we think of the Spirit in terms of that power within the believer which enables him to overcome evil and to produce the "fruit of the Spirit," many early Christians just as naturally thought of Him as the producer of ecstatic manifestations of various kinds, speaking with tongues, prophesyings, and the like. Both the ethical and the ecstatic are attested in the New Testament, and it is a question which of the two is meant here. The majority of commentators favor a reference to the ecstatic. They feel that we have a situation in Thessalonica the opposite of that at Corinth. There Paul had to restrain those who were going to excess. Here, it is said, those who delighted in the ecstatic manifestations had come under the censure of the more stolid, and there was a very real danger of their being discouraged. This may be so, but it seems to be reading a lot into the words of this verse. There is no other evidence that can be cited. In view of the very general character of the expression it may be well to understand the term more generally. In the second century Hermas maintained that both "the doubtful mind and the angry temper" grieve the Spirit, for He was given as a "cheerful" Spirit.[51] The same kind of thing may well be said here . Loafing, immorality, and other sins about which Paul has had occasion to warn his friends will quench the Spirit in a man's life, and result in the loss of spiritual power and joy.[52]

---

[50] Both ϑυμός and ὀργή are used.
[51] *Mandate* 10:2, 3 (cited from Lightfoot's edition). The word for "cheerful" is ἱλαρόν.
[52] The use of μή with the present imperative and not the aorist subjunctive represents a command to cease quenching. It implies that some, at

175

20 Those who see in the injunction not to quench the Spirit a reference to esctatic manifestations usually understand the words about prophecy similarly. Some of the Thessalonians, they tell us, were like the Corinthians. They had been so carried away by the ecstatic gifts like speaking with tongues that they were despising more important things like prophecy. Paul then would be trying to restore a proper sense of values by insisting on the place of prophecy. This may be so, but, like the previous conjecture, this one seems to be reading a good deal into a rather simple expression. All that we can say for certain is that there were apparently some members of the church at Thessalonica who had come to think of prophecy more poorly than they ought. Paul accordingly urges that prophecy be not despised.[53] If we are to conjecture it seems more in accordance with what we know of conditions in this church to associate the despising of prophecy with second-advent speculations. We know that there was much interest in the Parousia among the Thessalonians, and we know that throughout the history of the church such interest has commonly gone hand in hand with prophetic outbursts. One result which has usually followed has been that the more staid have rejected with decision both the advent speculations and the prophecy that has gone with it. It may be that something of the sort had happened at Thessalonica, and that Paul was reminding the church of the very real value of prophecy.

It is often thought today that prophecy in the early church was more or less like preaching today. There is something to be said for this, but the essence of prophecy as the early church understood it appears to have been that the Spirit of the Lord spoke to and through men. A prophet spoke because "a revelation" (I Cor. 14:30) had been made to him. From the human standpoint this was completely unpredictable, so that the revelation might be made to a man "sitting by" (*ibid.*), and apparently not expected to prophesy. Since God spoke through men in this way no limits could be placed to what might be said. Modern discussions generally insist that a prophet's function was rather to "forth-

---

least, of the Thessalonians were quenching the Spirit. Paul calls on them to stop.

[53] The verb, ἐξουθενέω, is a strong one, with the meaning "to make absolutely nothing of." Findlay says it "denotes contempt *objectively*, as it bears on the person or thing despised; while καταφρονέω (1 Cor. xi. 22) describes contempt *subjectively*, as it is in the mind of the despiser" (CGT).

tell" than to "fore-tell." While there is truth in this, it should not be forgotten that on occasion the prophet would foretell the future. While this does not seem to have been his characteristic function it should not be overlooked. Prophets were held in high honor, and we find them mentioned along with apostles several times (e.g., I Cor. 12:28, Eph. 2:20, 3:5). It does not seem likely that the Thessalonians would be despising such exalted personages. But prophesying might be carried out occasionally by people who were not regular prophets (e.g., Acts 19:6), and the term here is wide enough to cover such phenomena. Wherever the Spirit might convey the revelation the Apostle counsels his friends to be receptive.

21, 22 Although in this last section of the Epistle Paul introduces very varied topics and treats them but briefly, it is interesting to see how they link up with one another. So as he turns from the thought of prophecy it is to that of testing out all things, and this in turn leads naturally enough to the retention of the good and the rejection of the evil. What he has said in the previous verse might be misconstrued as an injunction to accept without further ado any utterance by a man who claimed to be a prophet and speaking by the Spirit. This would open the door to boundless credulity and all manner of evils, and it was far from the Apostle's mind. So he makes it clear that he expects them to use their common sense in such matters and to apply the necessary tests.[54] At the same time the words he uses are quite general, and they must be held to apply to all kinds of things, and not simply to claimants to spiritual gifts. It is part of the process of living out the Christian life that constantly the servant of the Lord is called upon to discriminate between the base and the true, and to fashion his conduct accordingly.

From the earliest times there has been a tendency to interpret this passage in the light of the saying attributed to Jesus, "Be approved bankers" (or "money-changers," i.e., men who test coins).[55] There is more indication of a connection in the Greek

---

[54] The "but" (δέ) of ARV mg. should probably be read, for it has excellent manuscript attestation. It should be understood as adversative, contrasting the right procedure which follows, with the incorrect procedure of the preceding.

[55] The passages where the saying appears are given in Lightfoot. There are strong grounds for thinking it is a genuine saying of the Lord Jesus.

than in our English translations. The verb "prove" is often connected with the testing of metals, and it is not unlikely that this is the basic meaning of the verb. We see it applied to gold in I Pet. 1:7 ("gold that perisheth though it is proved by fire"), and often outside the Scriptures. It is used both of applying the test, and of approving as a result of the test. Though the word "good" is not as closely connected with metals as is the verb, yet it is the right term to designate the true coin over against the spurious.[56] It means that which is good or beautiful in itself. It is very close in meaning to the other word rendered "good" in v. 15.[57] But where the two have their distinctive meanings our present word seems to denote, as we have said, that which is inherently good, that which is good by its nature, whereas the other concentrates rather on that which is good in its results. A little thought will show how appropriate the two are in their respective places in this present passage.

The point of this injunction, then, is that the Thessalonians are asked to apply tests. There are things that appear on the surface to be good. There are manifestations which are claimed to come from God. Such are not simply to be accepted at their face value, for it is no part of Christian simplicity to be credulous. All things must be tested. And not simply tested, but accepted wholeheartedly or rejected decisively as a result of the test. "Hold fast" denotes the firm acceptance of the good.[58] There must be no half measures.

The verb "abstain" is likewise a strong one. It is the verb Paul has used in 4:3 of keeping clear of fornication (see note), and here, as there, it is reinforced by a preposition which emphasizes the separation. If a thing is evil then the believer must have no truck with it whatever.

There is some difference of opinion as to the meaning of the word rendered "form." It signifies basically "that which meets the eye," "the external appearance." But from this it develops the

---

[56] Rutherford brings out some of this in his translation: "Rather, assay all things thereby. Stick to the true metal; have nothing to do with the base."

[57] Frame (on v. 15) says, "It is questionable whether in Paul's usage τὸ ἀγαθόν and τὸ καλόν (v. 21) can be sharply differentiated."

[58] κατέχω is a word of many meanings, as the notes of Frame and Milligan, as well as the lexicons, show. Most of its usages, however, stem from the two main ideas, "hold fast" and "hold back." It is the former which is the meaning here.

secondary meaning of "kind" or "species." Thus it is possible to understand the present verse either as "avoid every visible form of evil," or "avoid every kind of evil." On the whole it seems likely that the latter meaning is to be preferred.[59] Yet if the former be accepted it must be borne in mind that where this word is used of outward form (as it generally is in the New Testament, e.g., Luke 3:22, 9:29, John 5:37) there is no suspicion that the outward form does not correspond to something real. The meaning will be "evil which can be seen," and not "that which appears to be evil."

VIII. CONCLUSION, 5:23-28

23 And the God of peace himself sanctify you wholly; and may your spirit and soul and body be preserved entire, without blame at the coming of our Lord Jesus Christ.
24 Faithful is he that calleth you, who will also do it.
25 Brethren, pray for us.
26 Salute all the brethren with a holy kiss.
27 I adjure you by the Lord that this epistle be read unto all the brethren.
28 The grace of our Lord Jesus Christ be with you.

23 The exhortations are concluded and Paul passes over to prayer for his readers. The way in which he effects the transition (with the use of an adversative conjunction[60]) indicates that it is only in the power of the God on whom he calls that his exhortations can be brought to fruition. "I have been urging you to do certain things, *but* it is only in God's strength that you will be able to do them."

The prayer is directed to "the God of peace himself." "Himself" reinforces what we have said above. It is only in God that the Thessalonians will be able to do what they have been asked. To describe Him as "the God of peace" is peculiarly fitting in the light of the exhortations of vv. 12 f., but we cannot feel that it was elicited solely by the situation presupposed there. Paul often uses

---

[59] Notice that while the good is viewed as a unity, evil is of many kinds. There is some dispute as to whether πονηροῦ should be taken as a noun (as ARV) or as an adjective ("abstain from every evil sort"). It is probable that ARV is correct, but there is no real difference of meaning.
[60] The conjunction δέ.

the designation, especially towards the end of his letters.[61] Peace
brings before us the prosperity of the whole man, prosperity in the
widest sense, especially including spiritual prosperity (see on 1:1).
That it should be associated with God in this way is a reminder
that true peace can come only from Him, and that He is such a
God that peace may be said to be characteristic of Him.

This Epistle has had important things to say about sanctification
(3:13, 4:3 ff.), and it is not surprising that in the concluding prayer
Paul returns to the thought. The essential idea in sanctification is
that of being set apart for God, but there is also the thought of the
character involved in such separation. In this place Paul has both
aspects in mind.[62] Moreover, while there is a human element, in
that a man must yield himself up to God (cf. 4:4), yet the primary
thing is the power of God which enables this to be made good.
Thus Paul's prayer is that God will bring about this sanctification.
It is doubtful whether ARV is quite right in rendering the next
word "wholly" (though such commentators as Milligan and Frame
accept some such meaning). The point is that the word is a compound[63] of which the first part has the meaning "wholly." If the
second part is to have its proper significance we need something
to bring out the thought of reaching one's proper end, the end for
which one was made. The meaning is qualitative and not quantitative only. We need something like "so that you may be
complete."

So important is this sanctification that Paul repeats the prayer
in another form, this time praying that the whole man may be
preserved entire and without blame. There are some who see in
the reference to spirit, soul, and body an indication that man is a
threefold being, and not twofold as a division into body and soul
would imply.[64] But this is probably to press the language beyond

---

[61] It is found in Rom. 15:33, 16:20, I Cor. 14:23, II Cor. 13:11,
Phil. 4:9, (also Heb. 13:20), while "the Lord of peace" occurs in II Thess.
3:16.
[62] Cf. Frame, "consecration includes not only religion, devotion to God,
but conduct, ethical soundness."
[63] The word is ὁλοτελεῖς. Lightfoot says that this word "not only implies
entirety (which exhausts the meaning of ὅλους), but involves the further idea
of completion."
[64] Frame thinks that "spirit" probably denotes the divine Spirit which
dwells in believers, and marks them off as different from unbelievers. Bicknell,
however, maintains that this idea is "surely absurd. To speak of a 'portion'
of the divine Spirit introduces an idea of spatial division which contradicts

what is warranted. Paul is not at this point giving a description of the nature of the human constitution, but engaging in prayer. He uses this graphic form by way of insisting that the whole man, and not some part only, is involved.[65] All our powers of whatever sort are to be sanctified, entirely set apart for God. This totality is brought out in another fashion in that the verb "be preserved" and the adjective "entire" are both singular, though they clearly are intended to apply to all three.[66] In different ways Paul emphasizes that sanctification applies to the whole of man, and is not to be restricted to any segment. The word "entire" does not differ very greatly from that rendered "wholly" in the earlier part of the verse, though there is probably some difference of emphasis. Whereas the former word brought us the thought of "that which has attained its end," this one signifies "that which is complete in all its parts."[67] It has interesting associations with sacrifice in the Greek Old Testament and elsewhere. It describes the "whole" stones that were used in making the altar. It is used also of the victims that were offered.[68] If Paul has this sacrificial usage in mind it would fit in very well with the entire surrender of the man to God which is involved in sanctification. If the completeness of

---

the essential nature of Spirit. Nor is it easy to see how the Holy Spirit can in any sense need to be kept entire."

[65] Cf. H. Wheeler Robinson, "this is not a systematic dissection of the distinct elements of personality; its true analogy is such an Old Testament sentence as Deut. vi. 5, where a somewhat similar enumeration emphasizes the totality of the personality" (*The Christian Doctrine of Man* [Edinburgh, 1926], p. 108).

[66] Hendriksen has a long note on this verse during the course of which he maintains there are two clauses here. He thinks that ὁλόκληρον applies only to πνεῦμα, something along the lines of the Berkeley version, "May your spirit be without flaw and your soul and body maintained blameless." I cannot see any real reason for breaking up τὸ πνεῦμα κὰι ἡ ψυχὴ καὶ τὸ σῶμα. The unemphatic possessive, ὑμῶν, applies to all three, and so it seems does ὁλόκληρον. It is not uncommon to see an adjective agree in this way in number and gender with the nearest noun in a list, the whole of which it qualifies. There is moreover the point that it is difficult to take the adverb ἀμέμπτως simply with τηρηθείη (how could God keep people other than blamelessly?). It must surely, as Findlay points out, define ὁλόκληρον, so that the sentence will mean, "In full integrity may your spirit and your soul and your body be preserved,—found blamelessly so . . ." (CGT). It is possible to agree with Hendriksen's main point, that the verse does not give us a trichotomist view of the nature of man, without accepting this piece of linguistics.

[67] It is found, for example, in Jas. 1:4, where its meaning is brought out by the following ἐν μηδενὶ λειπόμενος, "lacking in nothing."

[68] It is used of the stones of the altar in the LXX of Deut. 27:6, while Philo and Josephus use it of sacrificial victims.

the surrender is in view in this word, it is rather the result which is in mind in the adverb rendered "without blame" (found in this epistle only in the New Testament[69]). The character involved in being a Christian is one which admits of only the very highest standards. Paul prays, not simply that they may live good lives, but that they may be blameless.

It is characteristic of this Epistle that these words should be followed by "at the coming of our Lord Jesus Christ." It is clear from earlier passages that the thought of the Parousia loomed large in the thinking both of the apostles and their converts. They were looking for the coming of the day of the Lord, and it is entirely natural accordingly that Paul should refer to it. But his reference has added point, for it makes the sanctification spoken of very far-reaching. Paul is not thinking of a sanctification that may last but a little time here on earth, but of one which continues at the Parousia. Primarily his thought is not which will last until the Parousia (although that is implied), but which will exist *at* the Parousia. As we have seen, the thought of judgment is associated with the second coming. It is a fitting climax to his thought on the sanctification of these believers that he looks for them to be preserved blameless not only through the changes and trials of this earthy life, but also on that dread day when they stand before the eternal Judge.

24 Paul's prayer is no despairing wail, but a cry of faith. He is supremely confident that what he has asked will be done, and this verse reveals that the ground of his trust is the nature of God. As we saw on the preceding verse, Paul was sure that the Thessalonians would be able to obey his injunctions because their resources were in God. Now we see that he is sure that God will indeed supply their need in this matter, because He is "faithful." Centuries before, Abraham had asked, "Shall not the Judge of all the earth do right?" (Gen. 18:25). Through all the intervening years the conviction that God can be depended upon had sustained men of faith as, indeed, it does to this day. It is not in the unstable qualities of men that trust must be placed, but in the eternal faithfulness of God. Paul does not mention the name of God, but proceeds to characterize Him as "he that calleth you" (see on 2:12).

---

[69] Milligan draws attention to the fact that it is found in sepulchral inscriptions at Thessalonica, and he quotes one of them.

There may be something of a hint at the fact that God's call is always sounding in the ears of His people, so that the present call that they hear is their guarantee that God will see them through. Or it may be that God is being spoken of as "the Caller," the God who habitually calls to Himself those whom He will have.

But God, besides being a Caller, is a Doer. The end of the verse fastens attention on this aspect of His being. The verbal idea is emphasized in the Greek in two ways, by the addition of "also" (God not only calls, He also acts), and by the omission of the object (there is no "it" in the Greek). There is no real doubt as to what the object is, and its omission has the effect of fastening attention on the verb "do." The God to whom Paul prays is not a God who is inactive or ineffective. Paul thinks of Him as One who will certainly bring to completion that which He has begun. "Hath he said, and will he not do it?" (Num. 23:19). Because He is the faithful One, and because He is the One who has called them, they may know that He will do perfectly all that is involved in their call. It is profoundly satisfying to the believer that in the last resort what matters is not his feeble hold on God, but God's strong grip on him (cf. John 10:28 f.).

25 It is easy to picture for ourselves Paul as a very great Apostle ceaselessly occupied with his work of issuing directives to other people on how they should live out their faith, while he himself sits above the storm or calmly goes on his undisturbed way. Such, of course, is far from being a true picture. Paul was very much caught up in the hurly-burly. He found himself in situations where he did not know how to act. Sometimes when he did act he was not at all sure that he had done the right thing (in II Cor. 7:8, for example, he tells us that he wrote a letter which he came to regret, but later did not regret). He was very conscious of his own limitations, and knew that his only hope was in God. So quite often we find him seeking the prayers of his converts as he does here.[70] He knew that he needed their prayers just as much as they needed his. So, as for the last time in this Epistle he uses the affectionate address, "Brethren," it is to request them to pray continually (continuous tense) for him.[71]

---

[70] See Rom. 15:30, Eph. 6:19, Col. 4:3 f., II Thess. 3:1 f., and cf. Phil. 1:19.

[71] If the "also" of ARV mg. is genuine the meaning will be "pray for

26 "Salute" sounds rather formal to us, but the Greek underlying it is simply the ordinary word for greeting people. Paul
usually ends his letters by sending greetings. As a rule, when he
writes to a church he knows he does not greet friends by name,
which might have been invidious. As here, he sends his greetings
to all. The "all" ensures that none are to be left out. He has spoken
of some people who were loafers, and some who were weak. There
were possibly others with whom he was not well pleased. But in his
closing greetings he includes them all. Some have seen in the word
an indication that the church was seriously divided, and, indeed,
was split into two groups (see Introduction, pp. 34 ff.). But this is to
read far too much into the word. It is not in a specially emphatic
position, and is adequately understood as above.

The reference to the kiss means "Give everyone a kiss from me"
(cf. I Cor. 16:24). Paul could not be present in person to bestow
this greeting, so he wrote it. In some other places Paul urged his
readers to greet one another with a holy kiss (see below), but this is
not the thought here. Paul is not telling the Thessalonians how to
greet one another but sending his own affectionate greetings to all.
It is clear enough that this is not meant as anything more than a
customary mode of greeting, much as we today shake hands. Not a
great deal is known about kissing among the early Christians, but
the practice, first taken over from the ordinary usage of secular
society as a mode of greeting, in time came to have liturgical
significance. Probably this arose from the fact that the kiss would
naturally be exchanged on those occasions when the brethren came
together for worship. It is usually held that the kiss was exchanged
at first only between members of the same sex. But in course of
time men and women exchanged kisses. Understandably this led
to undesirable scenes, and the early church councils passed a
number of regulations governing the circumstances under which
the kiss should be exchanged. The "holy kiss" is mentioned in
Rom. 16:16, I Cor. 16:20, II Cor. 13:12, and a "kiss of love" in
I Pet. 5:14, so that the custom was evidently widely practiced in
New Testament days.

27 It is not surprising that Paul should ask for his letter to be

---

us as well as for yourselves and other people," or, "pray for us as we have
been praying for you."

read to all. The word "read" will here mean "read aloud."[72] We do not know how far the early church was literate, but it is not likely that all the artisan church members of Thessalonica could read for themselves, so that reading aloud was the way in which the contents would be made known to all. Whether this means that Paul intends the letter to be read during public worship is not clear. In time such reading came to be accepted as a mark of canonicity, a sign that the writing was accepted as sacred Scripture. But it is uncertain either how old the custom was of reading such letters during service, or how early this signified canonicity. On the whole the likelihood is that Paul did mean the letter to be read, if not at worship, at least on the occasion when people assembled for worship (perhaps before or after the service). The point is that opportunities for those who were not leisured folk to meet were not many, and the gathering for worship would be the logical time for such a communication to be read to them all. This probably established a precedent. In time the kind of letters which might be read at service was sharply delimited, and so only letters held to be canonical were read.[73]

But if it is not surprising that Paul should ask that the letter be read it is surprising that he does so in language of such vehemence. "I adjure you by the Lord" means "I put you on your oath as Christians."[74] This is something which comes from Paul himself, for he says "I" and not "we." Why should Paul be so very urgent about the letter being read to all?

Harnack thought it fitted into his picture of a church in two

---

[72] It is often said that ἀναγινώσκω always means to read aloud, but the examples cited by Milligan show that it sometimes means simply "to read." The same examples make it difficult to hold, as some do, that reading was always aloud in antiquity. While there is no reason to doubt that it was often aloud (cf. Acts 8:30) it is very difficult to believe that educated men had not learned to read silently. Lake and Cadbury think this "surely incredible" (on Acts 8:30).

[73] Some manuscripts insert "holy" before "brethren" (ARV mg.). This is unlikely to be the true reading for a number of reasons. The adjective is unnecessary, for all the brethren, as Paul's insistence on sanctification shows, were holy. The expression "holy brethren" is found in no other place. The better manuscripts omit "holy" here. Its presence is explicable in that it may well have crept in from the previous verse. It is not surprising, accordingly, that almost all commentators omit it.

[74] The verb he uses is the rare ἐνορκίζω (only here in the New Testament, and not often elsewhere). This seems to be a strengthened form of ὁρκίζω (Mark 5:7, Acts 19:13). It is an extraordinarily strong form to employ in such a connection.

sections, and was a way of ensuring that it was read to both. But, as we have seen in the Introduction, this solution to the problems of the Thessalonian correspondence is an unlikely one. Others, while rejecting Harnack's view, think that the strength of the language must point to the possibility of some of the Thessalonians withholding the letter from others, and thus to a deep division. Others again hold that some of the obdurate brethren were likely to absent themselves when the letter was read. The charge then is laid upon the elders to see that all come to know the contents. The objection to all such views is the cordial tone of the letter. Paul felt deeply on the subject of division among the brethren, as we see from I Corinthians. It is difficult to imagine him writing in the strain he has done if there were such deep and serious divisions within the Thessalonian church.[75]

It seems to me that the best explanation available to us arises from a consideration of such passages as 2:17 f. (where see note). Paul has several times used strong expressions in protesting his tender regard for them, and his desire to be with them. Apparently some had said that he had no real love for his converts, and that if he had wished to do so, he would have been able to return. The fact that he had not done so showed him to have his affections set elsewhere. In this situation the ideal thing would have been for Paul to have returned. But his circumstances made this impossible. He had to use this letter as a substitute. Accordingly it was important not only that it should come before the notice of all, but also that it be seen plainly to be intended to come before the notice of all. In this way his care for them would be manifest.[76]

28 It is characteristic of Paul that he brings his letters to an end, not with the customary "Farewell," but with a prayer for grace for those to whom he has written (see on 1:1 for the significance of "grace" in Christian greetings). Occasionally the prayer is shorter than this one,[77] and sometimes it is longer, the longest

---

[75] Lightfoot thinks that Paul had a presentiment of a misuse of his name, a presentiment which, in the light of II Thess. 2:2, we see to have been amply justified. In the nature of the case we cannot verify such a conjecture, but it seems better to look for another explanation.

[76] It has also been suggested that Paul had a tender concern for the bereaved. He feared that some of them might be absent when his words of consolation were read, and in this way he ensured that everyone came to hear what he had written.

[77] The shortest of all is in Colossians, ἡ χάρις μεθ' ὑμῶν (the endings of the Pastorals are similar).

being II Cor. 13:14 with its mention of each of the Persons of the Trinity. But characteristic in each case is the prayer for grace. It is the grace of the Lord which lingers in the Apostle's thoughts, just as it is the grace of the Lord with which he begins his letters.[78] His own hand would seem to have penned these words in each epistle (see II Thess. 3:17, and note), for he took the pen from the amanuensis somewhere before the conclusion. Just where he did so in this letter is not apparent, though the use of the first person singular in v. 27 makes it appear that he wrote that verse himself.

---

[78] Cf. Denney: "Whatever God has to say to us—and in all the New Testament letters there are things that search the heart and make it quake —begins and ends with grace.... All that God has been to man in Jesus Christ is summed up in it: all His gentleness and beauty, all His tenderness and patience, all the holy passion of His love, is gathered up in grace. What more could one soul wish for another than that the grace of the Lord Jesus Christ should be with it?"

THE SECOND EPISTLE TO THE THESSALONIANS

ANALYSIS OF II THESSALONIANS

I. GREETING, 1:1, 2

II. PRAYER, 1:3–12
1. Thanksgiving, 1:3–5
2. Divine judgment, 1:6–10
3. The content of Paul's prayer, 1:11, 12

III. THE PAROUSIA, 2:1–12
1. The day of the Lord not yet present, 2:1, 2
2. The great rebellion, 2:3–12
(a) The Man of Lawlessness, 2:3–10a
(b) The Man of Lawlessness' followers, 2:10b–12

IV. THANKSGIVING AND ENCOURAGEMENT, 2:13–17
1. Thanksgiving, 2:13–15
2. Prayer for the converts, 2:16, 17

V. THE FAITHFULNESS OF GOD, 3:1–5
1. Request for prayer, 3:1, 2
2. God's faithfulness, 3:3–5

VI. GODLY DISCIPLINE, 3:6–15
1. The disorderly, 3:6–13
2. The disobedient, 3:14, 15

VII. CONCLUSION, 3:16–18

COMMENTARY ON II THESSALONIANS

I. GREETING, 1:1, 2

1 Paul, and Silvanus, and Timothy, unto the church of the Thessalonians in God our Father and the Lord Jesus Christ;
2 Grace to you and peace from God the Father and the Lord Jesus Christ.

1, 2 The greeting at the head of this Second Epistle follows that in the First Epistle fairly closely, and the notes on I Thess. 1:1 should be consulted. The only differences are the inclusion of "our" before Father, and the addition of the words which follow "peace" in v. 2. When the New Testament speaks of God as Father it is sometimes God as the Father of our Lord Jesus Christ that is in mind, and sometimes God as the Father of believers. The inclusion of "our" shows that it is this latter which is the thought here. Paul is thinking of what God has come to be to the believers in Thessalonica and of the bond which unites them with the apostles. The words added bring the shorter form given in I Thessalonians up to that which became Paul's standard mode of greeting. It is found in all the other epistles with the exception of Colossians (from which the words "and the Lord Jesus Christ" are missing). The effect of it is to remind his readers of the divine origin[1] of that grace and peace that had come to mean so much, and also of the fact that the Apostle prayed for them that they might enjoy this grace and peace to the full.[2]

---

[1] Bicknell comments: "The Greek makes plain that the Father and Christ are one source. It is remarkable that even at this early date the Son is placed side by side with the Father as the fount of divine grace, without any need of comment."

[2] Findlay speaks of the Father as "the ultimate spring" and the Lord Jesus Christ as "the mediating channel" of grace and peace (CGT). While we may feel that this is the true position, yet it does not arise out of the expression used here. The Father and the Son are closely linked, and no distinction is made between them. It is pertinent to notice in this connection that, whereas Paul seems usually to link peace with the Father and grace with the Son, he does not differentiate between them in his salutations.

II. PRAYER, 1:3-12

1. THANKSGIVING, 1:3-5

> 3 We are bound to give thanks to God always for you,
> brethren, even as it is meet, for that your faith
> groweth exceedingly, and the love of each one of you
> all toward one another aboundeth;
> 4 so that we ourselves glory in you in the churches of
> God for your patience and faith in all your persecu-
> tions and in the afflictions which ye endure;
> 5 *which is* a manifest token of the righteous judgment
> of God; to the end that ye may be counted worthy of
> the kingdom of God, for which ye also suffer:

3 A thanksgiving was the common epistolary convention at
this point of a letter, but, as we saw in the First Epistle, Paul adapts
the conventional form to his own particular needs. Now he utters
a thanksgiving, but it is far from being a perfunctory compliance
with convention. Some have seen in "we are bound" and "as it is
meet" an indication that this Epistle is colder and more formal than
the former one. Besides overlooking the warmth of the expressions
which follow, this view fails to take into consideration the whole
context in which the words are set. Paul has already written a very
warm letter, containing some passages of high praise for the
Thessalonian church. It is probable that in the subsequent communication that they had had with him (whether by letter, or by
word of mouth) they had said that they were not worthy of such
praise. Paul strongly maintains that his words had not been too
strong. There is an obligation[3] resting on him, he says. The
implication is that it would be wrong not to give thanks to God in
such a situation. There is a certain emphasis on "we are bound,"
and this is reinforced by the adverb "always." The quality of the
Christian life of the Thessalonians imposed a lasting obligation on
the apostles to render thanks to God. Paul passes from personal
obligation to the fitness of things in the expression "as it is meet."[4]

---

[3] The verb he uses, ὀφείλομεν, is unusual in his thanksgivings (though it
occurs also in 2:13). It carries the idea of personal obligation, whereas δεῖ
would denote something more in the nature of external compulsion.

[4] καθώς, as Frame points out, "in Paul is slightly causal." Thus it must
be taken with ὀφείλομεν, and not as indicating the degree or the manner of
the thanksgiving.

In praising the advance of the Thessalonians in the faith he was doing no more than give due recognition to the existing state of affairs.[5]

In the First Epistle he had given thanks for their faith, love, and hope. The absence of "patience of hope" here is probably not significant, for as the letter proceeds it does not appear that Paul thinks the Thessalonians to be deficient in hope. Moreover, in v. 4 he says he boasts of their "patience." It is significant that the two matters for which he now gives thanks are both mentioned in the former letter as subjects for improvement. In 3:10 he had spoken of his desire to perfect what was lacking in their faith, and in 3:12 he had prayed that their love might abound. Now he is able to thank God for the growth of their faith and the abundance of their love. His verb for "groweth exceedingly" is an unusual one (here only in the Greek Bible), and gives the thought of a very vigorous growth. The verb "aboundeth" is the one he used in the prayer of I Thess. 3:12, so that he is recording the exact answer to his prayer.[6]

In several places in both Epistles Paul uses expressions which indicate that all the Thessalonians are being included in some word of praise or greeting. He seems to be at pains to include them all, making no distinctions. It is as though he insists that, while he must rebuke some for their failings, yet there are no such grievous offenses as put men beyond the pale. Here we have a typical example. Paul points out that the love of which he speaks is to be found throughout the whole community. It is "the love of each one of you all." The expression is a strong one. Clearly Paul is making no exceptions. Love was a bond uniting the whole church.

4 All this has a most unexpected result. "We ourselves" is a very emphatic expression, much more emphatic than we would have expected in such a connection. It implies a strong contrast. The difficulty is that there is no one mentioned with whom "we" is being contrasted. Some exegetes have thought that the apostles are being contrasted with the fainthearted among the Thessalonians,

---

[5] Phillips exactly reverses the meaning of the two expressions in rendering, "I thank God for you not only in common fairness but as a moral obligation!"

[6] Of these two verbs Lightfoot says, "The words ὑπεραυξάνει and πλεονάζει are carefully chosen; the former implying an internal, organic growth, as of a tree; the other a diffusive, or expansive character, as of a flood irrigating the land." Paul has a special fondness for compounds with ὑπέρ.

or with the whole church. This may be so, but there seems no real grammatical reason. The probability is against Paul's expecting any church to boast of its achievements. Our best understanding seems to be that it was very unusual for the founders of a church to boast of that church. Other people might do so (cf. I Thess. 1:9), but not the founders. Yet in the case of the church at Thessalonica the qualities of which Paul speaks had been displayed in such outstanding measure that even those whose preaching had brought that church into being could not forbear to utter its praises. They did not do this apologetically, for the word "glory" is not the usual one, but a strong compound (by the use of which, Frame says, Paul "intensifies the point"). In line with this is the fact that his boasting is carried out "in the churches of God." There is no limit to any one region. We are not, of course, to understand that Paul had systematically told every church in existence about the Thessalonians, but his choice of such an inclusive expression indicates that his praise of them had been completely uninhibited.

In the previous verse Paul found two things in particular for which he thanked God, and now he mentions two for which he boasted about the converts. "Patience" would be better rendered "steadfastness." It is an active, manly quality, rather than a passive resignation (see on I Thess. 1:3). It is closely linked with faith, there being a single article which unites them. We are probably to understand the former as the fruit of the latter. Calvin explains the passage thus: "We glory in the patience which springs from faith, and we bear witness that it eminently shines forth in you." He goes on to say, "the more proficiency any one makes in faith, he will be so much the more endued with patience for enduring all things with fortitude, as on the other hand, softness and impatience under adversity betoken unbelief on our part." Some have understood "faith" here in the sense of "faithfulness," but this does not seem warranted. The word can have this meaning, and when it refers to God it always does have it. But when it is used of men in the New Testament it always seems to have the meaning "faith," "trust." It is man's response to the faithfulness of God. There are good reasons for doubting the contention that here and there it means "faithfulness."[7] It is man's reliance on

---

[7] But see an article by T. F. Torrance, "One Aspect of the Biblical Conception of Faith" (ExT, Vol. LXVIII, pp. 111–14), the short reply by

God's faithfulness for all things. It is not any human virtue, be it constancy or any other. It is a concept central to Christianity, and occurs many times. The frequency with which it must denote "faith" is impressive. In this passage the Apostle appears to mean that the faith of the Thessalonians had not failed under the stress of persecution, and for that he gloried on their behalf. See further on 3:2.

The way of the Thessalonian church had been far from easy (cf. I Thess. 1:6, 2:14, etc.). The use of "all" shows that their troubles had been many, while the present tense in the verb "endure" makes it plain that their difficulties were not yet over. Of the two words Paul uses to describe their troubles "persecutions" is the more specific. It points to suffering endured on account of the faith.[8] "Afflictions" might mean troubles of any kind (see on I Thess. 1:6). In this passage there is not much difference between them. Both refer to the sufferings that the converts had had to endure as Jews and Gentiles alike tried to turn them from the faith. Paul boasted of their continuing endurance.

5 But God is over all, and neither their sufferings, nor their bearing under their sufferings should be interpreted other than in the light of this great fact. It is at first sight somewhat difficult to follow the Apostle's train of thought. To us the fact of suffering seems to deny, rather than to prove, that God is working out His righteous purpose. But there are two things that must be said here. The one is that the New Testament does not look on suffering in quite the same way as do most modern people. To us it is in itself an evil, something to be avoided at all costs. Now while the New Testament does not gloss over this aspect of suffering it does not lose sight either of the fact that in the good providence of God suffering is often the means of working out God's eternal purpose. It develops in the sufferers qualities of character. It teaches valuable lessons. Suffering is not thought of as something which may possibly be avoided by the Christian. For him it is inevitable.

C. F. D. Moule (*ibid.*, p. 157), and the further notes by both writers (*ibid.*, pp. 221 f.). Dr. Torrance speaks freely of the faithfulness of man, as well as that of God. But if I understand him aright, his "faithfulness" is a constant trust in God. He strongly emphasizes the priority of the faithfulness of God.

[8] This is its usual meaning in the Greek Bible. In non-Biblical writings it has other meanings, such as "pursuit."

He is ordained to it (I Thess. 3:3). He must live out his life and develop his Christian character in a world which is dominated by non-Christian ideas. His faith is not some fragile thing, to be kept in a kind of spiritual cotton wool, insulated from all shocks. It is robust. It is to be manifested in the fires of trouble, and in the furnace of affliction. And not only is it to be manifested there, but, in part at any rate, it is to be fashioned in such places. The very troubles and afflictions which the world heaps on the believer become, under God, the means of making him what he ought to be. Suffering, when we have come to regard it in this light, is not to be thought of as evidence that God has forsaken us, but as evidence that God is with us. Paul can rejoice that he fills up "that which is lacking of the afflictions of Christ in my flesh for his body's sake, which is the church" (Col. 1:24). Such suffering is a vivid token of the presence of God.

The second point we must bear in mind is that in this verse the "manifest token" is probably not suffering simply, but the whole of the previous clause. That is to say, it includes also the bearing of the Thessalonians under suffering.[9] The fact that they had been able to endure it so courageously, with unshaken steadfastness and faith, is evidence that God is working in them. It is a righteous thing with God to provide for His people all things needful for them. The plain fact is that He has done this for the Thessalonians.

All this is "to the end that ye may be counted worthy of the kingdom of God." Paul brings out the point that the sufferings of the Thessalonians had not been haphazard. The Greek construction indicates purpose.[10] God had used the persecutions and afflictions as the means of accomplishing that which He had pleased, namely, that the believers should be deemed worthy (or perhaps "be shown to be worthy")[11] of the kingdom (for "the

---

[9] Cf. Frame, "Since the object of boasting specified in v. 4 is not suffering, but the constancy of their endurance and faith in the midst of persecution, ἔνδειγμα is not to be taken with the idea of suffering alone . . . but with the idea of endurance and faith in spite of persecutions."

[10] The construction is εἰς τό with the infinitive. The weakening of the telic force of this construction in late Greek leads a few to think that it may denote here either the content of the righteous judgment or its result. But in Paul the construction usually denotes purpose, and there is no real reason for thinking that the telic force is lacking here. Way renders, "a token . . . of His purpose that you be adjudged worthy."

[11] RSV renders, "that you may be made worthy," and Moffatt, "he means to make you worthy." But the verb is καταξιόω. While it is true that

198

kingdom of God" see on I Thess. 2:12). There is no idea that their endurance of suffering constituted a merit which gained them membership of the kingdom. The thought is that all is of God. He called them, and then proceeded to lead them in the right way. This involved that suffering that was His Fatherly discipline. It helped to shape them into what He would have them be. He gave them all needed grace to endure. Then at the end it is not said that they are worthy, but that they are deemed worthy. It is still all of God. Now He is thought of as giving the verdict in accordance with His eternal purpose. The concluding "for which ye also suffer" brings their suffering into intimate relation with the kingdom. It does not modify the previous statement in the direction of attributing merit to suffering. The Greek preposition rendered "for"[12] has the meaning "on behalf of," perhaps "in the interest of," and not "with a view to," "in order to gain which." The addition of "also" raises a small problem. It may link Paul with the Thessalonians. He was suffering for the faith, and they were suffering also. Or it may link present suffering and future glory. "You are both suffering and also being deemed worthy" would then be the thought. Grammatically either is possible, but perhaps the former is slightly more probable.

2. DIVINE JUDGMENT, 1:6-10

6   if so be that it is a righteous thing with God to recompense affliction to them that afflict you,
7   and to you that are afflicted rest with us, at the revelation of the Lord Jesus from heaven with the angels of his power in flaming fire,
8   rendering vengeance to them that know not God, and to them that obey not the gospel of our Lord Jesus:
9   who shall suffer punishment, *even* eternal destruction

---

verbs in -όω often have a factitive meaning, this is not the case where moral qualities are in question. Then the meaning is declaratory (e.g., ὁσιόω, ὁμοιόω, δικαιόω, etc.). καταξιόω must be understood in this way. It is a strengthened form of ἀξιόω (the meaning of which is clear in Luke 7:7), and means "to declare to be worthy," "to deem worthy." Many commentators (e.g., Frame, Milligan, Findlay) declare expressly that the word does not mean "to make worthy," but "to deem worthy." Cf. its use in Luke 20:35, Acts 5:41, in both of which RSV and Moffatt translate correctly with "considered worthy," "accounted worthy."

12 ὑπέρ.

from the face of the Lord and from the glory of his might,

10 when he shall come to be glorified in his saints, and to be marvelled at in all them that believed (because our testimony unto you was believed) in that day.

6 The fact that God's righteous purpose is being worked out is reiterated in the enunciation of a great principle. That Paul puts it into a hypothetical form ("if so be") does not signify that the matter is open to dispute. It is rather his way of indicating that it is so sure that it can with safety be cast into this hypothetical mould. "If (as all agree)" is the sense of it.

This resumes what has been said in the previous verse, and, so to speak, gives the other side of it. The use of the term "righteous" shows us that we are in the same circle of ideas as when Paul spoke of "the righteous judgment of God." But now we have the negative aspect. Just as it is true that it is a righteous thing with God to bring believers to salvation and blessing in His kingdom, so it is a righteous thing with Him to bring punishment to those who persist in courses of evil.[13] This is sometimes thought to be so un-Christian that the hypothesis of interpolation has been resorted to. This, however, does not seem warranted. If it is true that the New Testament speaks much of the love and mercy of God it is also true that it does not gloss over the serious nature of moral issues. Our Lord spoke plainly of the fate of those who persist in ways of sin and impenitence (Mark 9:47 f.; Luke 13:3, 5; etc.).[14] Those who followed after did not slur over this truth. They said plainly that the evil-doer can look for nothing but the continuing wrath of God (Rom. 1:18 ff.). Often retribution is pictured as overtaking men in the world to come, but there are not wanting passages which indicate that it may operate here and now (e.g., Rom. 1:24, 26, 28). This verse ought not then to be dismissed as un-Christian, but recognized as giving expression to a well-defined strand of New Testament teaching (albeit one unpalatable to modern men).[15]

---

[13] The verb ἀνταποδίδωμι, "to recompense," is a compound which conveys the thought of a full and due requital. It is used in a similar way of God's judicial recompense in Rom. 12:19. For "affliction," see on I Thess. 1:6.

[14] Cf. the reactions assigned by Jesus to one and the same king, with regard to one and the same servant, "the lord of that servant, being moved with compassion, released him, and forgave him," "his lord was wroth, and delivered him to the tormentors" (Matt. 18:27, 34).

[15] Similar teaching may be found in the Dead Sea Scrolls, e.g., "with

7 God's recompensing activity is not confined to the repayment of the wicked. It has its application to the relief of the righteous as well. Paul looks to God to grant rest to the afflicted. This word "rest" is frequently used by the Apostle, and nearly always in contrast to affliction, as here. It denotes a freedom from restraints and tension.[16] The prospect of such relief given by God Himself is held out before the suffering Thessalonians as something which will strengthen their spirits in the trying times through which they are passing. There is a tendency in modern times to look askance on heavenly rewards and the like. It is true that the Christian must serve his God for what He is, and not from selfish motives. It is true, too, that he who serves in order to obtain a reward has not really caught the spirit of Christianity at all. He has simply exchanged one form of selfishness for another, and the result is not pleasing. Yet when full allowance has been made for that, it remains that the New Testament does speak of a rest for the people of God (Heb. 4:9). We are not being true to its teaching if we overlook this. While it may well be true to say that if we are still serving God with a view to something for ourselves we do not know much about the Christian faith, it is also true that the contemplation of the rest that God has reserved for them is a legitimate activity of the saints who are passing through trials.

Paul speaks of rest "with us,"[17] a little touch which reminds his readers that he is not delivering an academic disquisition on the nature of suffering and recompense. He is speaking out of his own difficult situation. Throughout his missionary career he was encompassed with trials, not least during his stay at Corinth when this letter was written.

There is a sense in which retribution takes place in the here and now. There is a fuller sense in which it is reserved for the last great day. It is this that Paul has especially in mind in the present passage, as he proceeds to make clear. The section which begins

---

God is the judgment of every living man; and he will repay to a man his recompense" (from the closing Psalm in "The Manual of Discipline," cited from Millar Burrows, *The Dead Sea Scrolls* [London, 1956], p. 386).

[16] As in the slackening of a taut bow string.

[17] Frame quotes E. von Dobschütz as saying, "these two little words belong to the genuine Pauline touches for the sake of which no one, with any feeling for the way in which the mind of Paul works, can give up the authenticity of this brief epistle."

"at the revelation" and goes on to the end of v. 10 is of such a rhythmical character that a number of commentators have felt that it is a psalm of some sort. A necessary corollary seems to some to be that Paul is quoting from some other writer. While acknowledging that the section is poetic we may feel that it does not follow that Paul is not the author. No valid reason has been adduced for doubting that Paul wrote it. He often employs a very elevated style, as I Cor. 13 (to name no other) amply shows.

There are various words used of Christ's appearing on that day. The typical word (see on I Thess. 2:19) stresses the idea of coming. The word used here[18] directs attention rather to the thought of uncovering what is hidden. Now the Lord is hid from the view of the world, and it is even possible for men to deny His existence. But in that day He will be revealed in all His glory. He will be shown to be what He is.

Paul proceeds to describe this revelation[19] in a series of three prepositional phrases. It will be (a) from heaven, (b) with the angels, and (c) in flaming fire. The first of these conveys the thought that the highest place of all is His and is His now. He is enjoying the glory of the Father. When He comes it will be with the very highest authority, and His task will be that divine task of judgment. This thought of His glory is continued in the reference to "the angels of his power." Some feel that "of his power" should be taken as equivalent to an adjective, and thus AV translates "his mighty angels." While this is a possible way of reading the Greek the probability is that it should be taken as ARV. The point is that the passage is dealing with the Lord, and it is His power rather than that of the angels that is likely to be spoken of. It is also the case that "angels of power" seem to be a definite class in apocalyptic literature. Frame is able to cite a passage from the Ethiopic Enoch in which they are expressly distinguished from "the angels

---

[18] ἀποκάλυψις. The preposition is ἐν (ἐν τῇ ἀποκαλύψει), which signifies rather more than "at." It is not simply that the retribution will take place "at" the revelation. It will itself form part of that revelation. G. Vos has an interesting note on ἀποκάλυψις in The Pauline Eschatology (Grand Rapids, 1953), pp. 77–79.

[19] On this whole description Neil comments, "The most notable feature is the reticence of the description. What in normal apocalyptic literature would have included a lurid picture of the tortures of the damned and the bliss of the righteous, in Paul's hands becomes a restrained background of Judgment with the light focussed on the Person of Christ as Judge."

of principalities."²⁰ Possibly the expression implies that they are to be the agents of the divine will.

Some commentators prefer to take "in flaming fire"²¹ with what follows as indicating the manner in which the vengeance spoken of will be visited on the wicked.²² It seems preferable to take it with the preceding, and as being the third in the series of prepositional phrases describing the Lord's revelation. In that case the majesty of the appearance of the Lord who is revealed is brought out by comparing it to that of flaming fire. This comparison is to be found in other places as Exod. 3:2, Isa. 66:15, Rev. 1:13 f. On outstanding occasions, like the giving of the law on Mt. Sinai or the coming of the Holy Spirit at Pentecost, fire is the symbol of the divine presence.

8 Having spoken of flaming fire as the robe of the returning Lord, Paul moves on to His function, namely, that of administering justice. The word rendered "vengeance" has no associations of

---

²⁰ In the expression ἀγγέλων δυνάμεως αὐτοῦ Frame takes αὐτοῦ with the whole of the preceding and renders, "his angels of power." However, as a number of commentators point out, the position of αὐτοῦ (after δυνάμεως) is a principal reason for rejecting this translation. In this position it is very difficult to take αὐτοῦ as applying principally to "angels." It seems better to read it with the noun which it follows, "the angels of his power."

²¹ The Greek is ἐν πυρὶ φλογός, "in fire of flame." We might have expected the simpler ἐν φλογὶ πυρός, "in flame of fire" (which is actually read by some of the inferior manuscripts). However, ἐν πυρὶ φλογός is well attested, and the expression is found in a few other places, e.g., Sir. 8:10, 45:19.

²² T. F. Glasson says: "The source of this doctrine is not the teaching of Jesus. We cannot conceive Him talking of Himself as coming with flaming fire rendering vengeance upon them that know not God. Nor is the conception due to Paul; there is nothing distinctively Pauline about it as there is in the case of Justification by Faith, 'in Christ', and 'the fruit of the Spirit'. This Parousia teaching was evidently part of the Christian tradition at that time and the language betrays its origin in the O.T." (*The Second Advent* [London, 1947], p. 168). He thinks that the connecting link between the eschatology of the Old Testament and that of the church was "the conviction that Jesus was Lord" (*op. cit.*, p. 171). It is true that the early church made good use of the Old Testament, but Glasson has to resort to a good deal of critical surgery to empty the teaching of Jesus of all idea of the second coming. T. W. Manson, *The Teaching of Jesus* (Cambridge, 1943), pp. 260 ff., shows conclusively from the standpoint of modern criticism that Jesus looked for His second coming in judgment. See also G. R. Beasley–Murray, *Jesus and the Future* (London, 1954). Dr. Beasley–Murray shows clearly that Paul's eschatology depends on that of Jesus, and that Jesus did teach that He would come again.

vindictiveness.'[23] It is a compound based on the same root as the word rendered "righteous" in vv. 5, 6, and it has the idea of a firm administration of unwavering justice. As Findlay says: "it is the inflicting of *full justice* on the criminal . . . nothing more, nothing less." He draws attention to the use of the term in Luke 18:3, 7; Rom. 12:19; II Cor. 7:11. The passage in Romans is a quotation from Deut. 32:35, where this process is assigned to Jehovah. Yet here it belongs to the Lord Jesus. It is yet another example of the ease with which the church, from the very first, assigned to the Lord the functions which the Old Testament reserved for Jehovah.[24]

The rest of the verse concerns the identity of those who will be the objects of this retributory justice. The use of separate articles in the Greek before "them that know not God" and "them that obey not the gospel" is most naturally taken as pointing to two groups of people. Some commentators accordingly understand the first expression to signify the Gentiles, and the second to refer to the Jews.[25] The objection to this is that the distinction is not made clearly enough, for the verse can be readily understood as an example of synonymous parallelism.[26] If this is what Paul meant there seems no reason why he should not have inserted another word or two to make his meaning clear. While it is true that the Gentiles are sometimes described as people who do not know God, the Jews could also be spoken of in this way (as in John 8:54 f.). Again, the Gentiles can be spoken of as disobedient to God (Rom. 11:30). Bearing in mind the Hebraistic coloring of this passage and the fondness for parallelism in elevated Hebrew style it seems more likely that we have here alternative designations of more or less the same group of people. There is nothing in the context to prepare us for an allusion to Jew or Gentile. "Them that know not God" refers, of course, not to people who have never heard of the true God, but to those who are culpably ignorant. It is the sort of

---

[23] See note on the cognate word "avenger" in I Thess. 4:6.

[24] For the close connection between the Father and the Son see the note on I Thess. 3:11.

[25] If this distinction can be sustained it will readily apply to the two groups of persecutors at Thessalonica.

[26] There is also the point made by Lightfoot, "But if by τοῖς μὴ εἰδόσι Θεὸν are meant the heathen who rejected the Gospel when offered to them, they are not distinct from τοῖς μὴ ὑπακούουσι; and if on the other hand the heathen world generally is signified, this is opposed to the doctrine which St. Paul teaches in Romans ii."

thing that Paul speaks of in Rom. 1:28, where he refers to men who "refused to have God in their knowledge." The second clause is then a specific example of this, and the most heinous of all, for it involves the rejection of the revelation that God has given in His Son. The gospel is a message of good news, but it is also an invitation from the King of kings. Rejection of the gospel accordingly is disobedience to a royal invitation. This is emphasized in the reference to Jesus as "Lord," a word which, in addition, has point in a second-advent setting.

9 The thought of merited punishment continues. Paul does not use the simple relative, but the relative of quality which has the force of "who are of such a kind as to."[27] His verb has a legal background. The word "punishment" is another word from the same root as "righteous" and "vengeance" in the earlier verses. It brings us the idea of a just penalty, of a punishment meted out as the result of an even-handed assessment of the rights of the case.[28] Paul leaves us in no doubt either as to the fact of the punishment of the wicked, or of the justice of this proceeding.

The nature of the punishment is "eternal destruction."[29] The noun is used in I Cor. 5:5 of the destruction of the flesh with a view to the saving of the spirit. In that passage Paul clearly does not view destruction as annihilation, for there is no likelihood that he thought of such a one as being saved in a disembodied state. This has its relevance to the verse we are discussing, for it indicates that the word does not signify so much annihilation as the loss of all that is worthwhile, utter ruin. The adjective "eternal" means literally "age-long," and everything depends on the length of the age. In the New Testament there is never a hint that the coming age has an end—it is the continuing life of the world to come.[30]

---

[27] Cf. Lightfoot, "While the simple οἱ would define the persons themselves, οἵτινες regards them as members of a class, and points to their class characteristics."

[28] The word is δίκη on which Findlay says, "It connotes *justice* in the penalty, punishment determined by a lawful process." He distinguishes it from other words for punishment thus: "Punishment is δίκη from the point of view of the dispassionate judge; κόλασις from that of the criminal; τιμωρία from that of the injured party" (CGT).

[29] The expression is found in the Dead Sea Scrolls, namely, in "The War of the Sons of Light with the Sons of Darkness." See Millar Burrows, *op. cit.*, p. 390.

[30] Cf. the discussion by G. Dalman, *The Words of Jesus* (Edinburgh, 1902), pp. 147–62.

When the life of believers beyond the grave is spoken of it is with the use of this same adjective. "Eternal life" is that life which belongs to the age to come. Therefore it has no end. At the same time "eternal" is a quality of life. It is not only that life in the age to come will be longer than life here: it will also be of a different quality. All of this has to be borne in mind when we consider the other expression "eternal destruction." It is the opposite of eternal life. It is the end of all that is worthwhile in life. As eternal life can be defined in terms of the knowledge of God and of the Lord Jesus Christ (John 17:3), so the eternal destruction which is here in mind is "from the face of the Lord." "From" appears to have the meaning "away from"[31] (contrast I Thess. 4:17). It indicates that separation from the Lord which is the final disaster.[32] The solemnity of this thought should not be minimized. Those who oppose the things of God here and now are not engaged in some minor error which can easily be put right in the hereafter. They are engaging in that defiance of the will of God which has eternal consequences. Life here and now has a high and serious dignity. In particular, the facing up to the gospel invitation is a choice fraught with the most solemn and lasting consequences.[33]

The Semitic expressions towards the end of the verse serve a twofold purpose. They stress the certainty of the destruction that is being spoken of, and in their insistence on the might of the Lord they bring a message of hope and cheer to the Thessalonians. It is as though Paul is turning their eyes away from the troubles through which they are passing to remind them that the power of their oppressors is as nothing to the might of the glorious Lord who is to be revealed. "The glory of his might" is a very expressive

---

[31] This is certainly the meaning of ἀπό in Isa. 2:10 (of which this may be a reminiscence), and I take it as the most likely meaning here. Others have suggested, however, that ἀπό may be temporal, "from the time of the Lord's appearance," that it may indicate the source, "proceeding from the face..," or that it may be causal, "by reason of the face."

[32] Way renders: "Irrevocable destruction that bans them the presence of the Lord."

[33] Cf. Denney, "If the gospel, as conceived in the New Testament, has any character at all, it has the character of finality. It is God's *last word* to man. And the consequences of accepting or rejecting it are final; it opens no prospect beyond the life on the one hand, and the death on the other, which are the results of obedience and disobedience .... What God says to us in all Scripture, from beginning to end, is not, Sooner or later? but, Life or death?"

phrase, and the choice of the word "might" in this context is suggestive.

10 With this verse we are right back at the thought of the coming of the Lord. When this comes about[34] it will be in order that (the construction is purposive[35]) he may be glorified in the saints. "Saints," of course, refers to all believers, those set apart for the service of the Lord. The idea here is not a common one, namely, that the glory of the Lord will be seen in His saints, but it is strongly expressed. The verb "glorified" is an unusual compound (only here and v. 12 in the New Testament), the preposition "in" being prefixed. Then it is repeated before "saints." The meaning probably is that He will not only be glorified "among" them, but "in" them. On the great day it is not only the Lord Himself who will be glorious, but His glory will also be seen in the saints.[36] The thought may be that they have been redeemed and indwelt by the Lord, and that this will cause the angels to ascribe glory to the Lord (so, for example, Frame). But it seems more likely that the idea is that of the Lord's glory being shared with or mirrored in His people. They are one with Him and they will share His glory.

This clause and that which follows are a necessary corrective to any idea that the Lord at His coming will be preoccupied with the necessity for dealing with the wicked, which has been the center of attention in the preceding verses. The Lord comes primarily for other purposes, and the dealing with the wicked is incidental to the establishing of the new order of things. This new order will far surpass anything that we can dream of, as will the Lord who establishes it.[37] Thus Paul can speak of Him as being marvelled at. The wonders of that day are not to be taken for granted. We might have expected him to say "in all them that believe," both from the general sense of the passage, and also from the fact that

---

[34] "When" is ὅταν, the indefinite conjunction. The fact of the Lord's coming is known; the time is not. Thus Paul says "whenever."
[35] The simple infinitive, which is common in this sense after verbs of coming and the like.
[36] Cf. Calvin, "Paul declares that our Lord Jesus in no sense reserves His glory to Himself but possesses it only in order to radiate it to all the members of His body" (cited in H. Quistorp, *Calvin's Doctrine of the Last Things* [London, 1955], p. 172).
[37] Cf. the chapter on "The Glory of His Coming" in L. Berkhof, *The Second Coming of Christ* (Grand Rapids, 1953).

it is the Pauline habit to use the present tense of this participle. But in this verse he wishes to draw attention to the decisive act of faith, rather than to the continuing belief. So he employs the aorist. He describes those who will marvel as, "all those who will have put their trust in Him."

"In that day" goes with the coming and its associated events. It makes clear to what they apply. Its detachment from the remainder of the expression gives it a certain emphasis. The intervening words are a parenthesis. They are not particularly easy to fit into the structure of the sentence, and it is not surprising accordingly that some have suggested excision, and others emendation. Even Hort, who was very conservative in these matters, resorted to a conjectural emendation of the text.[38] There seems no point in working over all the suggestions that have been put forward. The simplest explanation is that we need some such words as "you will be among them" to bring out the sense. Paul has been speaking of the glorious saints. He knows that there are some fainthearted souls among the Thessalonians, and on the spur of the moment and with scant regard for the niceties of grammar, he makes his interjection which will assure them they will be of the number of the glorified ones in that day. The "testimony" reminds us that the essential task carried out by Paul and his companions had been the bearing witness to the saving truths of the gospel. They had not expounded some philosophical or religious theory, but had testified to what God had done in Christ. "Was believed" is another aorist. It brings before us the thought of the decisive act of belief with which the Thessalonians had welcomed the gospel.[39]

3. THE CONTENT OF PAUL'S PRAYER, 1:11, 12

> 11 To which end we also pray always for you, that our God may count you worthy of your calling, and fulfil every desire of goodness and *every* work of faith, with power;

---

[38] He suggested emending ἐπιστεύθη, "was believed," to ἐπιστώθη, "was confirmed."

[39] ἐφ ὑμᾶς is not a usual construction after μαρτύριον with which most connect it here (in Luke 9:5 μαρτύριον ἐπ᾽ αὐτούς is "a testimony *against* them"). Indeed no instance parallel to this one appears to be cited. Milligan thinks that we must be content "either to regard this as a unique construction, intended to emphasize the direction the testimony took, or (with Lft.) connect ἐφ᾽ ὑμᾶς with ἐπιστεύθη in the sense 'belief in our testimony directed itself to reach you.' "

12 that the name of our Lord Jesus may be glorified in
you, and ye in him, according to the grace of our God
and the Lord Jesus Christ.

Paul has been holding out before his friends the prospect of
deliverance and glory at the coming of the Lord. But he is mindful
of the fact that they still have to live out their faith in the hard
world of men who oppose themselves to the things of God. This
they can never do in their own strength, but only in the strength
that God supplies. Easily and naturally then the Apostle passes
over into prayer for his friends that God will see them through to
the very end.

11 "To which end" is rather loosely attached to the whole of
the preceding section, and is probably not to be taken closely with
any particular word or words. It refers to the whole of the salvation which he has been holding out before them. The expression
conveys the idea of purpose. "In order that this may be" Paul
proceeds to pray for his friends. In his previous letter he had
counselled them to be unceasing in their prayers (5:17), and he puts
his precept into practice. The "also" may indicate that the Thessalonians were praying about this matter and Paul joins them in
this. But more probably it arises from the fact that Paul has been
thanking God for them (v. 3), and has been boasting about them
(v. 4), and assuring them of their place in the scheme of things at
the last day (vv. 7, 10). Not only does he do this sort of thing, but
he also prays for them.

The first point in his prayer is that[40] "God may count you
worthy of your calling." The calling of God is a leading thought
with Paul. Usually it denotes the decisive moment when God calls
men out of darkness into His glorious light, and we might cite
Rom. 8:30 as the typical example of its use: "and whom he fore-
ordained, them he also called: and whom he called, them he also
justified. . . ." The call is an effective call, and implies that the
man who is called obeys that call. The prayer here that God
would count the Thessalonians worthy[41] of the call does not carry

---

[40] ἵνα is probably to be taken not simply as giving the content of the prayer,
but with a telic force, "in order that."
[41] ἀξιόω means "to deem worthy," "to reckon as worthy." Cf. the note
on the compound καταξιόω in v. 5.

209

with it the thought that they might fall away from the status of called people. When men are called they are completely unworthy of their call (Gal. 1:13–15 is perhaps the classic instance of this). But God does not intend them to continue in such a state. They are to walk worthily of the calling wherewith He calls them (Eph. 4:1). It is this that Paul has in mind here. It is inspiring that God has called them, but they must not so exult in this thought that they grow slack in the way. They must seek to be worthy. Since this is not something that can be accomplished in any human strength Paul prays that God will count them worthy. That is to say, his prayer is that they may so live between this moment and the judgment that God will then be able to pronounce them worthy of the calling wherewith He called them. "You" is emphatic in the Greek, and indicates Paul's special concern for them.

The next point is that God would "fulfil every desire of goodness." There are some who take this to mean that God is being asked to work out His good pleasure. While there is nothing unlikely in such a sentiment, yet the Greek here does not seem to point to this as the meaning. The "work of faith" which is parallel to this expression is something which men perform, and the natural understanding is that men are to work what is laid down in the first part also. Again, the word for "goodness" in the New Testament is always used of human goodness. All in all it seems clear enough that it is a work of God in the Thessalonians which is in mind. Paul is praying that God will produce a goodness of will in his friends. ARV "desire" does not quite convey the force of the Greek which has more the idea of resolve than of mere wish. The parallelism with "work of faith" indicates that the meaning is "resolve proceeding from goodness," rather than "a resolve after goodness," "a resolve to do good."

Parallel is "work of faith." "Every" which precedes "desire of goodness" is rightly taken with this phrase also in ARV. The expression reminds us that faith is not simply an intellectual attitude which does nothing. Faith is always busy. A true faith will clothe itself in works. So Paul prays that his friends will produce in their lives the works that spring from faith (see on I Thess. 1:3).

When Paul asks that God would "fulfil" these things he implies that no human power is adequate. The divine is necessary. He reinforces this by adding "with power" with which the verse ends.

Paul is not seeking for some merely human reformation, nor for some pious thinking. He wants to see that fruit of goodness that can come about only when the power of God is operative in men's lives.[42]

12 The purpose of all this is now given: "that the name of our Lord Jesus may be glorified in you." The name in Biblical times was much more than a means of distinguishing one person from another. It summed up the whole character of a person.[43] An instructive verse for an understanding of the name is Rev. 2:17: "To him that overcometh, to him will I give of the hidden manna, and I will give him a white stone, and upon the stone a new name written, which no one knoweth but he that receiveth it." To our way of thinking a name that nobody knows is useless. The whole purpose of a name is to designate a man. But in the Revelation the name nobody knows is very much in point. It signifies a new character that is given to the person in question, something that is a secret between his Lord and himself.

Thus when the prayer is made that the Thessalonians may so live that glory may be brought to the name of the Lord the meaning is not that the angels may name His name "with loud acclaims" (Frame). Rather, it is that there may be such virtues manifest in the believers that glory will accrue to Him who is ultimately responsible for these virtues. The Thessalonians will be such a bright and shining testimony to the reality of their salvation that the Savior will be seen to be the wonderful Being He is. The character in which He will be glorified is the double one of Lord (appropriate in this context so full of allusions to the second advent), and Jesus (with all its associations of the human Jesus who stooped so low for men). Then there is another aspect to this glory. The Thessalonians, too, will be glorified. Their glory will result from their association with the Lord, and thus Paul speaks of their being "in"

---

[42] The thought that all a man's goodness comes from God occurs a number of times in the Dead Sea Scrolls, e.g., "For the way of a man is not his own, a man does not direct his own steps; for judgment is God's, and from his hand is blamelessness of conduct" (Millar Burrows, *op. cit.*, p. 388).

[43] G. B. Gray speaks of the Hebrew as frequently using "name" "as almost an equivalent of the 'personality' or 'character' or nature of the person or thing named; and consequently, when a writer wishes to express forcibly the nature of a person or place, he says he will be called so-and-so, or his name will be so-and-so" (DB, Vol. III, p. 478).

Him in this connection.[44] On that day, just as He will be glorified in them on account of what they have become, so they will be glorified in Him on account of what He is.

Again and again Paul comes back to the great thought that Christians owe all that they have and all that they are to God. So now he adds to this picture of glory the thought that all is according to the grace of God. Grace is one of the great Christian words, and Paul uses it often (see on I Thess. 1:1). It carries with it thoughts of the joyous free favor of God, and of His unmerited kindness to men. This is operative in the whole process of salvation, and if it is more usual in the New Testament to find it used of the initial stages of salvation, there is no reason for thinking that it will be absent from the final stages. The glory of the last time will be due to God's grace to man.

It seems likely that ARV is correct in its rendering of the closing words of this chapter. But, since there is an article before "our God" and none before "Lord Jesus Christ," it is grammatically possible to understand the expression to mean, "our God and Lord, Jesus Christ." However, the expression "Lord Jesus Christ" occurs so frequently that it has almost the status of a proper name. Therefore when "Lord" is used of Jesus it is not necessary for it to have the article. This being so, it seems likely that we should understand the present passage to refer to both the Father and the Son. At the same time we should not overlook the fact that Paul does link them very closely indeed. The fact that there can be this doubt as to whether one or both is meant is itself indicative of the closeness of their connection in the mind of Paul. He makes no great distinction between them (see further on I Thess. 3:11).

---

[44] It is, of course, possible to take αὐτῷ as neuter, referring to the Name, when the translation would be "in it." Frame adopts this view, and understands ἐν "of ground." However, it is much more usual in the New Testament to speak of believers as being "in Christ" than to use the expression "in the Name" in such a connection as this.

Notice that believers are said to be glorified "in" Christ, and not simply "with" Him.

COMMENTARY ON II THESSALONIANS

CHAPTER II

III. THE PAROUSIA, 2:1-12

1. THE DAY OF THE LORD NOT YET PRESENT, 2:1, 2

1 Now we beseech you, brethren, touching the coming
of our Lord Jesus Christ, and our gathering together
unto him;
2 to the end that ye be not quickly shaken from your
mind, nor yet be troubled, either by spirit, or by word,
or by epistle as from us, as that the day of the Lord is
just at hand;

Paul had spoken a good deal about the second coming during his
mission at Thessalonica, but it is clear that not all of his teaching
had been grasped. New converts, full of enthusiasm, perhaps
emotionally unstable, but as yet imperfectly instructed in the deep
things of the faith, not unnaturally went astray in some points in
this important, but intricate, subject. Paul had had occasion to
refer to the Parousia in his first letter. This, however, did not clear
away all doubts. He felt, accordingly, that he must deal with the
subject again. Indeed, in II Thessalonians it forms the principal
part of the Epistle. Our big difficulty in interpreting what he says
is the fact that it is a supplement to his oral preaching. He and his
correspondents both knew what he had said when he was in
Thessalonica. There was no point in repeating it. He could take
it as known, and simply add what was necessary to clear up the
misunderstandings that had arisen. We find it very difficult to fill
in the gaps, and to catch his allusions. So difficult indeed, that
many and various suggestions have been put forward in the
attempt to elucidate the Apostle's meaning. We must bear in mind
the gaps in our knowledge, and not be too confident in our interpretations of this notoriously difficult passage.

1 Paul begins, not by pontificating, but by making request of
his friends. The verb he uses is not a common one in his writings
(though it is far from being an unusual word). It is appropriate to
a respectful request (see note on I Thess. 4:1), as is the affectionate

"brethren." The subject[1] of his request is twofold, but the coming of the Lord and the gathering of the saints are regarded as closely connected, as the use of a single article shows. They are two parts of one great event. For "coming" see the note on I Thess. 2:19. The assembly of the saints does not seem to be vitally related to the coming of the Antichrist, the subject Paul is beginning to discuss, but characteristically he includes it. It is so important, especially to his friends who had been in doubt about their loved ones who had died, and so very much a part of the coming of the Lord. The "gathering together" is the "muster" (Moffatt) of the saints. This may well have been something of a technical term. The cognate verb is used in Matt. 24:31, Mark 13:27 of the gathering of the elect at the Lord's coming. The noun occurs again in the New Testament only in Heb. 10:25. There it is the assembling of believers for worship that is in mind[2] (though it should not be overlooked that that verse also looks for the coming of the Lord). Notice the significance of "unto him." It is not simply that the saints meet one another: they meet their Lord and remain with Him for ever (cf. I Thess. 4:17).[3]

2 Always, it would seem, there have been some Christians who have let their imagination rather than their reason dictate their understanding of the Parousia. This was true of the earliest days of the church, just as of more recent times. The content of Paul's appeal accordingly is that his readers should retain their mental equilibrium. He employs two expressions for the kind of weakness he wants them to avoid. The first, "that ye be not quickly shaken from your mind," directs attention to the possibility of being caught up by a sudden excitement. The adverb "quickly" does not mean, "after a short period," as though pointing to their forsaking

---

[1] The preposition rendered "touching" is ὑπέρ, which usually means "on behalf of." Here it is more or less equivalent to περί, but it has its own particular emphasis. It signifies something like "in the interests of the truth concerning." Lightfoot (on Gal. 1:4) discusses these two prepositions and remarks that ὑπέρ has "a sense of 'interest in,' which is wanting to περί." This probably accounts for its use here.

[2] Deissmann notes the use of the term (ἐπισυναγωγή) for a collection of money. He thinks it differed from the more common συναγωγή scarcely more than "collecting" from "collecting together." He adds, "the longer Greek word was probably more to the taste of the later period" (LAE, p. 103).

[3] Of II Thess. 2:1 ff. J. E. Fison says, "It should be faced up to for what it is, a downright apostolic condemnation of all strictly realized eschatology" (*The Christian Hope* [London, 1954], p. 162).

the true position soon after reaching it. Rather, it has reference to the quality of the action. Its force is "hastily," "precipitately" (cf. its use in I Tim. 5:22). The verb is in the aorist, which points rather to a sudden action than one that is continuous. It is a verb which is often used of literal shaking, the motion produced by wind and wave, and especially violent motion. Its use of a ship driven from its mooring shows us the kind of thing Paul has in mind. He is thinking of people who lack a secure anchorage, and are readily tossed here and there.[4] His word for "mind" is one which can on occasion be near in meaning to "spirit" (as Lightfoot points out). Properly it directs attention to man's reasoning faculty. For example, it is used in distinction from "spirit" in I Cor. 14:14, "For if I pray in a tongue, my spirit prayeth, but my understanding is unfruitful." In the present passage "mind" stands for the whole mental balance of the man (Findlay, "the regulative intellectual faculty," CGT). Putting all this together then, Paul is urging them in the first instance to that stability, which will enable them to withstand any sudden shock or discovery. Men taken up with advent speculations may easily take an unbalanced interest in the latest idea. Their conduct will be adversely affected thereby. But those whose views on the second coming are more stable are not easily thrown off balance.[5]

The second weakness is that of being "troubled." This time the verb is in the present and denotes a continuing state. Our Lord used it, saying, "when ye shall hear of wars and rumors of wars, be not troubled" (Mark 13:7).[6] It describes a state of "jumpiness," or of worry. Just as some are easily thrown off balance, so others can fall into a state of constant fretting. Paul wants neither of these states in his converts.

He speaks of three possible ways in which they might be

---

[4] Knox's translation, "do not be terrified out of your senses all at once" (following the Vulgate *terreamini*) is not quite what is wanted. The verb σαλεύω refers to motion, rather than to terrifying.

[5] The preposition ἀπό, "from," adds the thought of the mind departing "from" the normal.

[6] This is not the only place where Paul's words remind us of expressions used by our Savior. See H. A. A. Kennedy, *St. Paul's Conceptions of the Last Things* (London, 1904), pp. 167 f., for a number of striking verbal coincidences with Christ's great eschatological discourse. This is not only a matter of verbal agreement; there is a unity of underlying ideas. G. R. Beasley-Murray also makes this point in *Jesus and the Future* (London, 1954), pp. 232 ff.

affected.[7] "Spirit" must be understood in the light of the fact that the early church expected supernatural communications from time to time, as through the ministry of prophets (cf. I Cor. 14:29 f., I John 4:1). It means some revelation divinely communicated. "Word" may refer to a sermon, though the term is wide enough to cover all manner of oral communications. Some have felt that "epistle" means I Thessalonians, but this is far from having been demonstrated. The expression is general, and might refer to that letter, or to another that Paul had written, or had been said to have written, or to a forgery. There are all kinds of possibilities. Nor is the matter rendered any easier by the following "as from us,"[8] for this expression, too, is rather indefinite. It indicates that Paul feared that a communication of some kind had been reputed to have come from him (and his assistants?). But he writes in general terms, and we are probably justified in inferring that he was not quite sure of exactly what had happened. Either that, or else he felt it not wise to refer to it too directly. But he is making it quite clear that he accepts no responsibility whatever for the report. However it had come, and however it had been attributed to him, he had had nothing to do with it. He did not want his friends to be worried by these speculations, and he completely renounces them.

The content of the particular report was "that the day of the Lord is just at hand" (for "the day of the Lord" see on I Thess. 5:2). There is no word for "just" in the Greek. By inserting it ARV brings out the point that the Parousia, according to the report, was on the very point of occurring. The verb does not really mean "to be at hand," but rather "to be present."[9] It is sometimes

---

[7] The construction, employing $\delta\iota\acute{a}$, brings the thought of the means "through" which the result is effected.

[8] $\dot{\omega}\varsigma$ $\delta\iota'$ $\dot{\eta}\mu\omega\nu$ is to be taken with all three of the preceding, which are closely linked. Paul is denying that the report emanated from a revelation made to him, or from any words of his, spoken or written. Some feel that it is only the letter which purports to come from Paul, but there seems no good reason for restricting the application of the phrase in this way.

[9] Cf. Frame, "$\dot{\epsilon}\nu\acute{\epsilon}\sigma\tau\eta\kappa\epsilon\nu$ means not 'is coming' ($\check{\epsilon}\varrho\chi\epsilon\tau\alpha\iota$ I–5:2), not 'is at hand' ($\mathring{\eta}\gamma\gamma\iota\kappa\epsilon\nu$ Rom. 13:12), not 'is near' ($\dot{\epsilon}\gamma\gamma\acute{\upsilon}\varsigma$ $\epsilon\sigma\tau\iota\nu$ Phil. 4:5), but 'has come,' 'is on hand,' 'is present.'" Later he cites Lillie as maintaining that those who favor the meaning "is at hand" do so "from the supposed necessity of the case rather than from any grammatical compulsion." Bicknell gives "is now present" as "the only possible translation of the Greek." B. B. Warfield, by contrast, uses strong language to indicate his disagreement with such views. He holds that the verb signifies "is upon us" (*The Expositor*, 3rd Series, Vol. IV, p. 37).

contrasted with verbs expressing the future idea, e.g., Rom. 8:38, I Cor. 3:22. Moreover, Paul could, and did, say that the Parousia was "at hand" (Phil. 4:5). It seems that the verb ought to be given its usual sense here, rather than to have the idea of imminence imported into it. Obviously the Lord had not returned in the full sense which Paul had described in his teaching to the Thessalonians, and outlined in the First Epistle. But the day of the Lord was a complex idea. It included within it quite a number of events, as we see from the various passages of Scripture which refer to it. To say that the day of the Lord had come did not mean that it was completed, and that all the glorious events associated with it had occurred. That was so obviously untrue that it needed no refutation. What it did mean was that that day had dawned. They were even then living in it.[10] This being so, the climax must infallibly be reached, and that within a very short space of time.[11] We can easily picture the effect such news would have on those who were not well grounded in the Christian faith, and who were given to excitability. Paul proceeds to show the complete falsity of such an idea.

2. THE GREAT REBELLION, 2:3–12

a. *The Man of Lawlessness, 2:3–10a*

3 let no man beguile you in any wise: for *it will not be, except the falling away come first, and the man of sin be revealed, the son of perdition,*

---

[10] There is a sense in which Christians are even now living in the end time. The decisive victory has been won. Cf. O. Cullmann, "Just as the 'Victory Day' does in fact present *something new* in contrast to the decisive battle already fought at some point or other of the war, just so the end which is still to come also brings something new. To be sure, this new thing that the 'Victory Day' brings is based entirely upon that decisive battle, and would be absolutely impossible without it. Thus we make for the future precisely the same confirmation as we did for the past. It is a unique occurrence; it has its meaning for redemptive history in itself; but on the other hand it is nevertheless founded upon that one unique event at the mid-point" (*Christ and Time* [London, 1951], p. 141). Those in error at Thessalonica, however, were not thinking of the decisive event as having occurred, as much as that "Victory Day" had already dawned.

[11] Cf. the remark of Origen cited by J. Jeremias, "It may be—in view of the fact that there were people among the Jews who claimed to know from books either of the time of the destruction (of the universe) or about other secret things—that therefore he (Paul) wrote this (2 Thess. 2. 1sq.), warning his followers not to believe the claims of these people" (*The Eucharistic Words of Jesus* [Oxford, 1955], p. 76, n. 1).

4 he that opposeth and exalteth himself against all that
is called God or that is worshipped; so that he sitteth
in the temple of God, setting himself forth as God.

5 Remember ye not, that, when I was yet with you, I
told you these things?

6 And now ye know that which restraineth, to the end
that he may be revealed in his own season.

7 For the mystery of lawlessness doth already work:
only *there is* one that restraineth now, until he be
taken out of the way.

8 And then shall be revealed the lawless one, whom
the Lord Jesus shall slay with the breath of his mouth,
and bring to nought by the manifestation of his
coming;

9 *even he,* whose coming is according to the working of
Satan with all power and signs and lying wonders,

10 and with all deceit of unrighteousness for them that
perish;

3 Paul is desperately anxious that his friends do not fall into
error. "Let no man beguile you in any wise" is not only an
exhortation, but a reminder of the folly of being led astray in this
way. The verb is a compound, the thought being that to be taken
in by the kind of thing he has outlined is not only to be deceived,
but to be badly deceived. The addition of "in any wise" extends
the possible ways of bringing about the deception. Paul objects to
the conclusion. He therefore excludes all ways of reaching it.

Now we come to the great fact which proves conclusively that
the day of the Lord has not yet arrived. That day will not come
about until the "falling away" takes place, and a certain evil
figure, "the man of sin" has made his appearance. Since neither is
yet in evidence, the argument runs, the day of the Lord cannot
possibly have come. There is some difficulty about our understanding of both these expressions. What is beyond doubt is that
Paul expected his allusion to be so clear to the Thessalonians that
they would see the folly of their error and return to sanity.

The term rendered "falling away" more properly signifies
"rebellion." It is used, for example, of political rebellions and
military rebellions. The characteristic thought of the Bible is that
God rules. Thus the word is appropriate for a rebellion against
His rule. In a way I suppose "falling away" points to this sort of
thing. It includes the idea of forsaking one's former allegiance.

But the expression is too negative to bring out the thought at all adequately. It is not so much forsaking one's first love and drifting into apathy that is meant, as setting oneself in opposition to God. Neil speaks of "a widespread and violent defiance of the authority of God." It is the supreme effort of Satan and his minions to which the word directs us.[12] Paul does not speak of "a" rebellion, as though introducing the topic for the first time, but of "the" rebellion, i.e., the well-known rebellion, that one about which we had already instructed them.

He speaks of the rebellion coming "first." But he does not say what it is to precede. There can be no doubt that ARV is correct in supplying "it will not be," with "it" referring to the day of the Lord. The omission of the words shows that the writer is excited and is not paying much attention to the strict rules of grammar,[13] which adds to our difficulties. This phenomenon helps us to see something of the importance Paul attached to the subject. It was desperately important that the Thessalonians get the thing straight. He cannot keep calm about the matter.

Associated with[14] the rebellion is the person who is traditionally known as "the man of sin."[15] This title is so universally used that it is probably impossible to substitute another. But the

---

[12] This is not to deny that there will be an apostasy in the last times, and one of considerable proportions, as we see from Matt. 24:10-12. All that I am maintaining is that in the present passage the emphasis is on the revolt against God, rather than on the falling away from the church which will be part of the picture.

Hendriksen sees in the absence of any adjective to qualify ἡ ἀποστασία an indication that practically the whole church will apostatize. This seems to be reading a good deal into the text. Lightfoot maintains that the word might apply to Christians or Jews, either of whom might be said to depart from God, but it can have no reference to Gentiles. Denney thinks that Paul is describing events in which the church is but a spectator, and that the term applies accordingly to the Jews. H. A. A. Kennedy says the word "can only mean a revolt against God. Therefore it must take place among the people who acknowledge the true God, i.e., the Jews" (*op. cit.*, p. 218). Such views may be a little too confident. If the word means "rebellion" it may well apply to the rebellion of the creature against the Creator. It is thus not impossible to envisage its use of others than Jews.

[13] "His style is that of a speaker, not of a studied writer; such broken sentences are inevitable, and explain themselves, in animated conversation" (Findlay, CGT).

[14] It is not certain whether the καί indicates that the rebellion and the revelation of the Man of Lawlessness are to be thought of as simultaneous, or whether the second is to follow the first. They are obviously closely connected, though not identical.

[15] Knox renders "the champion of wickedness."

better manuscripts read "man of lawlessness" instead of "man of sin." This fits in with the words used in vv. 7, 8, whereas the traditional rendering obscures the connection of thought. However, the difference in meaning between the two terms is not great. Lawlessness must be understood as failure to conform to the law of God, and this is what sin is (cf. I John 3:4). In the last resort sin is the refusal to be ruled by God. It is the assertion of the creature against the Creator, the self against the God of grace. All of this fits in with the great rebellion which had just been mentioned. The individual in mind is seen against the background of the rising of Satan against the power of God.

Who is this Man of Lawlessness? A common identification is with the Roman Emperor, either with an individual, or with the line of emperors. In favor of this can be urged the claim that the emperors were divine, and the demand that they be worshipped. The attitude of the persecuting emperors such as Nero must have led many Christians to see in them some of the attributes of the Man of Lawlessness. But against all such identifications is the fact that Paul seems to be speaking of the last and supreme embodiment of evil, one who will make his appearance only in the last time. There seems no evidence that he really thought that either a present or a future Roman emperor, or the whole line of emperors, was this supreme representative of Satan.

A variant of this view is that the whole idea is derived from the concept of Nero *redivivus*. After Nero's death more than one man arose claiming to be the dead emperor, and aroused men's fears. When it became accepted that Nero was indeed dead the expectation took shape that one day he would come back in supernatural fashion. The suggestion is made that the present passage is not due to the Apostle Paul, but to some later writer who has taken up facets of the Nero legend, and woven them into his conception of the Antichrist, the Man of Lawlessness.

Against this, more than one objection can be urged. One is that every indication seems to show that the letter is too early for it to be dependent on the Nero legend. If it is an authentic writing of Paul, then the Man of Lawlessness owes nothing to Nero. In any case the thought of Antichrist in some form is very old, as Bousset has shown conclusively in *The Antichrist Legend* (London, 1896).

From the Reformation onwards there have been many who have identified the papacy with the Man of Lawlessness (the Preface to the Authorized Version calls the pope "that Man of Sin"). But it is difficult to think of a line of popes as constituting the Man of Lawlessness. He seems rather to be an individual. No one would gather from reading the words of Paul that he was referring to a line of ecclesiastics. This view seems to have arisen more from hostility to the papacy than from exegetical considerations.

All attempts to equate the Man of Lawlessness with historical personages break down on the fact that Paul was speaking of someone who would appear only at the end of the age. The Man of Lawlessness is an eschatological personage. Paul wrote that he will appear just before the Lord comes again. Accordingly it seems futile to try to identify him. The Scripture tells us that there are many Antichrists (I John 2:18).[16] It does not surprise that through the ages of history many have appeared whose evil lives remind us of this or that trait of the Man of Lawlessness. But that does not give us grounds for identifying the supreme embodiment of evil with any of Satan's lesser lights by the way.[17]

Paul speaks of this figure as being "revealed," just as in 1:7 he has spoken of the revelation of the Lord Jesus. The position of the verb in the Greek gives it a certain emphasis, as does its repetition in vv. 6, 8. It indicates that the Man of Lawlessness will exist before his manifestation to the world. It may also point us to something supernatural about him. This would be natural enough, from his close association with Satan. It seems unlikely, however, that Paul means us to understand that the Man of Lawlessness was in existence at the time he was writing (as Frame, for example, holds).

---

[16] T. F. Glasson thinks of the figure of the Man of Lawlessness as being derived ultimately from the Old Testament. Some early Christians took certain ideas from the Old Testament, modified them, and produced this figure (see *The Second Advent* [London, 1947], pp. 180 ff.). It is well that we bear in mind that this concept is Biblical, whether we call the being Antichrist, Man of Lawlessness, Man of Sin, or anything else. There is no warrant for thinking it derived from current mythological speculations, or from extra-canonical Jewish literature (see G. Vos, *op. cit.*, pp. 94 ff.). But that does not mean that the idea was a novelty fashioned by the early church in isolation from the Master and such great figures as St. Paul. The teaching of Daniel was taken up by our Lord (Mark 13:14), and it is from Him that it becomes Christian tradition. From the first, Christians understood that the appearing of this evil being in the end time was inevitable.

[17] From the time of Theodore of Mopsuestia on many have held that the Man of Lawlessness is practically an "incarnation" of Satan, somewhat analogous to Christ's incarnation.

The Man of Lawlessness is further described as "the son of perdition"[18] a description which Jesus applied to Judas Iscariot (John 17:12). This type of genitive has a Hebraic twist. It denotes "characterized by" the quality in the genitive (cf. Isa. 57:4). So here it means that the Man of Lawlessness will certainly be lost. As Moffatt puts it, he is "the doomed One."

4 The description of the evil personage is continued.[19] "He that opposeth and exalteth himself" is our translation of two participles united under a single article, which thus form a third way of describing this being. The former of the two participles might be rendered "the adversary." It is often used of Satan. In this place it does not, of course, mean Satan, but the associations of the term were evil, and it stresses the evil character of the man to whom it refers. He sets himself against God, and the present participle indicates a continuing attitude. It is no passing phase. The second participle (also present continuous) deals with the exalted position the Man of Lawlessness arrogates to himself. He puts himself in the highest possible place. This is brought out by the express mention of "all that is called God or that is worshipped." He is not content with supreme political position. He insists on having the place reserved among all mankind for the supreme object of worship. He demands religious veneration. More exactly, he insists that no god nor anything bearing the name of God, nor any object of worship whatever[20] should be allowed pride of place. The Man of Lawlessness must be first of all.

The climax to all this is the explicit claim to deity.[21] He is to sit in the temple proclaiming himself to be God. There are some interesting touches here. "So that" is a conjunction indicating

---

[18] Deissmann explains this as due to "an echo of LXX Is. 57:4 τέκνα ἀπωλείας "(*Bible Studies* [Edinburgh, 1901], p. 163).

[19] The language resembles that in a number of passages in Daniel, notably Dan. 7:25, 8:9 ff., 11:36 ff. It is not likely that Paul was quoting. He had so often read and pondered the sacred Scripture that his language was naturally that of the Old Testament.

[20] Paul uses a rather rare word, σέβασμα, which includes anything at all that can be worshipped. It is used of gods and images, but also of shrines, altars, etc. Taken in conjunction with the preceding, "all that is called God," it emphasizes the complete refusal of the Man of Lawlessness to brook any rival of any kind at all.

[21] Some have felt that the religious associations of the Man of Lawlessness imply that he will be claiming to be the Christ, that is, a Hebrew pseudo-Messiah. Vos has shown this to be untenable (*op. cit.*, pp. 114 ff.).

result. This action is not unconnected with the preceding. It grows out of it. "He sitteth" is the aorist infinitive pointing to the single act of taking the seat, rather than the continuous action of sitting. It is in accordance with this that the preposition "in" is that naturally used of motion towards. The "temple" is the inmost shrine, and not the temple as a whole. It is not that he enters the temple precincts: he invades the most sacred place and there takes his seat. His action is itself a claim to deity,[22] and the verb "setting himself forth" may imply an explicit claim in so many words (several translators render "proclaim"[23]).

Most commentators draw attention to the attempt by Caligula to set up an image of himself in the temple at Jerusalem, an attempt which was frustrated only by his death. This took place in A.D. 40. The attempt aroused widespread horror among the Jews. It may well be that Paul has this incident in his mind in writing these words. At the same time, what he says goes beyond anything Caligula attempted. The Man of Lawlessness is not pictured as setting up a statue of himself, but as taking his seat in person (cf. Ezek. 28:2).

The question arises of what should be understood by "the temple of God." There are passages where such an expression means the Christian church (I Cor. 3:16 f.). Some have understood this sense here. The meaning then would be that the Man of Lawlessness makes the church his base of operations. He establishes himself there, claiming to be divine. This is rather a difficult concept (would not the church by that very fact cease to be the *Christian* church?). While the New Testament speaks of many falling away in the last days, it does not appear to envisage the church as such becoming apostate. There is, moreover, the vivid language already noted. This seems to mean that he will actually take his seat in a formal way in a sanctuary. Some suggest that it is heaven that is meant (cf. Ps. 11:4). Frame, for example, sees the possibility of a reference to the ancient tradition of the Dragon that stormed the heavens. The difficulty is that Paul pictures the Man of Law-

---

[22] E. Stauffer cites similar claims from the apocalyptic literature, as "I am the anointed one" (*Apocalypse of Elijah* 31:40), "I am God, and before me there has been no God" (*The Ascension of Isaiah* 4:6). These are cited in *New Testament Theology* (London, 1955), p. 215.

[23] Milligan cites examples of the verb in the sense "'nominate' or 'proclaim' to an office."

lessness as actually taking his seat in the shrine, and not merely as attempting to do so. It is like our Lord's "when ye see the abomination of desolation standing where he ought not" (Mark 13:14; the masculine shows that a person is in mind). While the temple is not easy to identify, the best way of understanding the passage seems to be that it is some material building which will serve as the setting for the blasphemous claim to deity which the Man of Lawlessness will make as the climax of his activities.

5 Frame speaks of "a trace of impatience" (as do others), and Findlay by contrast says that Paul "gently reproves" his readers. It is probable that neither suggestion exactly meets the case. As we have had occasion to notice before, this section is extremely lively, and throughout we get the impression that Paul was dictating animatedly with scant regard for grammatical niceties and the exact balance of phrase. The previous sentence is not really finished, and his thought rushes on. He vividly recalls what he had said when he was among them. Although throughout most of the letter the plural is used, here Paul replaces it with the singular as he recalls what he had done in Thessalonica. What he has just written is by way of reiteration of the oral teaching. The tense of the verb seems to imply that he had dealt with the subject often.[24] Thus he is able to content himself with the barest of outlines. Now his question obviates the need for a fuller explanation. Paul simply jogs their memory. He says, in effect, "It is as I told you before."

6 With "and now" Paul passes from a consideration of the future to the present state of affairs.[25] Once again he directs attention to a fact well known to the Thessalonians, and which, accordingly, he has no need to enlarge upon. His allusion is so general that commentators through the centuries have been baffled as to just exactly what he did mean. Many conjectures have been put forward. Sometimes they have been supported by ingenious

---

[24] The verb is ἔλεγον. The imperfect form favors the continuous sense, though, since, in the case of this verb, the imperfect is often used in a sense close to the aorist, it cannot be pressed. Most commentators favor the continuous sense.

[25] Some understand καὶ νῦν as logical, and marking simply the transition to a new stage of the argument. The temporal sense, "as to the present," however, seems much more to the point.

arguments. But we cannot feel at all sure that we have the clue to the situation. It is best to face the fact. We should take notice of the conjectures that have been made by earnest and scholarly souls, for one of them may conceivably be correct. But we should maintain a reserve in what we claim for our own particular interpretation.

"That which restraineth" is the neuter participle of a verb whose masculine participle is found in the next verse, where it is rendered "one that restraineth." Our first problem is the meaning of the verb rendered "restraineth." It is usually accepted that it means "hold back," "restrain." But it can also signify "hold fast," as it does, for example, in I Thess. 5:21 ("restrain" is an impossible meaning for it there). Sometimes the verb is intransitive, when it means "hold sway" (though it does not appear to have this meaning anywhere in the New Testament). While the probabilities are that the meaning assigned to it by ARV is the right one, we must not overlook the fact that our ignorance of the circumstances precludes us from ruling out the other meanings entirely.[26]

Some person or thing at the moment the Epistle was written was holding something fast, or exercising sway, or restraining (presumably restraining the Man of Lawlessness). Many commentators have seen a reference to the Roman Empire, which might be referred to as neuter, or, in the person of the emperor, as masculine. It would be dangerous to talk openly of the state or its ruler, and this oblique method is the result. Those who hold such views usually think of one of the emperors (usually Nero) as the Man of Lawlessness, whose appearance was held back by the existence of his predecessor. When the predecessor was removed the Man of Lawlessness would appear. It is difficult to carry this understanding through. There is no reason for thinking that Paul saw in any Roman emperor (Nero or any other) the Man of Lawlessness. Moreover the Roman Empire in due course passed away without the events that Paul here associates with the End.

B. B. Warfield thought of the restraining power as the Jewish state.[27] The masculine "restrainer" he thought might be James of

---

[26] Vos has an interesting note on the possibility of taking the verb in the sense "to hold in possession" (*op. cit.*, p. 133, n. 20).

[27] The restraining power "appears to be the Jewish state. For the continued existence of the Jewish state was both graciously and naturally a protection to Christianity, and hence a restraint on the persecuting power"

Jerusalem. Warfield was a great exegete, and all his opinions must be carefully weighed, but this is one in which few have been able to follow him. It is hard to see how the Jewish state could restrain the Man of Lawlessness (even if we accept Warfield's other idea that this was the line of Roman emperors). It is even more difficult to see the apostle James fulfilling this role.

A favorite view among many modern scholars is that Paul is here referring to some contemporary eschatological speculation. Babylonian and other myths are cited to show that at the end of the age it was thought that there would be a gigantic conflict between good and evil. There were various reasons urged for the postponement of this conflict. The suggestion is that Paul was alluding to some such idea, known to and held by the Christians at Thessalonica. This is not impossible. There is every reason for thinking that a great deal of early eschatological literature has perished, and we do not know what was in it. But that is just the point. We do not know. If Paul was alluding to some such idea we have no means of knowing what it was. Under the circumstances there seems no point in postulating this as the solution to our problem.

Cullmann strongly opposes the view that the restrainer is the Roman Empire. He suggests that "there is a reference to the missionary preaching as a sign pointing to the end."[28] The gospel must first be preached to the Gentiles. This sounds attractive while Cullmann is dealing with the neuter "that which restraineth." But when he moves on to the masculine participle he regards it as "a self-designation of the apostle."[29] This seems most improbable. It would be an extraordinary way for Paul to refer to himself. Nothing in the passage gives countenance to the idea that he felt that he himself was holding back such a being as the Man of Lawlessness.

Better than any of these speculations seems to be that which favors the principle of order which restrains the working of evil. This might be referred to in the abstract as neuter, or it might be personified, when it would be masculine. It might be illustrated by the system of law in the Roman Empire, or in other systems of law

---

(*The Expositor*, 3rd Series, Vol. IV, pp. 40 f.; *Biblical Doctrines* [New York, 1929], p. 611).
[28] *Christ and Time* (London, 1951), p. 164.
[29] *Ibid.*, p. 165.

which have succeeded to that. It is when law is taken out of the
way that the Lawless One will rule.[30]

But this, too, is speculation. The plain fact is that Paul and his
readers knew what he was talking about, and we do not. We have
not the means at our disposal to recover this part of his meaning.
It is best that we frankly acknowledge our ignorance.

The important thing is that some power was in operation, and
that the Man of Lawlessness could not possibly put in his appearance until this power was removed. The Thessalonians knew this.
Therefore they should have known that speculations about the
presence of the day of the Lord were necessarily false. Necessary
preconditions had yet to be fulfilled.

An important aspect of the teaching of this whole passage is pin-
pointed in the expression "in his own season." Paul is not describing some great series of events which take place in violation
of the will of God, while He, so to speak, has to work out some
plan as a counter. Paul thinks of God as being in control of the
whole process. While there are mysteries here, as there must be
whenever we contemplate the workings of evil in a universe
created by a God who is perfectly good, yet what is abundantly
plain is that God is over all. No wicked person, be he Satan, be he
the Man of Lawlessness, be he anyone else whatever, can overstep
the bounds which God has appointed him. The Man of Lawlessness will be revealed only as and when God permits. He is not
to be thought of as acting in complete independence. Throughout
this whole passage the thought of God's sovereignty is dominant.
Evil is strong, and will wax stronger in the last times. But God's
hand is in the process. Evil will not pass beyond its limits. God's
purpose, not that of Satan or his henchmen, will finally be seen to
have been effected.

7 "The mystery of lawlessness" is an unusual expression.[31]

---

[30] Cf. E. Stauffer, "The civil power is set up as a bulwark against the
powers of chaos, but it can only keep these powers in check, never really
subdue them. The fight against them will never come to an end, and in the
end it must succumb to their final onslaught" (*op. cit.*, p. 85). Dietrich
Bonhoeffer speaks of "the restrainer" as: "the force of order, equipped with
great physical strength, which effectively blocks the way of those who are
about to plunge into the abyss .... The 'restrainer' is the power of the state
to establish and maintain order "(*Ethics* [London, 1956], p. 44).

[31] A somewhat similar expression occurs in the Thanksgiving Psalms in the
Dead Sea Scrolls, namely, the "mystery of evil" (Millar Burrows, *op. cit.*, p. 333).

"Mystery" in the New Testament has nothing of the mysterious in our sense of the term about it. It rather denotes that which is secret, which is hidden from men, and which men, for all their searching, will never find by their own efforts. Usually there is the added thought that the mystery has now been made known. It is not surprising that it is usually employed of the purposes of God in salvation and the like. The gospel is something which was not known and could not be known until God pleased to reveal it in Christ (e.g., Rom. 16:25 f.). But the use of the term here reminds us that there are secrets also in sin. Man can never, by his own reasoning, plumb the depths of iniquity, the reason for its existence, or the manner of its working. Paul points out that even as he writes there is a secret activity of lawlessness at work. The explanation of it all is not open to men, but the fact of its being in operation is clear enough. The use of the term "lawlessness" connects it with the Man of Lawlessness. Though that individual has not yet been revealed, the principle that governs his operations is already at work among men (cf. I John 2:18). It is probable that Paul does not mean simply that evil is at work. That has always been true. It is rather "the spirit of the anti-christ" (I John 4:3) that is in mind, a special form of evil which is hostile to all that Christ stands for. We can hardly be more specific in view of the reserve with which Paul writes. The verb rendered "doth work" usually denotes some supernatural force (see note on I Thess. 2:13). Here it is Satan who sets the "mystery of lawlessness" in motion.

The animated style we noted in v. 3 continues. Once again Paul rushes on without completing his sentence.[32] His point is that although the lawless principle is at work already it cannot reach its climax at present because of the restrainer. That climax will be reached only when the restrainer is "taken out of the way." This is not explained. Even so it seems definite enough to exclude some suggestions as to the identity of the restrainer, e.g., that which thinks of the Holy Spirit (e.g., the Scofield Reference Bible). While

---

[32] The ellipsis can be filled in in more ways than one. Most have some such sense as ARV, but Lightfoot gives the meaning as: "Only it must work in secret, must be unrevealed, until he that restraineth now be taken out of the way." He points out that Gal. 2:10 affords "an exact parallel both to the ellipsis after μόνον, and to the position of ὁ κατέχων ἄρτι before the relative word ἕως for the sake of emphasis."

it would be easy to think of the Spirit as restraining the forces of evil it is impossible to envisage Him as being "taken out of the way." Such an idea does not appear in Scripture.

8 It is only then, after the restrainer has been removed, that the "lawless one" will be revealed. This is the high point in the unfolding of wickedness. It takes place only in its due order. The "lawless one" is another way of referring to the personage who has already been called the Man of Lawlessness. It is more terse, but hardly differs in significance. This is the third time that Paul has spoken of him as being revealed. The repetition gives emphasis to the thought. This is no ordinary being making an appearance in the normal course of events. He has supernatural associations. In the providence of God his appearance is withheld as yet. But in due course he will be "revealed" to the sons of men.

It is likely that the Man of Lawlessness will have something of a career. The general impression given by the Scriptures which speak of the last days is that he will have a large following. But Paul's interest is not in the course of the rebellion, nor in the Man of Lawlessness as such. He puts his emphasis on the over-riding sovereignty of God. He is convinced that all men and events are in the hand of God.[33] As he contemplates the happenings of the end time it is not with the eager eye of one who seeks to trace out the course of events and follow the progress of the Man of Lawlessness. Rather, he looks with joy on the revelation of the mighty hand of God. His purpose is to meet the need of his friends, not to gratify their (or our) curiosity. His unfolding of the picture is not with a view to providing them with a timetable of events at the last so that they will be in a position to anticipate the course of events step by step. He writes to assure them that whatever happens God is over all. He writes to assure them that God is working His purposes out and will continue to do so to the very

---

[33] Cf. A. E. J. Rawlinson, "The eschatological element in the Christian creed gives expression not only to the Christian conviction of the reality of the world to come, but also to the recognition (*a*) that the ultimate verdict upon human life and its issues is the verdict of God, (*b*) that the ultimate victory in the struggle between evil and good is the victory of God, and (*c*) that the ultimate satisfaction of the human spirit is not to be found in the sphere of things visible and temporal but in the sphere of the things eternal and invisible" (*The New Testament Doctrine of the Christ* [London, 1926], p. 123, n. 1).

end. The Man of Lawlessness and the great rebellion must be mentioned. But Paul's interest is not in them but in God. So no sooner has he come to the appearance of the Lawless One than he proceeds to his destruction.

This is to be accomplished by the Lord Jesus. The term "Lord" is significant and appropriate in this context, with its emphasis on the glory of Him who first came in lowliness. Though He had once been despised and rejected, at the supreme moment of history He will be seen in all His glorious majesty. His splendor is brought out by the use of words reminiscent of the sacred Scripture to indicate the manner in which He will deal with the Lawless One (the passage recalls Isa. 11:4, where similar words are used of Jehovah Himself). The picture is further strengthened by the ease with which the Lord will destroy this terrible being. "The breath of his mouth" will be sufficient (cf. Luther's hymn, "A word shall quickly slay him").

Not even an action on His part is necessary. It is enough for Him to manifest Himself to render the Man of Lawlessness powerless.[34] "The manifestation of his coming" combines two words associated with the second advent. The former refers on one occasion to the first coming of the Lord (II Tim. 1:10), but everywhere else in the New Testament to the second coming. It usually has some idea of striking splendor (its root meaning has to do with conspicuousness). Grimm–Thayer say the word is "often used by the Greeks of a glorious manifestation of the gods."[35] For

---

[34] The verb rendered "bring to nought" is καταργέω. Something of the difficulty of translating this verb is seen in the fact that AV employs seventeen different ways of rendering it in its twenty-seven occurrences. RV gets rid of seven of these, but introduces three new renderings. To complete the confusion the English and American revisers do not always agree. The verb has the basic meaning "to render idle" (ἀργόν = ἀ + ἔργον). Thus it comes to signify "to nullify," "to rob of force and effectiveness." C. Clare Oke thinks that "our modern totalitarian word 'liquidate' is an exact equivalent" (ExT, Vol. LXVII, p. 368, n. 1). This seems, however, to be going a little too far. In the present passage the verb refers to the robbing of the Man of Lawlessness of all significance, rather than to his destruction (which is the meaning of ἀνελεῖ).

[35] The word is ἐπιφάνεια. "It adds here the idea of a conspicuous manifestation of God to help His people by His presence" (Bicknell). A. Deissmann speaks of it as "another cult-word," and gives an example of its use of the "Epiphany of Augustus" (i.e., the coming of the emperor) (LAE, p. 373). Similarly E. Stauffer cites an inscription referring to "the first year of the Epiphany of Gaius Caesar" as showing "the way the inhabitants of Cos calculated their time after the visit of a prince of the house of Augustus" (op. cit., pp. 314 f., n. 709).

"coming" see on I Thess. 2:19. The combination heightens the idea of the splendor and majesty of the Lord at that day. This has point in the present context. The Thessalonians need not fear, however illustrious evil men might be. Even the most outstanding of them all would be far outshone by the Lord of these lowly believers when He returns.

9 Paul does not underestimate the Man of Lawlessness. His confident assertions of the last couple of verses spring from recognition of the splendor and the power of the Lord Jesus, not from any failure to appreciate the power of the opposition. He concludes his words on the Man of Lawlessness by showing that he fully recognizes his stature, and the majesty that will be his when he comes on his evil mission.

He speaks of this man as having a "coming." The word is that which has just been used of the second advent of the Lord Jesus. It is the characteristic word for that advent. The Man of Lawlessness will come[36] with splendor, and with power. That power is associated with Satan, whose representative he is. The verse strongly suggests that we are confronted with a parody of the incarnation. The Man of Lawlessness is not simply a man with evil ideas. He is empowered by Satan to do Satan's work. Thus it is that he comes "with all power and signs and lying wonders." All three of these words are used of the miracles of Christ. They are probably used for that reason. They help us to see the counterfeit nature of the ministry of the Man of Lawlessness. The first term denotes the supernatural force which actuates the miracles. The second points to their character as directing attention to something beyond themselves. The third, "wonders," reminds us that miracles are things which man cannot explain. He can only marvel at them. "Of falsehood" (ARV, "lying") follows in the Greek. It should probably be taken with all three of the preceding, and not simply with "wonders" as ARV. The thought is not that the miracles are counterfeit (cf. RSV, "pretended signs and wonders"), so that there is no real miracle at all. Their reality is conceded (would Satan do less?). What Paul is contending is that they are wrought in a spirit of falsehood. They are the miracles which befit

---

[36] Paul uses the present tense, ἐστιν, which stresses the certainty of the coming.

one who seeks to deceive men, just as Christ's miracles befitted Him who came to save men.

10ª The melancholy catalogue of this man's wickedness continues. Whereas before Paul has been concerned with his outward, objective show, now he turns to the effect of all this on men. The Man of Lawlessness will come expressly to deceive men. He will be well equipped to do this. He will have "all" deception. "With evil's undiluted power to deceive" (Phillips) is hardly a translation, but it conveys Paul's thought. The Lawless One will be out to lure men to their destruction. To that end he will be armed with every weapon of Satan.

This deceit is "for them that perish." There may be the thought here that those in Christ have nothing to fear. But the primary emphasis is on the fate of those who are deceived. The Man of Lawlessness will gain a following. He will be welcomed by many. But his dupes will find in the end that they have followed him to their own irreparable loss.

b. The Man of Lawlessness' Followers, 2:10b–12

because they received not the love of the truth, that they might be saved.
11 And for this cause God sendeth them a working of error, that they should believe a lie:
12 that they all might be judged who believed not the truth, but had pleasure in unrighteousness.

10ᵇ Paul leaves the subject of the Man of Lawlessness in the middle of this verse, and turns his attention to that evil one's followers. Having said that they would perish, he goes on to the cause[37] of this, namely, their wrong attitude to the truth. "Truth" here, as elsewhere in Paul's writings, is not to be thought of simply as an abstract moral quality. It is intimately related to Jesus (cf. Eph. 4:21, "as truth is in Jesus"; John 14:6, "I am . . . the truth"). More particularly it is the saving truth of the gospel. This aspect is very marked in the present passage. Receiving it means salvation. This truth should have been received with warm affection (as

---

[37] "Because" is ἀνθ' ὧν. The preposition ἀντί often has the thought of correspondence, and this may well be in view here. "In requital of their refusal to entertain the love of the truth" as Findlay puts it (CGT).

every one who has welcomed it knows). Thus Paul speaks not simply of "the truth," but of "the love of the truth," an expression found here only in the Greek Bible. The whole bent of the people he is describing is away from all the things of God, and therefore away from the truth of God. They gave the truth of God no welcome (this is the force of the word rendered "received"; see on I Thess. 2:13), that truth of God which is expressed in the love which brought about the gospel. This is a deliberate action. It expresses the attitude of their heart. And it is fraught with eternal consequences.

The verse concludes with a clause of purpose which emphasizes the magnitude of the gift these men rejected. Other men love the truth with a view to their salvation. It was this upon which those who perish had turned their backs.

11 God is not to be thought of as sitting passively by while all this is going on. Invariably the Bible pictures Him as taking part in the world's drama. Indeed, the world's drama is nothing other than the working out of His purposes. He has created this universe, and set it running on His own principles. He orders the affairs of man in the way He chooses. And one of the things He chooses is that an inevitable retribution overtakes the sinner. Sometimes men today refer to the inevitability of the moral law. But the Bible picture is truer. There is no self-acting moral law. There is a moral God who is operative in the working of moral law.[38] In this verse the word "God" is in an emphatic position. Paul wants there to be no doubt but that God Himself is responsible for the action of which he writes.

There is a backward look, "for this cause." What follows is due not to any caprice on the part of God, but to the culpable failure of the men in question to welcome the saving truth that was offerred to them. The certainty of the result is underlined with the use of the present tense "sendeth." Paul sees it before his very eyes, so sure is its coming.[39] God sends "a working of error." The

---

[38] Cf. Neil, "Men start by rejecting the Gospel voluntarily; they then reach the stage when they are unable to tell what is gospel and what is fallacy. This is the powerful 'delusion' which Paul rightly regards as an Act of God."

[39] The present may also carry a hint that what will take place on the grand scale when the Man of Lawlessness comes, is even now at work in principle in the case of lesser men. Whenever men refuse the truth God sends the working of error.

genitive is the objective genitive, with the meaning, in Frame's words, of "an energy unto delusion." God will send a power which will operate to bring about in them a delusion. This is further explained, "that they should believe a lie." The last expression is really "the lie." It is not just any lie that these people accept, but Satan's last and greatest effort: the lie that the Man of Lawlessness is God. They refuse to accept the truth and they find themselves delivered over to the lie.

The principle underlying this verse is of great importance for the understanding of the moral government of the universe. From the foregoing verses it might perhaps be thought that there is a contest in which Satan on the one hand, and God on the other, make their moves, but with God somewhat the stronger. But Paul has a much grander conception. God is using the very evil that men and Satan produce for the working out of His purpose. They think that they are acting in defiance of Him. But in the end they find that those very acts in which they expressed their defiance were the vehicle of their punishment. Paul has the same truth in other places. For example, in Rom. 1:26 God gave up certain sinners "unto vile passions." They thought that they were enjoying their sinful pleasures. They turned out to be "receiving in themselves that recompense of their error which was due." The same truth is found in other parts of the Bible also.[40] God is sovereign. No forces of evil, not Satan himself, nor his Man of Lawlessness can resist His might. He chooses to use men's sin as the way in which He works out their punishment.[41]

12 The judicial purpose of God in thus using evil as His

---

[40] Notably in God's putting a lying spirit into the mouths of the false prophets (I Kings 22:23; cf. Ezek. 14:9). Similarly an action of Satan (I Chron. 21:1) may be ascribed to God (II Sam. 24:1). God is sovereign and no evil power has independent existence. God uses evil to forward His purposes, and thus, in a sense, may be said even to originate it.

[41] An interesting partial parallel is to be found in the "Habbakuk Commentary" among the Dead Sea Scrolls. On Hab. 2:12 f. the commentary begins: "This saying means the preacher of the lie, who enticed many to build a city of delusion in blood and to establish a congregation in falsehood for the sake of its honor, making many grow weary of the service of delusion and making them pregnant with works of falsehood, that their toil may be in vain, to the end that they may come into judgments of fire" (Millar Burrows, *op. cit.*, p. 369). In "The Manual of Discipline" God is thought of as creating the evil spirit as well as the good (*op. cit.*, p. 374). In the closing Psalm we read, "apart from thy will nothing will be done ... everything that has come to pass has been by thy will" (*op. cit.*, p. 389).

instrument is made clear. "That they should believe a lie" is followed by "that they all might be judged," the construction indicating purpose. There is method in all that God does in this situation. The word "judged" in this context implies condemnation (Rutherford and Moffatt both translate, "doomed"). But the use of this term rather than one which signifies condemnation and nothing more stresses the judicial purpose of God. His act is just. The section concludes with a further characterization of the condemned, bringing out the nature of their offense. Paul returns to their wrong attitude to the truth. Whereas previously he has complained that they had no welcome nor love for the truth, now he says that they did not even believe it. Once more it is the saving truth of the gospel that is in mind, but these sinners would have none of it. Paul employs a construction which is unusual with him[42] (elsewhere it occurs only in quotations) to emphasize their position. His more usual construction has the thought of personal trust, as in the case of faith in Christ. This one denotes simply credence. The dupes of the Man of Lawlessness are so blinded to realities that they do not even realize that the gospel is God's truth. So does sin blind men.

Not only did they not believe the truth, but they "had pleasure in unrighteousness."[43] There is a sharp contrast in both parts of this clause. "Had pleasure" contrasts with their attitude to the truth. There was no warmth in their attitude to the gospel, no welcome, no love, no belief even. But they actively rejoiced in unrighteousness, they inclined towards it, they regarded it with favor and good will. So, too, "unrighteousness" is contrasted with "truth." This word has been connected with "deceit" in v. 10. It is a general term for all manner of wickedness. The stark contrast reminds us that ultimately we must belong to one or other of two classes, namely, those who welcome and love God's truth, and those who take their pleasure in wickedness. Those who begin by failing to accept God's good gift end by setting forward unrighteousness. Notice the way they become perverted. These men are not

---

[42] πιστεύω followed by the dative, as also in v. 11. The more usual construction is εἰς with the accusative.

[43] εὐδοκέω also has an unusual construction. This is the only place in the New Testament where it is construed with the simple dative. Elsewhere we find ἐν, pointing to that "in" which the good pleasure lies. The dative will denote "inclination towards," "favor to."

described as sinning through force of circumstances or any form
of compulsion. They now find their pleasure in sin. They delight
in wrong.[44] For them evil has become good.

IV. THANKSGIVING AND ENCOURAGEMENT, 2:13-17

1. THANKSGIVING, 2:13-15

13 But we are bound to give thanks to God always for
you, brethren beloved of the Lord, for that God chose
you from the beginning unto salvation in sanctification of the Spirit and belief of the truth:
14 whereunto he called you through our gospel, to the
obtaining of the glory of our Lord Jesus Christ.
15 So then, brethren, stand fast, and hold the traditions
which ye were taught, whether by word, or by epistle
of ours.

13 It was necessary to deal with the Man of Lawlessness and
his detestable enormities, but Paul's real interest lay elsewhere.
The advent speculations of his Thessalonian friends had made it
essential for him to say enough to set them right. That done he
turns to a more congenial subject, the divine choice of the Thessalonians to salvation. In language reminiscent of his words in
1:3, perhaps intentionally so, he says that he and his friends are
"bound" to thank God for them. He wants his readers to be in no
doubt as to the justice of the thanksgiving that he offers. So he
repeats the word indicative of obligation, and he reinforces it this
time (as he did not do in the opening part of the Epistle) with the
emphatic pronoun for "we."[45] The Thessalonians can after this
be in no doubt at all that Paul thinks highly of their Christian
profession. Notice the insertion of "always." His impression of
the Thessalonians is of men whose Christian life is consistent.
Accordingly he must be thanking God for them all the time.

He employs the affectionate address "brethren," and adds to it
"beloved of the Lord." The addition is not usual. In I Thess. 1:4

[44] Way's rendering, "but have actually gloated over iniquity," is probably
too strong. But it brings out the point of their delight in evil.
[45] Cf. Bicknell: "In the Greek *we* is as emphatic as the language can well
make it." He thinks that this is "best explained as reiterating the fact that
their founders are bound to thank God for their condition in spite of the
discouragement of some of their converts."

he has used the similar expression "beloved of God." There, as here, the thought of election was present. Election and the love of God are connected. The perfect participle, "beloved," brings the two thoughts of an action in time past and a continuing result. This is, of course, very appropriate in proximity to the concept of election. "The Lord," in conformity with Pauline usage, will here denote the Lord Jesus rather than the Father. There is probably no significance in the change from "beloved of God" to "beloved of the Lord." The use of the title "Lord," however, is possibly evoked in this context by the preceding mention of mighty ones among the evil beings. Just as in v. 8 there is significance in referring to Jesus as the Lord (for He is mighty to destroy the Man of Lawlessness), so here the title is not otiose. In the face of the might of evil the Thessalonians may well be calm, for they are beloved of the mighty Lord.

Paul thanks God because He has chosen the converts unto salvation. "Chose" is one of a number of words used to convey the idea of election.[46] This is the only place where it is used in this sense in the New Testament (though it is found with this meaning in the Greek Old Testament[47]). There is no one word which constantly expresses the idea of election, but the fundamental thought remains unchanged. The salvation of believers rests on the divine choice, not on human effort. Nor was this some afterthought on God's part. He chose them "from the beginning." Some have felt that this means no more than from the beginning of the mission to Thessalonica, but this is inadequate. The fact that this is an unusual expression in Pauline writings for "from the beginning of time" is not significant. We have just seen that Paul's election terminology is variable and the same goes for his time expressions. There are several of these without there being any real difference of meaning,[48] and we must feel that this is no more than a stylistic

---

[46] Thus we find ἐκλέγομαι, προορίζω, προγινώσκω, and words of more general meaning like τίθημι (as in I Thess. 5:9), ἀξιόω, καταξιόω, etc. The word here is εἵλατο.

[47] It is found in Deut. 26:18, and the compound προαιρέομαι in Deut. 7:6 f., 10:15.

[48] He uses πρὸ τῶν αἰώνων, πρὸ καταβολῆς κόσμου, and ἀπὸ τῶν αἰώνων. His expression here is ἀπ' ἀρχῆς, which is used of the beginning of things in Isa. 63:16, Matt. 19:4, I John 2:13. The variant reading, ἀπαρχήν, "as a firstfruit," is preferred by some commentators. The meaning would be first in contrast with others yet to come, or first in Greece. The former is not very

variant, all the more so since it is used elsewhere in the Greek Bible in such a sense. The meaning then is that God chose out the Thessalonian Christians from the very beginning of things. Their election was no recent innovation.

They were chosen out for salvation (the construction indicates purpose as in I Thess. 5:9). Two aspects are singled out for mention. "Sanctification of the Spirit" is by some understood not of the work of the Holy Spirit in the believer, but (giving "spirit" a small "s") of the sanctification of the believer's spirit. Against this we should notice that it is the whole man that is sanctified (I Thess. 5:23). This sanctification is effected by the Holy Spirit (cf. I Pet. 1:2). It is more likely, then, that the expression is to be understood of the work of the Holy Spirit in making holy the whole man.[49]

"Belief of the truth" is not an easy expression. As in vv. 10, 12, "truth" is not simply an ethical quality, but the truth of the gospel. It is that truth that is associated with Jesus Christ. "Belief" is better rendered "faith" as in the margin of the Revised Version. The expression points us to that faith in the truth of God which is the basis of Christian life.[50] At first sight it is surprising that this should be mentioned after "sanctification of the Spirit." It may be that we are intended to understand that this can only follow upon an activity of the Spirit. The order may also point us to the truth that the faith being spoken of is not simply one initial act. It is a continuing habit.

---

natural, and against the latter is the fact that the Philippians were converted before the Thessalonians.

Both variants have good manuscript support. Transcriptional probability may be held to favor ἀπ' ἀρχῆς, for this is not a typical Pauline expression, while ἀπαρχή is. Moreover, while Paul employs the concept of firstfruits on a number of occasions he never connects it with election. On the other hand, he often associates election with some expression rooting it in the beginning. A further point militating against ἀπαρχήν is the absence of a qualifying genitive, which, as Frame points out, is usual in Paul's use of that noun.

[49] Notice that in this verse all three Persons of the Trinity are mentioned. This is not yet the official statement of the doctrine, but it represents such an understanding of the Persons and work of Father, Son, and Holy Spirit as was bound, in the end, to give rise to the dogma.

[50] Cf. T. F. Torrance, "In Greek 'faith of the truth' is an awkward expression, but it is clear from the Old Testament background that for St. Paul neither *pistis* nor *aletheia* will express fully what he is after, and so he puts both words together to convey what the Old Testament means by '*emeth* and/or '*emunah*" (ExT, Vol. LXVIII, p. 113).

14 "Whereunto" is to be taken with the whole of the previous expression "salvation . . . truth," and not with any one member of it. The thought is that God calls men into a state of salvation. He calls them with a view to salvation. With the idea of call Paul moves from the pre-temporal election by God to His effectual calling of men in history. The idea of the divine call is a favorite one with the Apostle. There are other passages where he connects it with the thought of election as he does here (e.g., Rom. 8:30). We have already seen references to God's call in I Thess. 2:12, 5:24, in both which places the call is present. In the present passage it is in the past tense. This points to the time when the Thessalonians had responded to the gospel. This is made quite clear by the addition of "through our gospel." The gospel Paul and his companions had preached had been the instrument of God's call. The personal touch is to be discerned in the possessive adjective, appropriate in a passage like this where the writer is concerned to stress his care for his converts. For the expression "our gospel" cf. I Thess. 1:5, and the note there.

Salvation is not confined to its present aspects and Paul moves on to the future glory. This, he says, is that "of our Lord Jesus Christ." The thought that the glory of the believer is closely associated with that of the Savior is one which recurs. We have met it, for example, in 1:10 (where see note). Those who are in Christ share the glory of Christ. For them there is no other glory. In I Thess. 2:12 Paul had written of the Thessalonians as being called into the glory of God. The fact that he can here speak of the glory of Christ in a similar fashion illustrates the closeness of the relationship between the Father and the Son. Cf. also Rom. 8:30. For "obtaining" see the note on I Thess. 5:9. It is not a usual word in this kind of context. It may be meant to stress the reality of the possession of this glory in face of the fact that some at Thessalonica all too readily became downhearted.[51]

15 "So then" represents a pair of inferential conjunctions which indicate that what follows is the logical consequence of the

---

[51] Denney draws attention to "the new world which the gospel created for the mind of man." The profound thoughts in these two verses were "addressed originally to a little company of working people, but unmatched for length and breadth and depth and height by all that pagan literature could offer to the wisest and the best."

preceding. Paul has been pointing out something of the evil power of the Man of Lawlessness and of the terrible times ahead. But he has also been careful to interweave with this the thought of the might of the Lord who had loved the Thessalonians and had chosen them and called them. All this means something. Paul proceeds to draw out something of its relevance to the situation in which his readers find themselves. They should not "be shaken" (v. 2), but contrariwise they should "stand fast." His verb here is an unusual one with an emphasis on the firmness of the stand.[52] Cf. its use in I Thess. 3:8, and the note there.

Linked with this is the injunction to "hold the traditions." The verb is used by Paul elsewhere only in Col. 2:19 (of holding fast to Christ the "Head"). It is often used in the literal sense as of holding with the hand. It then denotes a firm grip. It is used of holding the traditions of the elders in Mark 7:3, 8. "Traditions" is a word which points us to the fact that the Christian message is essentially derivative.[53] It does not originate in men's fertile imaginations. It rests on the facts of the life, death, resurrection, and ascension of Jesus Christ. Paul disclaims originating these things, and expressly says that the things he passed on he had himself first received (I Cor. 15:3). For us these traditions are embodied in the documents of the New Testament. But for Paul's readers there was no such volume. For them the Christian traditions were principally those which they had received by word of mouth. Paul also associates "epistle of ours" with the spoken word. By this he probably means I Thessalonians. He puts no difference between the authority of the written and the spoken word. Both alike were in very deed the word of God, as we see from I Thess. 2:13 and I Cor. 14:37. As in the case of election which we were considering a verse or two back, the handing over of the Christian message is expressed with quite a variety of terminology.[54] But the underlying idea is always the same. It is a message which comes from God. It must therefore be accepted with humility and

---

[52] Like the following "hold fast," the verb is present imperative, signifying continuity. "Stand firm continually . . . keep holding fast."

[53] Cullmann has an important chapter on "The Tradition" in *The Early Church* (London, 1956), pp. 59–99. He argues that the tradition which is passed on by the apostles "is not effected by men, but by Christ the Lord himself" (p. 73).

[54] Verbs used of delivering it include, δίδωμι, παραδίδωμι, διδάσκω, γνωρίζω, παραγγέλλω.

transmitted faithfully. The derivative nature of the message is a reminder that men ought not to depart from it in any way. Since the traditions were not of human origin they must stand fast in them.

2. PRAYER FOR THE CONVERTS, 2:16, 17

16 Now our Lord Jesus Christ himself, and God our Father who loved us and gave us eternal comfort and good hope through grace,
17 comfort your hearts and establish them in every good work and word.

16-17 The "Now" with which this section begins is the translation of an adversative conjunction. It might better be rendered "but." Paul has been urging his friends to action. But they can do nothing effective in their own strength. Thus Paul directs them to that one source of strength that will see them through. He does more. He prays for them, just as he did in the first letter (I Thess. 3:11 ff.). The prayer is at about the same stage in the argument, and there are coincidences of language between the two.

This prayer is notable for the place it assigns to Jesus Christ. He is given the full title "Lord Jesus Christ," where each word has its full weight (see on I Thess. 1:1 for the force of each of these). Ever since he got on to the subject of the Man of Lawlessness Paul has used every opportunity of insisting on the superlative worth and might of the Savior. He is linked with the Father, and, what is unusual, He is placed before the Father. This sometimes happens elsewhere (Gal. 1:1, II Cor. 13:14), but the more usual order is to place the Father first. Although the subject is in this way a double one, yet the two verbs "comfort" and "establish" are singular.[55] We have seen this done by Paul in the earlier Epistle (see note on I Thess. 3:11). All this combines to give the highest place imaginable to Christ. Paul is not giving a formal account of his understanding of the nature of deity, but this incidental allusion in an informal act of prayer is all the more revealing for that reason. It is clear that he made no sharp distinction between the Son and the Father.

---

[55] Cf. Lightfoot, "There is probably no instance in St Paul of a plural adjective or verb, where the two Persons of the Godhead are mentioned."

It is not quite clear whether the clause "who loved us," etc. is to be taken only with the Father, or with both Persons. On the whole it seems more likely that it refers to the Father only (though Frame prefers the other view). Nothing much hinges on the point. Either way the acts of love and giving are divine in origin, and if they are thought of as emanating from the Father they are certainly brought about through the Son. "Loved" and "gave" are both aorist participles. The probability accordingly is that they refer to definite actions. "Who loved us" will have primary reference to the love of God shown in the cross. "Gave us eternal comfort" is rather the good gift of God when He brought us into the state of salvation.

The content of the gift is hardly "comfort" in our sense of the term. The word is from the root which we examined in the note on I Thess. 3:2, where we saw that the idea is that of encouraging or strengthening. "Eternal" encouragement is particularly appropriate in this context where the thought is much of the troubles of the last days. Come the Man of Lawlessness, come the Parousia of our Lord, come the day of Judgment, come anything else whatever, their encouragement will abide. Linked with it is "good hope." This is another concept which is very much in place where the interest is so highly eschatological. The Christian hope is good, as Frame points out, both in contrast with the empty hope of those who are not believers, and also because it will endure till it is realized at the coming of the Lord.[56]

"Through grace" is not to be taken with "hope" but with "gave." The encouragement and the hope are both the products of the grace of God. It is because of this divine origin and backing that they are valid.

Both the verbs "comfort" and "establish" were used in I Thess. 3:2, where see notes. The combination of the English "comfort" with the following "hearts" suggests irresistibly the thought of

---

[56] The importance of a "good" hope should not be overlooked in the light of our contemporary situation. J. E. Fison has reminded us that hope is a necessity for any movement that would grip men's hearts (*The Christian Hope* [London, 1954], pp. 16 ff.). One reason for the success of the Communists in many areas is that to men who have no hope they bring hope. But their hope is not a "good" hope. It is illusory. The first Christians were outwardly "of all men most miserable." But they had a good hope, that sure and certain hope of the return of their Lord in glory. It transformed for them the whole of life.

consolation. But this is not the right way to understand it. The verb has the thought of strengthening. The noun "heart" stands for the whole of the inner life of man, and not particularly for his emotional life as with us (see note on I Thess. 2:4). The prayer, then, is for inner strengthening with a view to faithful Christian living. Usually when "word" and "work" are put together in this way "word" precedes. Possibly the order in this passage is due to the stress on the doing which will proceed from the divine strength for which the Apostle prays.

COMMENTARY ON II THESSALONIANS

CHAPTER III

V. THE FAITHFULNESS OF GOD, 3:1–5

1. REQUEST FOR PRAYER, 3:1, 2

1 Finally, brethren, pray for us, that the word of the
Lord may run and be glorified, even as also *it is*
with you;

2 and that we may be delivered from unreasonable and
evil men; for all have not faith.

1 Paul was a very great apostle. But his greatness consisted
not so much in sheer native ability (though he had his share of
that) as in his recognition of his dependence on God. It arises out
of this that he so often requests the prayers of those to whom he
ministers. He did not feel himself as high above them, but as one
with them. He valued their intercessions and sought their prayers.

Thus, as he passes from the major section of his letter to that
which follows,[1] he does so with a request for prayer. He puts his
imperative "pray" in an emphatic position, which leaves no doubt
as to the importance he attaches to it, and he puts it in the present
continuous tense, so that it means "pray continually." He looks not
for a perfunctory petition, but for continuing, prevailing prayer.
In I Thess. 5:25 he had simply requested prayer. Now he specifies
the objects for prayer. The first of them concerns "the word of the
Lord." This means the preaching of the Apostle, as in I Thess.
2:13. Paul wants it "to run," a piece of lively imagery which may
have reference to the games (as often when Paul speaks of contests
of various kinds). There is also a reference to a strong man running
his course in Ps. 19:5, but the imagery of our present verse probably
goes back ultimately to Ps. 147:15, "His word runneth very
swiftly." It is clear that when Paul first preached at Thessalonica
there were spectacular results. Many were speedily converted. It
is this kind of free movement of the word of God that he has in

---

[1] For τὸ λοιπόν see the note on λοιπὸν οὖν in I Thess. 4:1. It marks the
transition from the main section of the Epistle.

mind. With this he couples the idea of the word's "being glorified." Men are led to glorify the word when they see what it does. There may also be a glance at the idea that, when the word is operative in the way spoken of, it displays its glories before men. Both verbs are in the present subjunctive, and the significance of this continuous tense should not be overlooked. Paul is not looking for a single striking manifestation of the word, but for its continuous swift advance, and for its continual arousing of admiration.

"Even as also it is with you" reminds us of Paul's difficulties at the time of writing. Since his departure from Thessalonica he had been compelled to leave Beroea, he had had little success at Athens, and was striking trouble at Corinth. He recalls the glorious days in Macedonia, days which were continuing, judging from the reports Paul was receiving. There is no "it is" in the Greek (ARV puts these words in italics), and it is not required. The statement is very general.[2] Paul is probably including both the first days of the mission in Thessalonica, and the days when he was writing.

2 The second petition is that Paul may be delivered from his enemies. Both the use of the aorist tense in the verb "delivered"[3] and the article with "unreasonable and evil men" point to a definite situation. Paul is not asking for prayer that he might be kept safe in his constant journeys and preachings. He writes in the light of his particular situation. He writes knowing that his friends are aware of his difficulty. He looks to them to join him in prayer that he may be delivered out of it. It seems most natural to understand his enemies as those Jews who opposed his preaching. We know that they dogged his steps at Corinth as elsewhere (Acts 18:12 ff.). His request reminds us of similar words in Rom. 15:31.

The word rendered "unreasonable" is used of persons only here in the New Testament (it is used of things in Luke 23:41, Acts 25:5, 28:6, in each place being rendered "amiss" by ARV). Basically it signifies what is out of place. When it is used in an ethical

---

[2] RSV "as it did among you" limits the meaning of the expression unduly, just as ARV does in another direction.

[3] The verb ῥύομαι is a general term for rescue, whereas verbs like "redeem" are more restricted ("redeem" = free by the payment of a price). In the Bible ῥύομαι often has the idea of deliverance with power. Milligan suggests that the use of the preposition ἀπό here, rather than ἐκ (as in I Thess. 1:10) lays stress "perhaps on the deliverance itself rather than on the power from which it is granted."

sense it denotes that which is improper, and so unrighteous. Joined with "evil" it refers to the malignant temper of those who were setting themselves in opposition to the Apostle as he sought to propagate the faith.

The meaning of "faith" at the end of the sentence is not beyond dispute. The Greek word it translates may mean "faithfulness," "fidelity." It always has this meaning when it is used of God, but never, it would seem, in the New Testament when it is used of men. Or it may mean "faith" in the sense of "trust." With the article (which it has here) it may also signify "the faith," i.e., the body of Christian teaching. The first meaning is obviously unsuitable here, but it is difficult to decide between the other two. In either case the meaning is much the same in this place. There is not a great deal of difference between "Not all men believe in Jesus Christ," and, "Not all men embrace the Christian faith." It makes it clear that the men opposing Paul were outside the church, and not believers. On the whole it seems a little more likely that we should understand "faith" rather than "the faith," for the former would lead more naturally into the thought of the next verse.[4]

2. GOD'S FAITHFULNESS, 3:3-5

3 But the Lord is faithful, who shall establish you, and guard you from the evil *one*.
4 And we have confidence in the Lord touching you, that ye both do and will do the things which we command.
5 And the Lord direct your hearts into the love of God, and into the patience of Christ.

3 As so often in his writings Paul turns away from the difficulties of man to the God on whom all men must depend. He does not shut his eyes to the very great difficulties of his situation, as his request for prayer plainly shows. But he knows that the really significant factor is the character of his Lord, not the might of the enemy. His usual practice is to refer to the faithfulness of God

---

4 Notice that the πίστις which ends this verse is immediately followed by the πιστός which begins the next. Paul is fond of such word plays. Knox tries to bring out the connection by rendering, "the faith does not reach all hearts. But the Lord keeps faith."

(I Cor. 1:9, 10:13, II Cor. 1:18).[5] It is quite in keeping with the whole drift of the present passage, however, for him to speak of "the Lord." From the time of the mention of the Man of Lawlessness onwards Paul has been constantly referring to "the Lord." The repetition is part of the way in which he seeks to inspire his converts. The reiteration of the lordship of their Leader means a corresponding belittlement of the forces of evil. Paul emphasizes the faithfulness of the Lord as an existing reality by inserting the verb "is." Normally in Greek this would not be necessary in a sentence of this kind. In none of the three pasages listed above, for example, where God is said to be faithful is the verb inserted. Its presence here gives emphasis and certainty to the thought. The Lord is really faithful.[6]

There are two things which he looks for the Lord to do, and it is a little unexpected that he speaks of them being done to the Thessalonians rather than to himself. He has been speaking of his own difficulties and requesting their prayers. We expect accordingly that he will go on to say that he is confident that the Lord will deliver him. But the concern of the pastor for his flock rises above any personal considerations. Paul speaks of what the Lord will do for them and not of what He will do for him. First, the Lord will "establish" them. For this verb see on I Thess. 3:2. The faithfulness of the Lord means that His people will not be left to the mercy of any and every temptation that may assail them, but they will be settled in the faith.

Secondly, the Lord will guard them. The verb hardly calls for comment, though it is not very common in the Pauline writings. It is not joined with the verb for "establish" anywhere else in the Greek Bible. It is not certain whether the last expression in this verse should be understood as ARV, "the evil one," or as AV, "evil." The Greek could mean either. We have the same problem in the Lord's Prayer, and elsewhere in the New Testament. Most commentators agree that the reference to a person is probable here. It fits the context better, for the preceding chapter has been

---

[5] Cf. this statement from the closing Psalm of "The Manual of Discipline" from among the Dead Sea Scrolls, "For the faithfulness of God is the rock I tread, and his strength is the staff of my right hand" (Millar Burrows, *op. cit.*, p. 387). The Scrolls often express man's complete dependence on God.

[6] Cf. the vision recorded in Acts 18:9 f., where the Lord encouraged Paul to continue his work at Corinth.

concerned with evil persons, not with the general concept of evil (cf. Findlay, "The passage depicts a personal conflict, not a war of principles," CGT). There is also the point made by Calvin, "I prefer, however, to interpret it of Satan, the head of all the wicked. For it were a small thing to be delivered from the cunning or violence of men, if the Lord did not protect us from all spiritual injury."

4 From the thought of the faithfulness of the Lord Paul proceeds to express his confidence, a confidence which rests in the Lord, that his friends will do what he enjoins them. The connection of thought is not obvious, but then the connection of thought is not obvious in a number of places hereabouts. It is a true letter. Paul writes to his friends as his thoughts come to him, and there is not the carefully marshalled argument of the theological treatise. These words show us something of the tactfulness of Paul. Though the things he speaks of are not defined, it seems fairly clear that he is leading up to the injunctions of vv. 6 ff. He wants the Thessalonians to obey his directions. But he begins by expressing his complete confidence in them. Always he loves to praise where he can. His confidence does not rest in them as men: "in the Lord" shows clearly where the basis of his certainty lies. It is not absolutely certain whether "in the Lord" is to be taken with "confidence" as ARV, or with "you" (as, for example, Moffatt, "we rely upon you in the Lord"), though the word order favors ARV. But in the end they come to much the same. Paul is putting his trust basically in the Lord. But he is expecting the Lord so to work in the lives of his friends that they will respond to the commands laid upon them.

He says they "both do and will do" the things in question. The emphasis is probably on "will do." As Findlay points out, had he been thinking only of their present or past performances he would probably have used a verb like "know" instead of "have confidence," as he does, for example, in II Cor. 9:2 (CGT). He is preparing the way for the commands which follow. The verb "command" denotes an authoritative command (see the note on the cognate noun, I Thess. 4:2). It is probably not without significance that this is the verb he is to employ in vv. 6, 10, 12.

5 This verse has important links of thought both with what precedes and what follows. Paul has been speaking of his confidence in the Thessalonians, but it is a confidence in the Lord and what He will do in them, and not simply a confidence in men. Thus immediately after his expression of confidence he breaks into prayer. It is only as the Lord works in them that his confidence will prove to have been justified. And if the fact that he prays follows significantly on the preceding verse, the content of the prayer has an important bearing on what follows. Paul is about to deal with certain people who are idle and insubordinate. He never shirks an issue, and his directions when he comes to them are blunt enough. But it is no part of his plan to give needless offense, and the reference to the love of God is timely.[7] It reminds them that Paul speaks as one who himself owed everything to the love of God and loved God himself, and also that they are in the same position. There should be no resentment among men whose thoughts are fixed on God's love. Similarly the reference to "the steadfastness of Christ" is in point when the idleness of men is about to be rebuked.

"The Lord" here is Jesus, and we have another indication of the place Paul accorded Him in this prayer addressed to Him. For the verb "direct" see note on I Thess. 3:11, and for "heart" see on I Thess. 2:4. The verb signifies the removal of all obstacles so that the way is cleared. The noun stands for the whole of the inner life. Paul's prayer then is that the Lord will lead his friends to concentrate their thinking, their emotions, and their will on the love and steadfastness to which he refers.

There is some difficulty in knowing exactly what the following expressions signify. An expression like "the love of God" might mean in Greek either God's love for us or our love for God. Our first difficulty is that the logic of the prayer seems to require some such meaning as "The Lord lead you to love God," but in Paul's writings "the love of God" always seems to mean God's love for man. Lightfoot is probably right in suggesting that "the Apostles availed themselves . . . of the vagueness or rather comprehensiveness of language, to express a great spiritual truth." He goes on to suggest that the two senses are "combined and interwoven." If we may accept this, then the primary idea will be that of God's love

---

[7] The Dead Sea Scrolls often speak of the steadfast love of God. For example, in the closing Psalm in "The Manual of Discipline" we read: "on his steadfast love I will lean all the day," "As for me, if I slip, the steadfast love of God is my salvation forever" (Millar Burrows, *op. cit.*, pp. 386, 388).

to us, but there will be also the secondary idea of our love to Him. Paul's prayer then will be that the inner life of his friends be so concentrated on God's love for them that this will evoke an answering love for Him.[8]

Conformably to this, "the patience of Christ" will denote first the attitude of Christ, and then the answering attitude on the part of the Thessalonians. "Patience," here as elsewhere, will denote not so much "patience" in our sense of the term, as "steadfastness" or "endurance" (see note on I Thess. 1:3). The Thessalonians are being reminded of the constancy exhibited by the Master, which forms the pattern on which they should model themselves.

VI. GODLY DISCIPLINE, 3:6–15

1. THE DISORDERLY, 3:6–13

6 Now we command you, brethren, in the name of our Lord Jesus Christ, that ye withdraw yourselves from every brother that walketh disorderly, and not after the tradition which they received of us.

7 For yourselves know how ye ought to imitate us: for we behaved not ourselves disorderly among you;

8 neither did we eat bread for nought at any man's hand, but in labor and travail, working night and day, that we might not burden any of you:

9 not because we have not the right, but to make ourselves an ensample unto you, that ye should imitate us.

10 For even when we were with you, this we commanded you, If any will not work, neither let him eat.

11 For we hear of some that walk among you disorderly, that work not at all, but are busybodies.

12 Now them that are such we command and exhort in the Lord Jesus Christ, that with quietness they work, and eat their own bread.

13 But ye, brethren, be not weary in well-doing.

In the First Epistle Paul had mentioned some who would not work, but were disorderly (4:11 f., 5:14), but it is evident that his brief exhortations had not produced the desired effect. He felt

---

[8] Cf. Moffatt, "It is by the sense of God's love alone, not by any mere acquiescence in His will or stoical endurance of it, that the patience and courage of the Christian are sustained."

strongly on the matter as we see from the fact that in this Epistle he devotes so much space to this problem. Next to the section on the coming of the Lord this is the longest section in the Epistle. Paul is most anxious that these friends should come to their senses. It is noteworthy that he continues to treat them as friends. For all the authority that he knew he possessed, and for all the authoritative tone of some of this section, he yet bears well in mind that these are brethren. He appeals to them as such.

6 Tenderness is blended with authority in this opening exhortation. Paul addresses the church as "brethren" and refers to the erring as "every brother." But his verb is the strong one he has used in v. 4. He commands, he does not simply advise. Moreover, he speaks "in the name of our Lord Jesus Christ." This is at once a reminder of the very real authority that Paul exercised, and of the seriousness of any refusal to obey. Paul was not giving some private ideas of his own when he spoke "in the name."

The substance of his command is that they "withdraw" from the erring. In view of v. 15 this does not mean "abstain from all intercourse," but it stands for the withholding of intimate fellowship. The verb has the idea of a retreating within oneself (cf. its use of furling sails). Such a line of conduct is meant as would impress on the offenders that they had opened up a gap between themselves and the rest. They had to be made to see that complete fellowship is possible only when there is complete harmony. The workers had a responsibility to the offenders. For, as Frame says, "Idleness is an affair of the brotherhood (I, 4:9–12, 5:12–14), and the brethren as a whole are responsible for the few among them who 'do nothing but fetch frisks and vagaries' (Leigh)" (on v. 11). It is an aspect of the Christian life that is but little observed today.

The offenders are characterized as being "disorderly" and as not following the "tradition." "Disorderly" is the adverb from the same root as that which we examined in the note on "the disorderly" in I Thess. 5:14. It shows us that the same people are in mind as in the former passage, and, as we saw there, that their offence was idleness. In view of the nearness of the Parousia (as they thought) they were refraining from doing any work. They would find such conduct all the easier in view of the Greek idea that labor was degrading. It was a menial occupation, fit for slaves only, not for free men. But this kind of conduct could not be overlooked as due to ignorance of the obligations of Christian discipleship. It was contrary to the "tradition," which indicates that Paul had given instruction on this specific point (cf. v. 10). For the word see note on 2:15. "Received of us" shows that the particular teaching Paul has in mind is the teaching that he had given on the original visit.[9]

7 By using the emphatic pronoun "yourselves" Paul stresses that his friends had all the knowledge that was necessary on this point. He was not giving them any new teaching, but simply directing their attention to what they knew quite well already.

Almost frightening is the way in which Paul continually appeals to the force of his own example. Here his "ought" is a strong expression. It is often translated "must." The imitation of the Apostles is not optional, but Paul regards it as imperative on the converts. While we feel some diffidence today about appealing to our own example, and while we must recognize that dangers lie there, yet it still remains true that no preaching of the gospel can ever be really effective unless the life of the preacher is such as to commend his message. Those who hear must feel that they are listening to one whose life shows his sincerity and the power of the message he brings.[10] See further on I Thess. 1:5, 6.

Paul relates this general duty of imitation to the present circumstances by reminding them that he and his fellows "behaved not ourselves disorderly among you." This is a classical understatement in view of what we know of Paul's life among the

---

[9] There is a textual problem as to whether we should read "they received" (παρελάβοσαν), or "ye received" (παρελάβετε). Not much hangs on the decision, for in either case Paul is directing his readers' attention to the original proclamation. Each reading has good, though not decisive attestation. παρελάβοσαν is favored by many as the harder reading. It is possible, however, that it arose by what Westcott and Hort call "an ocular confusion" with the ending παράδοσιν in the corresponding place in the line above (*The New Testament in the Original Greek*, Introduction [London, 1907], Appendix, p. 172). On the whole it seems likely that παρελάβετε is to be preferred. This would lead more naturally to the οἴδατε of the next verse, where the other reading would look for οἴδασιν. Moulton thinks it "more than doubtful" whether παρελάβοσαν can be accepted, since the termination is so very rare at this period (*Proleg.*, p. 52).

[10] The expression πῶς δεῖ μιμεῖσθαι ἡμᾶς is, as Lightfoot points out, an abridgment for πῶς δεῖ ὑμᾶς περιπατεῖν ὥστε μιμεῖσθαι ἡμᾶς, how ye ought to walk so as to imitate us" (cf. I Thess. 4:1). The present expression, besides being more terse, puts an emphasis on μιμεῖσθαι and thus keeps the thought of imitation prominent.

Thessalonians. As the succeeding verses make plain he had toiled hard among them, both at his trade and in preaching. His life had been highly disciplined. He had not allowed even the importance of preaching the gospel to prevent him from giving a good witness by earning his living. His behavior under those circumstances was the strongest rebuke to those who had no such excuse for not working, but who nevertheless had given themselves to idleness.

8 "To eat bread" is evidently a Semitism. It means not simply "get a meal," or even "meals," but rather "get a living" (cf. Gen. 3:19, Amos 7:12, etc.). Paul does not mean that he had never accepted a hospitable invitation, but that he had not depended on other people for his means of livelihood.[11]

Paul employs a strong adversative conjunction (rendered "but") to show that his conduct was the very opposite of that which he has just disclaimed. Far from being idle and imposing on others for his living, he and his friends had worked hard, and constantly, and purposefully. He had made these three points in the First Epistle (see I Thess. 2:9, a verse very similar to the present one). Then he had been demonstrating that he was no charlatan, but that his motives in seeking to win the Thessalonians had been of the purest. Now he appeals to those same facts as being an example to his converts. He had shown them the way a Christian ought to support himself. Paul's toil had been laborious, the conjunction of the two words he uses being emphatic. He had not shrunk from toiling through long hours ("night and day"). He had done it with the set purpose of refraining from imposing a burden on any other.[12]

9 Characteristically Paul adds to his description of his conduct a statement of his rights. He was an apostle with all that that meant in terms of prestige and the right to maintenance. He knew that our Lord had ordained that preachers of the gospel might live from their preaching (I Cor. 9:14; the whole passage I Cor. 9:3 ff. should be consulted as the fullest statement of Paul's views on this subject). Paul would never let it be forgotten that he possessed such prestige and such rights. But just as it is characteristic of him to assert that he had full rights, so is it for him to waive those

---

11 "For nought" is the translation of δωρεάν, "gift-wise," "by way of gift."
12 See the notes on I Thess. 2:9 for the force of the language employed both here and there.

rights whenever he judged that to do so would forward the cause of Christ. One such occasion had been when he preached in Thessalonica. Then his refusal to accept maintenance had demonstrated the purity of his motives and had given his converts an example. This latter point he proceeds to underline. He speaks of his friends and himself as being an "ensample" (for this word see on I Thess. 1:7). He speaks of their purpose that the Thessalonians should imitate them.

"To make ourselves" is literally "in order that we might give ourselves." This form of expression brings out something of the self-abasement implied in Paul's action. It reminds us of his other statement that "we were well pleased to impart unto you, not the gospel of God only, but also our own souls" (I Thess. 2:8). "Ourselves" is emphatic. They gave not only a message, but themselves. They did not only what was required, but more. They went the second mile. The Thessalonians are reminded that this was not a piece of pageantry or showmanship, but was very purposive. They should follow the example thus set.

10 Not only[13] did the apostles set an example: they embodied their teaching in a pithy precept which Paul now reproduces. The origin of this precept is a matter for speculation, and the most diverse sources have been claimed. Findlay derives it from Jewish sources, others claim a Greek provenance, while Deissmann sees in it "a bit of good old workshop morality, a maxim applied no doubt hundreds of times by industrious workmen as they forbade a lazy apprentice to sit down to dinner."[14] The plain fact is that this is the oldest passage we have which contains it. Parallels have been adduced from various sources, but they lack the idea of labor as a moral duty which is the very root of the matter (they are of the "he who doesn't work doesn't eat" variety). It may have been Paul who originated the saying: it was certainly he who made it part of the Christian view of labor. The saying emphasizes the will[15]—"If any one *won't* work, refuses to work"—and the con-

---

[13] καὶ γάρ ("for even") should be taken in the sense "for also."
[14] LAE, p. 314. Neil thinks that "It belongs to the universal realm of common sense."
[15] "Οὐ θέλω is not the mere contradictory, but the contrary of θέλω . . . not a negative supposition (εἰ μή), but the supposition of a negative" (Findlay, CGT).

tinuous tense gives the thought of the habitual attitude.[16] The concluding clause is not a statement of fact, "neither shall he eat," but an imperative, "let him not eat." Paul is giving the clearest expression to the thought that the Christian man cannot be a drone. It is obligatory on him to be a worker.

The importance of this to Paul is manifest in many ways. There is the force of his own example, to which he has appealed in the previous verses. There is also the use of the same authoritative verb "commanded" that we have already noticed in vv. 4, 6. It is here in the imperfect tense, which indicates continuous action. Paul had repeatedly used this injunction in his preaching.

11 Paul comes out into the open. He has not been speaking simply in general terms, laying down precepts against some possible future need. He has in mind a definite situation. He writes to correct known errors. How he knows he does not say. The verb "we hear" is usually used of hearing by the ear, and thus might well point to information received by word of mouth. But the word is capable of wider use, and Frame cites examples of its use of information received by letter. The present tense might indicate repeated information, "we keep on hearing." Or, it could just as well be equivalent to "we have heard."[17] He does not say who the offenders are. But, though his language is purposely indefinite, the impression the Greek leaves is that he knows quite well their identity. He just prefers not to give their names. He speaks of these people as being "among you," and it may be significant that he does not say "of you." Their conduct had removed them from their full status in the church and set up something of a barrier between them and their fellows.

These people are characterized as "disorderly," the same word as in v. 6 and the same root as in I Thess. 5:14 (where see note). It indicates that they were loafing and not doing any work for their living. This Paul brings out further with his "that work not at all, but are busybodies." This embodies a play on words which we miss in our usual translation (Moffatt's is perhaps the best attempt to reproduce it in English, "busybodies instead of busy").

---

[16] Cf. Rutherford, "Why, when we were with you, we were always telling you that there should be only one rule, 'No work, no bread.' "
[17] For this construction of the present tense as equivalent to the perfect, see Burton, *Syntax*, p. 10.

These people were not simply idle, they were meddling in the affairs of others. We may conjecture that they were trying to do one or both of two incompatible things, namely, to get their living from others, and to persuade those others to share their point of view about the second advent, and so persuade them to stop working also.

12 Paul now interjects an exhortation directed at the offenders, though he employs a very oblique way of referring to them. He does not say "you loafers," or even "those loafers." He uses instead an expression which means "people of this kind," "men who answer to this description." It is part of the tactfulness that we see displayed throughout this whole section. Paul leaves us in no doubt but that he reprobated their conduct, but his tone is always brotherly. He is anxious to secure not condemnation but reconciliation. He wants them to be won back into the fellowship of the church, and all his exhortations have this in mind. So here he addresses them in this very roundabout way. He uses the authoritative verb of commanding (see vv. 6, 10), but he softens it with the addition of "exhort," making a combination unique in the Pauline writings. Whereas he had earlier commanded them in the name of Christ (v. 6), now he exhorts them "in Christ." This gives a note of authority, it is true, but they as well as Paul were in Christ. The expression has a brotherly ring, and at the same time it has the effect of drawing attention to the obligations consequent on the fact that they were in Christ.

Paul urges them to work "with quietness."[18] The root trouble apparently was their excitability. The thought of the nearness of the Parousia had thrown them into a flutter, and this had led to unwelcome consequences of which their idleness was the outstanding feature. So Paul directs them to that calmness of disposition which ought to characterize those whose trust is in Christ.[19] They are to earn their living. For the force of "eat bread" see on v. 8. Paul inserts an emphatic "their own" with bread. These people had existed on the bounty of others. They are urged to exist on the fruits of their own labors.

---

[18] μετὰ ἡσυχίας. The μετά marks the attendant disposition.

[19] Cf. Bicknell, quietness "probably is in contrast not to the meddlesomeness of the idle, but to the restlessness of mind that they fostered in themselves and in others." Milligan says that ἡσυχία "differs from ἠρεμία in denoting tranquillity arising from *within* rather than from *without.*"

13 Paul turns back to the majority of the church members, with an emphatic "but ye" (i.e., whatever the recalcitrant may do), and an affectionate address "brethren." The exhortation is couched in general terms. It is broad enough to cover the whole of life, but probably there is meant particularly the obligation to do everything possible to bring back the erring brethren. Such a task is never easy, hence the exhortation not to be weary.[20] Some have felt that the majority had not been exactly tactful of the minority, and their impatience had only widened the breach. This may well be so, though we have no means of verifying it. If it is the case Paul's words are more than ever in point. Calvin draws a wide moral, "however ingratitude, moroseness, pride, arrogance, and other unseemly dispositions on the part of the poor, may have a tendency to annoy us, or to dispirit us, from a feeling of weariness, we must strive, nevertheless, never to leave off aiming at doing good." Paul's word for doing good is found here only in the New Testament, though the two components which together make up the word are found as separate words several times. In accordance with the basic difference of meaning between the two words for "good" which we noted in I Thess. 5:21, the word used here will mean rather doing the thing that is right in itself, the thing that is noble, than conferring benefits (which would be the compound used in Luke 6:9).

2. THE DISOBEDIENT, 3:14, 15

> 14 And if any man obeyeth not our word by this epistle, note that man, that ye have no company with him, to the end that he may be ashamed.
> 15 And yet count him not as an enemy, but admonish him as a brother.

Paul anticipated that some might not obey his instructions. So he gives direction as to the way they are to be treated. It is most probable that it is some among the idlers that he has in mind, though his words are general enough to cover disobedience to anything he has said throughout the Epistle.

14 The use of the present tense, "obeyeth," views the matter, as is common in Greek letters, from the point of view of the

---

20 The use of μή with the aorist (μὴ ἐγκακήσητε) implies that they had not begun to grow weary.

recipients. By the time they get to this point they have read the letter, they have heard the injunctions, and any refusal to obey is present, not still future. "By this epistle" is literally "through the epistle." The occurrence of "epistle" with the article towards the end of a letter almost always means the letter just being written. Thus ARV almost certainly gives us the sense of it. We should perhaps notice that there are some who prefer to take this expression with the words that follow, giving the meaning "designate that man by letter." They understand Paul to mean that he wants to be informed in writing about such a happening. However, it is not likely that this interpretation is correct. We have already noted that the usual Greek usage is against it. So also are the word order, and the general sense of the passage. Paul is telling the church members what action they should take, not asking for an opportunity of taking action himself. "Note that man" means more than simply "notice" him. It means "mark him out," though the means whereby this is to be done is not specified. The word originally was neutral, and might mean mark out for good as well as for ill, but in time it came to have a somewhat sinister significance. It came to mean marking out for blame, as here.[21]

The treatment of such a person is the withdrawal of fellowship. This is in a limited degree compared with the procedure laid down in I Cor. 5:9-13. There, too, the withdrawal of fellowship is spoken of (the verb used is the same as that here,[22] these being the only two places in the New Testament where it occurs), but it is much more far-reaching. It is specifically laid down there that they are not to eat with such a man, and that they are to put him away from among them. Here the man is still to be regarded as a brother (see the very warm statement of v. 15). The treatment is primarily intended to bring him back to his rightful position. At the same time it is a punishment. He is one who has ignored the teaching originally given by word of mouth, then the injunctions of the First Epistle, and now those of the Second. Clearly this shows a measure of obduracy. It is no longer possible to regard such a person as being in good standing with the church. He must be disciplined.[23]

---

[21] Grammarians used the term in the sense *nota bene* (see MM). It meant more than just a passing notice, and implied serious attention.

[22] συναναμίγνυμι is an expressive double compound, with a meaning like "mix up together."

[23] There are many examples in the Dead Sea Scrolls of the withdrawal of fellowship, especially in "The Manual of Discipline." Exclusion for varying

The object of the discipline is "that he may be ashamed." Always Paul has in mind his repentance and reinstatement. Findlay draws attention to the fact that the verb is the passive (as it usually is in the New Testament), with the meaning "to be turned in (upon oneself)" (CGT). It is this process of reflection on the enormity of one's actions that Paul wishes to see effected in the unruly.

15 Paul's thought that the offender must still be regarded as a brother now becomes explicit. The "yet" of ARV should probably be omitted. While it could possibly be understood from the Greek[24] it is more natural to take the connective as meaning simply "and." The point is that Paul is not contrasting the behavior outlined in this verse with that in the previous one. He is carrying on a consistent line of thought. Throughout this whole section he aims at having the dissident reclaimed in a spirit of love. The actions enjoined in v. 14 are just as kindly intentioned as those in this verse.

It is noteworthy that Paul puts the injunction not to treat him as an enemy before that to admonish him. He is eager to protect the brother's standing, and to see to it that what is done to him is from the best of motives, and that it secures the desired result. The enforcement of discipline is a difficult matter. It is easy for men to become censorious and unnecessarily harsh in the process. Paul's words are directed against any such eventuality. The "but" between the two clauses of this verse is a strong adversative. They are to be far from treating the offender as an enemy. On the contrary, they are to admonish him in brotherly fashion. For this verb see on I Thess. 5:12. It contains the idea of a rebuke for wrongdoing, but Paul always uses it with a certain tenderness. It is the rebuke of a friend. It is most appropriate here with its combination of the two ideas of a steady refusal to have any truck with the evil thing, and a genuine concern for the well-being of the wrongdoer.

---

periods is the penalty for a number of offenses (one which is not without its interest runs: "One who lies down and goes to sleep during a session of the masters [shall be punished] thirty days" [Millar Burrows, *op. cit.*, p. 380]. A curious provision in the two-year punishment of a traitor is that he may not "touch the sacred food of the masters" during the first year, while "during the second he shall not touch the drink of the masters" (Millar Burrows, *op. cit.*, p. 381).

24 Taking καί in the sense of καίτοι.

VII.   CONCLUSION, 3:16-18

16   Now the Lord of peace himself give you peace at all
times in all ways. The Lord be with you all.
17   The salutation of me Paul with mine own hand,
which is the token in every epistle: so I write.
18   The grace of our Lord Jesus Christ be with you all.

16 Paul usually has a short prayer towards the close of his
letters, and not uncommonly it includes a reference to "the God of
peace." Because of this it is probably wrong to place a great deal
of emphasis on the occurrence of "peace" just here. Yet at the
least we may notice that it is appropriate immediately following
his references to the unhappy division in the church. The Lord
they serve is a Lord of peace, and those who serve Him should be
likewise characterized by peace. At the same time we must bear in
mind that peace in the Bible is not simply the absence of strife (see
on I Thess. 1:1). It means prosperity in the completest sense, and
its association here with the Lord is a reminder that such a state
comes only as the gift of God.

Though a prayer with a reference to "the God of peace" is
common in Paul, one mentioning "the Lord of peace" is not.
"Lord" with Paul usually means Jesus Christ, and there is every
reason for thinking that it is Jesus who is in mind here. The
"himself" gives it a certain emphasis, as is the case elsewhere in
these Epistles. The whole expression is a reminder to his Thessalonian friends that the solution to the problems before them,
including those of the idlers and disobedient, rested not in their
own efforts, but in the help which the Lord would bring them.[25]
"At all times" is not quite the force of the Greek, which is rather
"continually" (as Moffatt renders it). The thought is not that of a
peace which comes on a series of occasions, but that of a peace
which is unchanging. It abides continually. The thought of a
peace which is present no matter how the circumstances may
change is contained in the following "in all ways." The last word
literally means "turning." It has within it the idea of the way in
which conditions alter. For the Christian no change in that which

---

[25] Cf. Lightfoot, "The disjunctive particle δέ is slightly corrective of the
preceding. It implies: 'Yet without the help of the Lord all your efforts will
be in vain.'"

is outward can interfere with his deep-seated peace. His peace is not a matter of equilibrium with the tensions of the outward. It is the gift of his Lord, and comes independently of outward circumstances. This is put in another way when Paul prays, "The Lord be with you all." The peace which a Christian has is not something which is ever independent of the Lord. It is the gift of the Lord, and it is impossible apart from the Lord. Indeed, it is the presence of the Lord. It is only as the Lord is present in the heart of the believer day by day that he knows this peace. It may be an example of the way Paul enjoyed this peace that he puts "all" at the end of his prayer. There is no resentment against those who disobey his injunctions. He prays for all the Thessalonians, those who were out of step as well as those who were in perfect harmony with him.

17 As the letter draws to its close Paul gives the method he employs to authenticate his writings. It seems to have been his custom (as with most other people of antiquity) to dictate his correspondence while an amanuensis wrote down what he said. Thus in Rom. 16:22 we have a reference to Tertius "who wrote the epistle." The Apostle would take the pen himself, however, towards the close of the letter and the few verses in his own characteristic handwriting would show that the letter came from him. The stage at which Paul took the pen seems to have varied. He wrote quite a few verses at the end of Galatians (Gal. 6:11), but shorter amounts in other letters (see I Cor. 16:21 and Col 4:18 for other places where he draws attention to what he was doing). It is possible that in the case of a short letter like that to Philemon he wrote the whole (Philem. 19). We do not know why on some occasions he drew attention to the autograph and on other occasions did not. There is no reason for thinking that he penned his salutation only in the cases where he specifically calls attention to it. He tells us here that it is his custom "in every epistle." Deissmann has given us an interesting example of this practice in the letter which he reproduces from a gentleman called Mystarion to a priest.[26] The letter is written in one hand, but the final greeting and the date are in another hand. There is no reasonable doubt that this latter is the hand of Mystarion himself. The interesting thing is

---

[26] LAE, pp. 170 ff.

that Mystarion says nothing about this. He just does it. If we had only a copy of his letter, and not the original itself, we would not know what had happened. And what Mystarion did, so also did Paul the Apostle.

Paul proceeds to tell us that this is his customary "token," i.e., means of authentication. This is the way he indicates that his letters are genuine. Some have thought that this shows this to be the first letter Paul wrote to the Thessalonians. They argue that such a statement would be necessary in a first letter but not after that. This, however, is to go too fast. Paul may well have simply followed his normal practice in his first letter. However, there arose circumstances in which men were not certain about a letter from Paul, though it purported to come from him, as we see from 2:2. Now he makes it quite clear. They may know that this letter is authentic because they can recognize his handwriting. And in the future that applies to any other letter he may write. Incidentally, the way he puts it, "the token in every epistle" makes it seem as though he wrote other letters which are now lost. "So I write" probably means, "This is what my writing is like," rather than "This is my custom" (cf. Knox, "This is my handwriting").

18 The letter concludes in exactly the same fashion as the First Epistle (see the notes there), with the exception that the word "all" is added. Twice in the last three verses we have seen this reference to the whole membership, and we can only feel that Paul's tenderness for his entire flock carries through to the end. He has had some hard things to say about those who were offending, but he closes on an inclusive note. *All* his friends were included in his final prayer.[27]

---

[27] That is if we assume that the addition of "all" is significant, and is in view of the specific disturbances noted earlier. This is likely, yet we should notice that Paul could use a similar expression in Rom. 15:33, where no such inference is to be drawn.

INDEX OF CHIEF SUBJECTS

INDEX OF PERSONS AND PLACES

INDEX OF SCRIPTURE REFERENCES
OLD TESTAMENT

INDEX OF SCRIPTURE REFERENCES
NEW TESTAMENT